"Finely attuned to the myriad ways in which individuals voice their complaints in marital, cross-cultural, and corporate settings, Lachkar offers us a treasure trove of insight and interventions, as she delineates communicative patterns across the globe within a dyadic context. She also introduces original concepts like the 'V-spot' (the point of our greatest vulnerability). Noting changes in the nation's demography, she offers a cultural ear for discerning cultural rationalization from neurotic conflicts. Her writing is firmly anchored in theory and yet eminently accessible to readers at all levels of experience."

—**Salman Akhtar**, MD, Thomas Jefferson University, and Supervising and Training Analyst, Psychoanalytic Center of Philadelphia

"Joan Lachkar's genius for learning from her patients is matched only by her talent for organizing her insights and sharing them with her readers. In *Common Complaints in Couple Therapy*, she explores the common but frequently overlooked symptomatic styles of the complainer, through which she threads such key modalities of narcissism, borderline conditions, and obsessive-compulsive neurosis, all deftly framed within current theories and therapeutic interventions."

—**Dan Dervin**, PhD, author of *Creativity and Culture*, and of the forthcoming *The Evolution of Inwardness*

"Joan Lachkar once again has written an excellent guide for psychologists engaged in conjoint therapies. While she speaks directly to the modern American psychologist, she goes beyond the usual middle-class situations to examine cross-cultural relationships, artists with their special needs, and even the new sensibility toward gays, lesbians, and transsexuals. To other readers, including lay persons outside of the United States, the author offers an unabashed insight into the problems of one key culture, and especially opens the conversation to international conflict-resolution, the control of terrorism, and other psycho-historical themes."

—**Norman Simms**, PhD, founding editor of *Mentalities/ Mentalites*, an interdisciplinary journal of the history of mentalities and psychohistory

"Lachkar captures the art of listening, distinguishing legitimate complaints, and how to respond. Moving from the domestic to the global, she has succinctly demonstrated the crucial importance of listening to the other as well as walking in their shoes. In this book she reintroduces the challenges that cross-cultural couples bring into today's ever changing world. This book is of utmost vital importance for all those who are involved in and committed to resolving family to global conflict."

—**Nancy Kobrin**, PhD, psychoanalyst

Common Complaints in Couple Therapy

Marriage and couple therapists see clients with broken relationships and bonds all the time; those who were once madly in love can grow indifferent, people change, and couples go into sessions feeling depressed, traumatized, and sometimes abused by their partners. Joan Lachkar examines the vicissitudes of love relations by taking into account aspects of aggression, cruelty, sadism, envy, and other primitive defenses lurking in the shadows of love and intimacy. Each chapter revolves around a specific situational conflict, with guidelines and treatment suggestions offered to the therapist. Numerous vignettes and detailed descriptions of theoretical technique, methodology, and diagnostic distinctions are included throughout the book to help readers see theory in action. The theoretical concepts drawn on include psychoanalysis, object relations, self-psychology, attachment theory, dialectical behavioral therapy, mindfulness, and others, with a heavy emphasis on listening and non-verbal and verbal communication throughout.

Joan Lachkar, PhD, is a licensed marriage and family therapist in private practice in Sherman Oaks, California. She teaches and practices psychotherapy using a psychodynamic approach. She is the author of numerous publications on marital conflict, is an affiliate member and instructor at the New Center for Psychoanalysis, is a master presenter at numerous conferences, and is on the editorial board of the *Journal of Emotional Abuse*.

Common Complaints in Couple Therapy

New Approaches to Treating Marital Conflict

Joan Lachkar

Routledge
Taylor & Francis Group

NEW YORK AND LONDON

First published 2014
by Routledge
711 Third Avenue, New York, NY 10017

and by Routledge
27 Church Road, Hove, East Sussex BN3 2FA

Routledge is an imprint of the Taylor & Francis Group, an informa business

Library of Congress Cataloging-in-Publication Data

Lachkar, Joan.
   Common complaints in couple therapy : new approaches to treating
marital conflict / Joan Lachkar. — 1 Edition.
      pages cm
   Includes bibliographical references and index.
   1. Couples therapy.   2. Marital psychotherapy.   I. Title.
   RC488.5.L3473 2014
   616.89'1562—dc23
   2013050994

ISBN: 978-0-415-83605-0 (hbk)
ISBN: 978-0-415-83606-7 (pbk)
ISBN: 978-0-203-42815-3 (ebk)

Typeset in Berkeley
by Apex CoVantage, LLC

Contents

About the Author

Joan Lachkar, PhD, a licensed marriage and family therapist in private practice in Sherman Oaks, California, is an affiliate member of the New Center for Psychoanalysis and the author of *The Narcissistic/ Borderline Couple: Psychoanalytic Perspective on Marital Treatment, The Many Faces of Abuse: Treating the Emotional Abuse of High-Functioning Women, The V-Spot, How to Talk to a Narcissist, How to Talk to a Borderline,* and *The Disappearing Male.* In addition to being a communication specialist, Dr. Lachkar is considered one of the foremost experts on marital and political conflict. She has taught courses both locally and internationally at universities, psychoanalytic institutes, and major conferences throughout the world. Dr. Lachkar has integrated her work on emotional abuse, terrorism, and counterterrorism with the political arena and presented a paper on "The Psychopathology of Terrorism," written from a psychodynamic perspective, at the Rand Corporation.

Acknowledgments

I would like to pay special tribute to the many steadfast friends and colleagues who have remained patient and loyal during this continuation of my publishing journey.

The readers of this book, which is an extension of my previously published works, may see normal-looking pages. However, I still see endless lines of red, green, and blue markups, and editorial comments peppering the margins. For this I am grateful to my superb editor, Joanne Freeman, whose razor-sharp eye has guided me through this and other volumes, keeping me focused on the task at hand. As a plus, her background in music allows her to intrinsically understand and share in my artistic proclivity.

As a classically trained dancer, I find the subtle blending of ballet technique and discipline priceless in understanding psychoanalytic principles. To this I owe a debt of gratitude to the ballet masters with whom I have studied. These include Margaret Hills, Nader Hamed, Mark Anthony, Sven Toovald, Alan Kirk, the late Carmelita Maracci, Stanley Holden, Yvonne Mounsey, and those at Westside Academy of Ballet.

I also want to thank my three daughters—Dr. Pamela Brody, Sharon Stone, and Nicole Raphael—who in response to my announcement that I was writing a book about complaints said, "On this topic, Mom, you are a master!"

My work on cross-cultural couples would not have been possible without the contributions of Peter Berton, Professor Emeritus at the University of Southern California—an expert in international relations and a foreign affairs scholar whose vast knowledge of East Asia has been enormously helpful in understanding shame cultures. In the same vein, I owe much gratitude to Dr. Nancy Hartevelt Kobrin, whose collaboration as political analyst, psychoanalyst, and scholar has greatly contributed to my work on the study of terrorism, counter-terrorism, and cross-culture from a psychodynamic perspective.

I am immensely grateful to the following friends and colleagues for their continual support, encouragement, and insight: Drs. Nina Savelle-Rochklin, Orli Peter, Mara Thorsen, Norman Simms, Jamie Glazov, Irene Harwood, Robert Baker, Sherry Siassi, Roberta Rinaldi, Myrna Goodman, Vera Hamilton, and the late Dr. Shelley Ventura.

Special tribute goes to Peggi Ridgeway, my computer and website specialist. I am also indebted to my UCLA research assistants, Simone Dvoskin, Alexander Sokhis and Rafi Raffe, as well as many others who have now moved on to become successful professionals in their own right.

I give thanks for my amazing editors past and present for their encouragement and willingness to allow me to roam beyond the usual parameters of psychoanalysis into the world of creativity, art, music, and culture: Associate Editor Marta Moldvai, Editorial Assistant Elizabeth Lotto, Production Editor Hannah Slater, Associate Marketing Manager Julia Gardiner, Marketing Assistant Alexa Tarpey, Cover Designer Sally Beesley, and Publisher George Zimmar at Routledge; Project Manager Sheri Sipka and the team at Apex CoVantage; Publisher Jason Aronson and Editor Amy King at Jason Aronson; and Lloyd deMause, publisher of the *Journal of Psychohistory*.

Of course, there are the great masters—Drs. Otto Kernberg, Salman Akhtar, James Grotstein, Marvin Osman, Robert Kahn, Sam Vaknin, and many others—whose contributions have enriched the analytic literature.

Special gratitude to all those at the New Center for Psychoanalysis for their continual support and to Bernd Leygraf and Jaap Westerbos for their welcoming kindness and generosity in inviting me to teach a master class at the NAOS Institute in London. It was a most memorable experience.

My great appreciation also goes to all my friends, colleagues, and patients who have shared their complaints with me, leading to insights that have made me a better listener and a more enlightened clinician.

Introduction

This book has a different twist than my other publications. Rather than starting out by delineating the various diagnostic disorders (the borderline, the narcissistic, etc.) and illustrating how their corresponding defense mechanisms impede the capacity for intimate love relations and healthy object relations, this book focuses on the complaints themselves. Each chapter will revolve around a specific type of personality and the situational conflicts that ensue. Every individual, every patient, every couple, every culture has its own way of complaining. Individuals and couples often enter into treatment thinking their battles are over money, sex, children, and custody when they really are about betrayal, isolation, abandonment, entitlement, victimization, control, domination, and oedipal rivalry. Treating the emotional vulnerabilities within the context of these complaints makes it imperative to take account of these qualitative differences. The treatment for these conflicts requires a broad grasp of the psychodynamics within the constructs of various personality disorders and corresponding environments.

As it takes a serious look at the fine art of complaining, this volume delves beyond ethnic and religious borders to understand the dynamics of complaints from a clinical and cultural perspective. The descriptive titles outlined in this book—such as "the entitled" rather than the narcissist, the "promiser" rather than the borderline, or "the withholder" rather than obsessive-compulsive— are in no way intended to be pejorative. Rather, they are intended to make this book more accessible to a variety of readers. These titles are segues to understanding the kinds of conflict stirred up by various personality types and the reactions these individuals evoke in others. In many of the chapters, I take the liberty to speak in the voice of these actors. When examining the complaints that are presented, we need to be aware of the type of personality voicing the complaint. We need to understand "how to listen," to tell when we are hearing a legitimate problem and distinguish when a complaint is not a complaint. Finally, we must learn how to listen with a "cultural ear." (See Chapter Eight on cross-culture.)

Subsequent to my first publication, *The Narcissistic/Borderline Couple* (Lachkar, 2004a), I moved on to a variety of other kinds of dyadic configurations, which inspired me to focus more on "the complaints' than the disorders per se. My experience as a professional ballet dancer motivated me to use the metaphor of the dance for the often rondo-like choreography in which a couple engages when the partners stay in painful, conflictual relations that are ongoing, circular, and never-ending. Even when "good advice" is offered, these couples never seem to reach conflict resolution.

This book revisits various couples from my previous works—those experiencing early trauma and past archaic injuries that affect every aspect of their lives. Archaic injuries can be best explained by a concept I originated, the V-spot (Lachkar, 2008c). This term is tailor-made for homing in on the vertex of vulnerability. The V-spot is the epicenter of our most sensitive area of emotional vulnerability, which becomes aroused when one partner hits a raw spot or "pushes the other's buttons." It is the product of early trauma that each partner unwittingly and voraciously holds on to. The archaic injury or V-spot is what causes our suppressed feelings to explode to the surface at the least provocation. When the V-spot is provoked, even the most innocent remark can be a recipe for disaster. The V-spot is the precise point where a complaint often hits, causing an out-of-proportion reaction.

> I told my boyfriend I had a backache. He tells me to go and get a massage. That's when I blew. He is just like my mother, always telling me what to do with no compassion for how I feel.

Using the common complaints abstracted from these couples as a starting point, I began to see not only the qualitative differences but also the variations in their behavior. For example, the way a narcissist complains when not properly mirrored or admired or when his self-objects become depleted is quite different than complaints from a borderline, who bonds through pain, victimization, and revenge. This is in contrast to someone like the obsessive-compulsive, who complains when his object world is in a state of disarray. The actions of these complainers greatly affect the people who live with them and love them.

The interacting dramas enacted by the couples are illustrated throughout the text, along with many case examples. Each chapter includes case illustrations/vignettes, specific theoretical technique, theories and methodology, diagnostic distinctions, and a detailed discussion and summary. Although my work is a distillation of concepts, ideas, and theoretical formulations from my previous publications, this book focuses specifically on the symptoms and mechanisms of defense that emerge, highjacking the couple from love and intimacy. These defenses include withdrawal, isolation, abandonment, anxiety, shame, blame, splitting, projection, and projective identification. These types of defenses are the viruses that infect and trespass on the capacity to maintain healthy love relations.

In my personal, clinical, and professional experience, I have worked with a number of couples who have been vastly frustrated and disappointed in their marriages. They were madly in love at the onset, but the loving feelings have vanished. Many of these couples come into sessions feeling depressed, traumatized and disappointed, and abused by their partners. Prowling in the shadows are undiscovered primitive defenses that attack and destroy the love bond. The mysteriousness of this was enough to motivate me to examine the vicissitudes of love relations, taking into account aspects of aggression, cruelty, sadism, envy, and other primitive defenses that threaten the capacity for love and intimacy.

I draw mainly from psychoanalysis, social psychology, behavioral psychology, group psychology, and psychohistory, using a metapsychological approach to study individuals, couples, and groups—including those in cross-cultural relationships. I have sometimes been criticized by professional colleagues, who claim that therapists have no business analyzing other cultures. I strongly disagree. Society has changed vastly in the past couple of decades. It has taken on new hues as interracial and cross-cultural marriages proliferate. Society has also assumed varying configurations as people come to accept and integrate the rights and needs of gay, lesbian, and transgender individuals and couples. It is imperative that in today's clinical practices we embrace this ever-changing society and learn to deal with the special needs of people from various cultures and ethnic groups.

Mental health professionals are now beginning to understand not only that the dynamics and ideology of people varies from culture to culture, but also that the degree of abuse and violations against women varies across borders. To penetrate seemingly impermeable borders, therapists must take into account religion, childrearing practices, ideology, and mythology, as well as psychodynamics such as shame, honor, saving face, guilt, dependency, envy, jealousy, devotion, and meaning of self. The knowledge of group psychology is important in understanding not only the dynamics of cross-cultural couples, but also those of nations, countries, and even institutions and corporations.

OUTLINE OF THE BOOK

Chapter One presents an overview of the psychological makeup of the complainer from a psychodynamic/psychoanalytic perspective. It offers various ways to listen to the complaint and discusses when a complaint is a complaint and when there is a complainer without a complaint. Common complaints that couples bring into treatment are listed, and tips on how to listen to a complaint are presented within various analytic modalities and styles.

Chapter Two concentrates specifically on various theoretical contributions and psychodynamics—from classical psychoanalysis, ego psychology, attachment theory, object relations, and self-psychology to more contemporary theories, including dialectical behavioral therapy. It also shows how each theorist would respond to complaints, given his or her theoretical framework.

Chapter Three focuses on the entitled complainer, one who has a grandiose sense of self and feels that the world is indebted to them. The title, "It Takes One to Tango," embodies the self-absorbed persona within a "me, me, and only me" personality, who is unaware of how this behavior impacts others.

Chapter Four presents another type of complainer—the "promiser," also known as the revenger, the betrayer, the Don Juan, the femme fatale, the womanizer, the victim, the abuser, the addict, the insatiable, and the saboteur. The promiser, unlike others in the book's cast of characters, has the ability through the false self to put on a face of loyalty and trust, but the drama ends in sabotage and betrayal, causing outrage and disbelief in those who trusted him or her.

Chapter Five describes the robotic personality, complainers unique from the others in that they are obsessed with objects rather than love and intimacy. Unlike the manipulator, the cheater, and the pathological liar, they do have a conscience and are possessed by a very harsh punitive superego that demands perfection.

Chapter Six examines the passive-aggressive, a procrastinator/mañana personality, one of the few who does not complain overtly but who unconsciously coerces others to become enraged with them. They insidiously and covertly project their helpless parasitic dependency onto others and coerce them to take on parental/caretaking roles. Joining the passive-aggressive in this chapter is the depressive or victimized "poor me" personality. What distinguishes this personality type from the other complainers is that complaints are leveled against the self—hatred turned inward, resulting in self-loathing and self-blame. The slightest sense of defeat sets these complainers on a downward path.

Chapter Seven discusses the antisocial and his or her "Life of Lies." This complainer is distinguished by the absence of a conscience. The most dominant trait is the lack of superego ego functioning and the lack of remorse and guilt for their wrongdoings and manipulative acts.

Chapter Eight examines cross-cultural complainers within the framework of cross-cultural couples, mainly those from the Middle East and Asia. These complainers relentlessly cling to their cultural flags, beliefs, and nationalistic pride. They refuse to adapt and will do anything to maintain their sense of identity, creating conflict in their relationships with others. This chapter extends the discussion of how to listen in Chapter One, showing how to listen to complaints with a "cultural ear."

Chapter Nine takes complaints to the corporate level. Professional people working in large corporations have complained of abuse, humiliation, and mistreatment by management. Using the formulations of group psychology, this chapter explains how an entire group, institution, or company joins in collusive bonds, finding scapegoats onto whom to project its problems.

Chapter Ten includes treatment suggestions and techniques, as well as discussion of the therapeutic functions, the three phases of treatment, suggestions for the partners in therapy, and a review of how to listen. It is recommended that the therapist provide a broad range of listening techniques and theoretical approaches not only for integration but also for the facility to target specific complaints by noting their qualitative differences and distinctions. Effective communication necessitates not only talking but also careful listening to ferret out the underlying meaning of the complaint. "One man's complaint is another man's need."

Finally, "Closing Thoughts" offers reflections on the nature of complaints in an ever-changing world.

Chapter *1*

∞✕∞

Complaints and the Art of Listening

According to *Merriam-Webster's Dictionary*, a complaint is a means to express grief, pain, dissatisfaction, or discomfort. A complaint also could involve a formal accusation or charge. It could also refer to a bodily ailment or a disease. The first known use of the word was in the fourteenth century—although I'm sure complaints date back to Neanderthal times. Synonyms for the verb *complain* include the following: beef, bellyache, crab, fuss, gripe, groan, growl, grumble, holler, kick up a fuss, kvetch, moan, nag, squawk, wail, whimper, and whine.

This may seem quite odd, but one of the most significant influences for my study of complaints began in a French restaurant that was owned by my ex-husband and his two brothers. While sitting there eating and sampling various wines, I began to observe the behaviors and interactions of different personality types that frequented the restaurant. As a new graduate with psychoanalytic training in marital therapy, I started to write down my observations of frequent customers as if I were doing a mental status evaluation. I noticed that each personality type would exhibit his/her unique way of complaining. The narcissistic customers would come in and complain about the seating, the chairs, and the noise, among other things, and whatever we did to accommodate them was never enough. The borderline personalities would come in and show extreme impatience, demanding to be seated and fed right away; if the server did not respond to their needs immediately, they would act out aggressively.

In doing my customer evaluation, I realized that the server became the bad-breast, non-feeding mommy, unresponsive to the borderlines' on-demand needs. In contrast, the passive-aggressive typically would come late, keeping everyone waiting with a barrage of excuses (got lost, forgot the directions, couldn't find his keys), then comply with the server's recommendations, return the food, and blame his wife for forcing him to go out when he really wanted to eat at home. The obsessive-compulsive would insist that the portions of fish, potatoes, green vegetables, and so forth should not touch one another; these foods had to be served on separate plates or set far apart to avoid "contamination." The schizoid customer would take forever to order, and when asked what he or she would like responded with "Whatever!" or "Well, I'm not sure; let me think about it some more." It didn't take much for me as an observer to note that this type of customer was not only disconnected to his emotional needs but his feeding ones as well.

Food is one of the earliest experiences the infant has with the maternal object. Through my psychological lens, I witnessed how the server became the mommy and the customers the children acting out their unconscious childhood fantasies. Who would ever have imagined that the confluence of my experience in a French restaurant would lead to a psychoanalytic study of complaints that appeared as an article, "Restaurant Theatrics," published in the 1983 View section of the *Los Angeles Times*?

HOW TO LISTEN TO COMPLAINTS

In clinical practice, we get an "earful." As a good friend and colleague quipped, "Why don't you put up a Complaint Department shingle?" It might be taken for granted that analysts listen to their patients' complaints: One person has the complaint, and the other listens to it. However, it's not quite that cut and dried. When is a complaint a complaint, and when is it an evacuation or a legitimate need? Listening analytically is an essential skill that takes the analyst years to learn. One of the most common complaints of patients entering treatment is, "He/she never listens to me."

Theodor Reik (1948) has given special meaning to listening with his innovative work, *Listening with the Third Ear*, and its relationship to the unconscious. Reik's third ear is inextricably linked to the unconscious and recognizes its intuitive messages. Unlike Klein's persecutory superego (1957), Reik's superego can also soothe, console, and forgive. It does not necessarily only punish, criticize, and admonish; it can also be benevolent and understanding. He contrasts this to the ego, which is an organ of perception capable of observing the self.

The road to listening is endless. Klein would listen through the patient's projections and projective identification, whereas Kohut would listen through the lens of empathic attunement. Most relevant, however, is how Wilfred Bion (1967), the champion of thinking, formulates and describes the concepts of alpha function versus beta elements. The beta element complaint might be conceptualized by Bion as a complaint made without thinking, used solely for evacuation, like idle whistling.

Kohut's self-psychology stance (1971, 1977) stresses the patient's subjective experience as reality and does not consider it to be a distortion or a projection. For Kohut, empathy is the ability to put oneself in the shoes of the other person, to see the world through the eyes of another for the purpose of understanding as a precondition to interpretation. To feel what the patient feels and to understand why the patient feels that way is what Kohut refers to as empathic immersion.

Klein and her followers, on the other hand, believe that patients with more severe symptomologies tend to distort reality, misperceive, deny, and do not see the objective reality. Although these two disciplines may sound worlds apart in the way they "listen," they miraculously are quite compatible in clinical practice.

Although the two languages I created—the language of empathology and the language of dialectics—were initially designed primarily for narcissistic and borderline disorders, they are broad enough in scope to have relevance for listening and responding to other types of complainers and complaints. Motivated by the works of Heinz Kohut (1971, 1977), I employed the need for empathic understanding and attunement in speaking with the narcissist, and I used Wilfred Bion and Marsha Linehan's (1993a, 1993b) concept of dialectics to address the splitting mechanism for the borderline in order to make communication more "user friendly." Without trying to sound too narcissistic myself, it is my hope that these concepts will also enhance the response methodologies used in the "listening and talking cure."

Is it fair to teach patients to "listen like an analyst?" At one time, I would have considered that to be an extra burden. My encouragement comes from well-known Indian analyst Salman Akhtar. In his latest book, *Psychoanalytic Listening* (2013), Akhtar does not specifically reference patient's complaints, but his listening techniques have profound application to this subject. Akhtar goes beyond "the talking cure" to the "listening cure," based on the premise that listening with no talking or talking with no listening can only go so far. He believes the analytic community has been short-sighted about the importance of listening. He believes that both talking and listening are crucial elements in effective clinical work. I would like to broaden this concept to include our patients; if it is good enough for us, it is good enough for them.

Akhtar describes four different kinds of listening approaches: (1) objective listening, (2) subjective listening, (3) empathic listening, and (4) introspective listening, which he outlines in *Psychoanalytic Listening*. To these, he also adds silence and non-verbal communication, as he demonstrates with great proficiency the multifaceted aspects of what seemingly is a simple therapeutic skill. In the following list, I have taken the liberty of expanding the various ways of listening that Akhtar laid out:

- Objective listening
- Subjective listening
- Empathic listening

- Introspective listening
- Intersubjective listening
- Listening to the silence; non-verbal listening
- Containment listening (holding the thought without response)
- Transference and countertransference listening
- Language of empathology listening (listening with empathy)
- Language of dialectic listening (listening to two sides)
- Listening to bad internal/external objects (identification/bonding with bad internal objects)

What follows are various ways of listening and responding to a common complaint, noting the distinctions and qualitative differences based on the type of listening that is being used.

The Sample Complaint: My Mother Abused Me!

Objective Listening

"I believe your mother abused you. Maybe this is why you are so hard on yourself and why you transfer to me the idea that I am abusive to you." The objective listener functions as the neutral, detached observer who listens without preconceptions and abandons all conscious memory—as opposed to the subjective listener who listens with preconceptions. The best way to describe this difference in listening is to discuss the differences between self-psychology and object relations. Self-psychology, including the field of intersubjectivity, offers a variety of listening stances. Self-psychology takes the position that the patient's reality is the "truth." It does not consider the patient's reality as delusional or distorted. In object relations, the patient's "distortions" and "misperceptions" are considered as part-object functioning, split off and projected.

Subjective Listening

"What did you do to make her so angry?" The therapist is aware that he is annoyed with the patient and can understand why someone would abuse her. "Even if you behaved in the way you said you did as a child, still no one has the right to abuse you." The subjective listener pays attention to his own feelings, overreactions, body movements and intuitions.

> A therapist was getting extremely weary of dealing with one particular patient, who was constantly yawning. When not yawning, he would talk in slow, excruciatingly long, drawn-out sentences, to the extent his analyst could hardly keep his eyelids open. The therapist finally interpreted what was going on and gave his insights to the patient: "You are letting us know what it feels like to have an empty, internal world where there is nothing going on."

Empathic Listening

"That was a violation and a terrible thing to go through. You have a right to feel everyone is going to be cruel and mean to you because that was what your early experience was." The empathic listener feels what the patient feels and understands why the patient feels that way.

Introspective Listening

"You need not be so hard on yourself because your mother abused you as a child. Now as an adult you abuse yourself."

Intersubjective Listening

"There is something that you do that makes people angry with you, but even so, no one has the right to abuse you. You feel that I am as abusive as your mother, but you are confusing my attempt to create boundaries and discipline here with abuse. My intent is not to punish or attack you, but to make the environment safe for both of us" (abuse within the experience of two). This is the point where two subjective realities come together in a collaborative effort, the final understanding when two unconscious minds meet. This type of listening can be most valuable in couple therapy.

> I remember a couple that came into session at the clinic, complaining about moving a box in the middle of their living room. They went on and on about who was to remove the box. I later discovered what moving the box meant for each partner. For the one more inclined toward narcissistic personality, it represented a sense of entitlement. "I'm a professional drummer and practicing is far more important than moving some goddam box." The other partner was more inclined toward borderline organization and felt, "I am always the one kowtowing to this narcissist! I'm fed up and won't do it anymore!"

Silent (Non-Verbal) Listening

"I can tell each time you think about the abuse because you start to wiggle your foot."

Different kinds of silence include the following:
- Part of the human mind that has no words, the unmentalized experience, or more commonly known as being out of touch. "You may be silent because you have something difficult to share or you don't know how to express the feelings about the abuse you experienced as a child."
- Part of the human mind that has words that are hidden (repressed thoughts often associated with shame). "For many years you thought you had to remain silent about your mother's abuse, but now you know you are not alone and should not be ashamed."

- Part of the human mind that speaks through non-verbal communication. This kind of listening requires response to gestures such as toe tapping, nail biting, avoidance of eye contact, as well as body position and movements.

Containment Listening

"Because you were abused as a child, you were left with feelings that are intolerable. In order to rid yourself of these feelings, you project them into me as the container for your unwanted parts." Bion's conception of containment is a very active process that involves feeling, thinking, and organizing, which leads to an action. For Bion, silence does not play a part within the reverie experience because it blocks the opening of a therapeutic alliance. In a way, this is a good thing because it enables the therapist to get into the experience with the patient (detoxification and transformation for a new experience).

Transference and Countertransference Listening

"When I told you about the increase in the fee, I knew you were not complaining about money. It is more about the feeling that I am going to be like your mother and abuse and take advantage of you. You have accumulated much wealth, and now you feel people take advantage of you." (Meanwhile therapist is struggling with his/her own financial issues.)

Language of Empathology Listening

"What I am about to say in no way invalidates the abuse you received as a child from your mother. No parents have the right to abuse their children, and I can understand how this affects your ability to trust in an intimate relationship."

Language of Dialectics Listening

"I can understand the confusion and ambivalence you feel because you were abused by your mother." One part of the mother who was loving and kind was the same mother who could be cruel, abusive, and sadistic.

Listening to Bad Internal/External Objects

"Yes, there can always be an external real mother who abused you as a child, and this, of course, is a violation and never should have been allowed; but there can be an internal abusive mother that can abuse you, such as when you put yourself down or deprive yourself, or never think you are good enough" (see Chapter Two for more examples of internal/external abusers).

DISTINGUISHING A REAL COMPLAINT FROM A NON-LEGITIMATE COMPLAINT

Although Akhtar (2013) does not address complaints per se, he offers us valuable tools that help us distinguish legitimate complaints that have to do with real needs, as opposed to illegitimate complaints. There is a profound

difference between patients showing concern for something that is genuinely disturbing and complaining for the sake of complaining. The beauty
of analytic work is the process of sorting out and weighing the real from the
not real, the objective from the subjective, and the reality based from the
intersubjective.

Let us say, for example, that an entitled narcissistic patient complains about
the fee being above her means and insists that the therapist reduce this fee.
However, at every session, she walks in with new designer clothing (a Chanel purse, Michael Kors shoes, and a Cartier watch). The therapist (using the
language of empathology as a precautionary measure to avoid a narcissistic
injury) compliments the patient on how lovely she looks but mentions that
how she looks is less important than her mental health. The patient's complaint
is obviously not legitimate. The expenditure on materialistic objects is used as
a defense against facing her real needs and internal issues. The therapeutic task
is to get the patient in contact with her real needs and not the defenses that act
as a protective shield to avoid introspection.

A legitimate complaint that frequently arises among couples who live
together is that one of the partners wants to get married, whereas the other
denies that marriage is important and claims it is "just a piece of paper." In this
instance, it is clear that one partner's desire for marriage trumps the other's dec-
laration that marriage means nothing, which can be not only a denial of reality
but also a defense against intimacy and commitment.

The complainer without a complaint is often one who is inextricably
bonded with the mother of pain. Parasitic needs become the replacement for
healthy dependency needs. These are frequently borderline personality types
who feel persecuted by their internal needs. I am reminded of a patient whose
response each time I asked her to express her needs directly was, "What and
open up that can of worms!" Unconsciously, these patients set themselves up
for failure, then blame the world for being a bad and destructive place. The following example shows how a patient's complaints sabotage her real needs while
she searches for the unavailable object.

> Ms. B. is a 60-year-old actress, who maintains she can get parts suitable for a
> far younger actress. She feels men of her age are too old for her and yearns for
> men in their late 30s or 40s. On weekends she complains of loneliness and
> is stressed out. She does not heed my advice about going to movies, operas,
> or the theater because she thinks that all movies, plays, and performances are
> terrible and not what they used to be. She opts to be alone all weekends except
> when her daughter comes to pick her up to take her to dinner. But because
> Ms. B is a vegan, it leaves them very little choices of where to dine. Yet she
> complains of her life as restricted and isolated.

The following are examples of "legitimate" complaints. Please keep in mind
that these are subjective, based solely on my professional, personal, and clinical
experiences.

- It upsets me that you never want to celebrate holidays.
- It upsets me that you never sit down and eat dinner with us.
- It upsets me that when we go to dinner you flirt with the female server.
- It upsets me that you dump me at the last minute to go out with your adult kids.
- It upsets me that you won't ever make plans and insist on doing things at the last minute.
- It upsets me that you let yourself get out of shape.
- It upsets me that you allow your mother to intrude into our relationship.
- It upsets me that you don't say loving things to me.
- It upsets me that you make important decisions without me.
- It upsets me that you withhold money, time, and attention from me.
- It upsets me that you don't see that my biological clock is running out.

COMMON COMPLAINTS

From the outside looking in, most complaints on the surface seem to revolve around children, sex, money, commitment, work, and outside intrusions (ex-spouses, in-laws, friends, sports, pets, and hobbies). However, the underlying issues are more about control, domination, envy, jealousy, shame, guilt, submission, victimization, and oedipal rivals. Many couples come into treatment confused and baffled. The female complains, "He pays more attention to his dog than to me. All my husband cares about is when he can play golf. When he's not playing golf, all he does is work, work, work. He doesn't spend time with me or the family." The male grouses, "All she cares about is getting her acting career on track."

Common complaints that bring couples into therapy are often conflicts over intimacy, time, financial stress, infidelities, and communication barriers. The degree of severity can range from issues around miscommunication to domestic violence to endless divorce and custody disputes. At the more severe end are the cheaters, the dreamers, the spendthrifts, the withholders, the pack rats, the messy ones, the perfectionists, the shopaholics, the alcoholics, the druggies, the lazy ones, the promisers, and others that can push the relationship over the emotional cliff.

Gottman (1995) identifies how such obstacles as avoidance, stonewalling, and denial break down the capacity for marital intimacy. Contrary to many beliefs, Gottman reports that complaining is often useful in marriages and distinguishes complaints from attacks and criticisms. When a partner withdraws, it often leaves the other feeling lonely, isolated, and depressed. Many wonder where the romance went. "Why can't we be the way we were before we were married and had kids? He used to treat me like a queen; now he barely acknowledges me." Couples often have difficulty maintaining the boundaries, time, and space to keep the romance alive. "We can't make love. As soon as we start our kids come barging in our room!"

Often one partner complains of feeling controlled and suffocated. "Why can't we get married? Why do you keep saying you need space?" One partner may want kids, whereas the other keeps putting the issue on hold. "My biological clock is running out, and you think I am just going to sit here and wait until it is too late?" Other complaints include stress about one partner not doing his fair share. "He lies on the couch all day while I work, take care of two kids, clean the house. He does nothing but offer false promises." It becomes a familiar litany: "He's a workaholic." "She obsesses over every little thing; I can't take it anymore." "I can't tell him anything without him getting into a competition. It's a no-win situation." Then there's the "Well, you do it, too" response; "She always has to be right. Even when she's wrong she's right. She never apologizes or admits she's wrong." "She's always sick, always the victim. If she's not sick, she's tired and exhausted, a real turn-off." "I know my wife is a wonderful musician and her teacher told her to practice more, but that's all she does!"

The list that follows contains some typical issues that bring couples into treatment. When these issues are not addressed, they bring about lack of trust and failure to provide a safe and reliable holding environment. One of my daughters, who happens to be a clinical psychologist, said, "Mom you're making this more complicated than it is. It is about sex, money, and kids; that's it." But hiding behind those basic issues is a battery of complicated reasoning and emotions.

- Lack of sex and romance
- Love and intimacy concerns ("Why can't it be like it was before?")
- Control, power, and domination
- Competition and tit for tat
- Failure to keep promises, false hopes, and lying or cheating
- Lack of trust
- Boredom, loss of attraction, growing apart, and isolation
- Infidelity
- Immaturity ("Why is he always the victim? He always gets into trouble, forgets his car keys, gets his car towed, and loses his wallet, and I have to take care of him.")
- Commitment, marriage, children, and having kids ("I know her biological clock is running out, but I don't want to get married or have kids, yet I want to stay in the relationship!")
- Stress ("He's always on the couch watching TV or getting loaded while I'm working my butt off.")
- Threats ("He keeps threatening me with divorce but doesn't do anything to work on our relationship.")
- Money ("She's a shopaholic; all she does is shop and spend." "He's not a good provider.")
- Control ("I can't do anything without his watching over me and criticizing my every move.")
- Entitlement ("He feels entitled to everything—a nice car, nice clothes, high-tech equipment—and when I need money to have my nails done, he makes me feel as though I am unrealistic.")

- Withholding ("He has to count every penny and thinks vacations, going out to dinner, and redoing the house are just a waste of time and money.")
- Attention seeking ("She always sick, tired, or exhausted. If it is not one ailment, it is another. It's a turn-off.")
- Self-absorption ("All he does is work." "All she does is obsess over her body and her looks.")
- Lack of romance, not enough sex, and exhaustion from work/kids ("She says she doesn't feel romantic after working hard all day, then dealing with the kids.")
- Lack of emotion ("He shows no emotion and has no desire to do anything; he is like a zombie.")
- Obsessiveness ("He threatens to kill me if I ever dare to throw any of his objects away, even a wire coat hanger. We can hardly get into the house anymore.")
- Perfection "(Everything has to be perfect—all the towels facing the same direction, perfect closets with everything labeled and covered with plastic— and if I have a hair out of place, he won't go out with me.")
- Nagging and blaming ("All she does is nag, nag, nag, with one complaint after another non-stop." "Everything is my fault.")
- Lack of caring/not invested in the relationship ("Why is it when things are going well he will always find excuses to sabotages our plans?")
- Flirting ("He was such a charmer in the beginning, and I really felt that he/she loved me. Now he's always on the prowl, looking for other men/women.")
- Addiction ("I feel so helpless; his addictions control our relationship.")
- Manipulation ("He fools the world; he is a real con artist and the biggest manipulator.")
- Psychopathology ("He has no regrets for any harm he has done to others except when he gets caught.")

Psychosomatic Complaints

It is not an easy task to address psychosomatic symptoms with patients who are in denial or totally convinced that their affliction is physiologically based. Even when their physician tells them, "It's all in your head," and that there is no medical evidence for their problems, they are still unconvinced. However, symptoms overlap and can range from mild to severe headaches, nausea, asthma, eczema, heart problems, hypertension, ulcers, migraines, insomnia, diarrhea, muscle pain, panic attacks, colitis, and more.

Psychosomatic symptoms differ from psychosomatic complaints. Psychosomatic symptoms are more physically based, whereas psychosomatic complaints are more emotionally based, resulting from the need for attention. Although there are a variety of theories to account for the development of psychosomatic symptoms, researchers are continually puzzled about how negative thoughts can produce feelings of real affliction. For example, a momentary and slight change in one's heart rate can precipitate an alarming reaction. "Call 911. I am having a heart attack!" One patient kept thinking he had a venereal disease each time he had an itch on his penis. Doctor after doctor reassured him there were no signs of infection or illness, yet at each itch he would go into panic mode.

This is where I conjure up my language of dialectics to address both the psychological and the physical. "Yes, your symptoms are real, but your fears and negativity are not!" A precautionary note: As mental health professionals who do not have medical degrees, we must safeguard against ruling out the medical aspects. The distinguished psychoanalyst Albert Mason (1981) wrote a paper, "The Suffocating Superego," employing psychoanalysis as an adjunctive treatment to asthma. He noted that when he interpreted the patients' closed, tightly restricted inner world, their airway passages began to open, and they could breathe better.

Consider this scenario. A patient comes to the therapist with the following complaint: "I've been to every specialist imaginable for my sinuses. I have tried rinses, antibiotics, and nasal sprays and still cannot breathe." Later the patient states, "My mother-in-law lives with us, and I feel as though she is everywhere. I feel blocked in every part of my own home." To this the therapist suggests that the patient may be suffering from a psychosomatic condition, her body reacting to a situation in which she feels helpless and where she feels her emotional airways are blocked and obstructed.

Many symptoms emerge from stress, guilt, depression, work, and relationship issues. Many of these include divorce, custody battles, finances, sleep deprivation, and so forth. The key is for the therapist to refine listening and communication skills. "During our last session, I noticed you had difficulty breathing and started to choke right when you were explaining how your mother suffocates you and never gives you a moment to breathe." At an early age, children are often punished for self-expression and learn to repress their feelings; later they often disguise their unexpressed negative thoughts though psychosomatic illness.

Our Complaint Society: Never Enough!

In a recent article in *Time* magazine, Joel Stein (2013) addressed the generation of kids who are at the heart of the new wave of social revolution. This generation's feelings of being entitled and preoccupation with self are unprecedented, as evidenced by their endless, self-centered Twitter and Facebook posts and photos of themselves, their friends, and their pets. Not a moment goes by without their feeling the need to check in with their friends. It is as though friends have become the replacement parents. Meanwhile, parents complain that their children's obsession with cell phones, iPods, and other forms of technology has replaced face-to-face social interaction and intimacy. Friend or follower, it's all about me for these kids. For them, nothing is ever enough. They are constantly wanting and searching for more, but the more they find, the less connected they are. Thus, we also need to "listen" to a new generation of young adults, who, with their superego-enforcing outlook, are instituting new forms of societal norms that in the future may well exacerbate the problems that occur between couples.

DEPRIVATION: MR. AND MRS. D

Mr. and Mrs. D came into treatment complaining that their marriage was lacking intimacy and respect for each other's needs. They were not listening or paying attention to the feelings of the other. For months I would hear bantering back and forth that included a barrage of complaints from one about the other—until one session when it all came to a head.

Therapist: We've been going back and forth, and I have been listening to each of your complaining about your spouse. Last week we discussed some individual issues that you both decided you would deal with in your individual therapy. But today I would like to focus on what you feel the goals of the marriage are while you are both in conjoint treatment.

Mrs. D: I feel deprived. We have some serious stuff going on. Basically, I would like a happier marriage, for us to be a happier family and have more intimacy and fun.

Mr. D: I would like a more positive connection, to feel happy and safe, and be more sexually attracted to my wife.

Mrs. D: I feel very upset with all the uprising—the bombings in Boston, the explosions in West Texas, all the bomb threats (this is all happening during our sessions). It's scary to go anywhere today.

Therapist: Sounds like there is something else scary going on. (Therapist listening with the Reikian "third ear")

Mrs. D: Yeah, we have a mortgage to pay and two kids starting college, and we don't know where to get the funds. We're both working, and it is not enough. I hope we don't go bankrupt. (Therapist hearing this also as emotional bankruptcy)

Therapist: What about your dad? Will he help?

Mrs. D: My dad! That's a joke. I still owe him for a loan he gave us years ago. Besides, he's supporting my alcoholic brother.

Therapist: Would it help not to repay him now, to buy some extra time?

Mrs. D: No, I can't do that. I have to pay him back.

Therapist: Yet, your dad can afford to wait. He has lots of properties, investments, and gives tons of money to your other siblings.

Mrs. D: But I feel so guilty.

Therapist: Guilty?

Mrs. D: When I was young I had terrible grades, smashed up two cars, and caused my parents a lot of problems.

Therapist: But that was then. Did they ever take you for counseling?

Mrs. D: No! But now I want to enjoy my life, give to my kids, and have a better relationship with my husband.

Mr. D: Are you saying she should not pay back her father?

Therapist: No! I am saying she should tell her dad that there will be a delay. Look, it is not my job to advise you on how to deal with your finances. There are financial planners for that. There can always be an external depriver like your dad, but there can also be an internal depriver. And when there is so much guilt, fear, and feelings of deprivation, it makes it harder to find a solution.

Discussion

This is an example of listening to unearth the problems beneath the verbally stated problem. Both Mr. and Mrs. D share the dynamics of guilt, shame, and deprivation. Mr. D feels sexually deprived because of Mrs. D's weight gain and loss of sexual attraction. She gained weight to soothe herself from feelings of deprivation. Aside from Mr. and Mrs. D's financial crisis, the therapist must listen carefully to get in contact with the underlying dynamic and illustrate how hard it is to find a solution when these defenses are operative. It is also important to make reference to the reverse superego—the child who is good gets punished while the child who is bad gets rewarded (the alcoholic brother). This is described further in Chapter Two, pointing out when the ego goes into dysfunctionality.

THE AFFAIR

Another, often life-shattering, complaint that gets revealed in conjoint therapy is cheating and infidelity. In the back of every therapist's mind is the fear that lurking in the shadows is the discovery of "the affair." There is not only the revelation of the affair, putting both therapist and the victim of the affair in a compromising position; there is also the problem of what to do after the revelation. A distraught wife comes into treatment after calling for an emergency session. "When I saw his telephone number on my iPhone, I just knew he was confessing to a long-term affair. My heart began to pound as I listened to the confession!" After the revelation, there is the problem of how to deal with the initial shock, how to explore the reasons for the affair, and how to deal with the threats of divorce or the reparative process. "All these years I had no clue he was screwing another woman."

The most common reasons for an affair are the following:

- The person falls madly in love with someone else.
- The person feels something is missing in the relationship.
- The person acts out of revenge or as an expression of anger.

- The person needs many different people for adulation and attention.
- The person is perverted and looks for excitement in lieu of love.
- The person has lost contact with his/her inner passion and turns to excitement as a superficial substitute.

Mr. and Mrs. A

Mr. and Mrs. A have been married for six years. They have a baby boy whom they both love and cherish. Mrs. A described her marriage as a storybook one.

Mrs. A: We have loving and supportive families, and we were childhood sweethearts. I am the love of his life, the one and only. When we are together, he cannot keep his hands off me. There isn't a day that goes by when he doesn't call me to tell me how he can't wait to come home to me and our baby. I don't know what got into me, but somehow I had a premonition to check his e-mail. I was shocked. For two years my husband has been fucking another woman! How is this possible? How can a man with any sort of conscience do that, then come home and sleep next to me? This woman he was sleeping with was the complete opposite of me, passive, compliant, needy, dependent. I just don't get it! I am the alpha woman—independent, self-sufficient. I don't need anything from anybody. Guess he must have felt that with all my strong attributes I was cutting his balls off. I don't know if I will ever take him back or forgive him, but if I do, I guess I will have to take some responsibility for making him feel like a nothing.

Therapist: Even if your behavior does play a part, it still does not justify his screwing around. I want you to know that what I am about to say in no way validates your husband's betrayal, but we do need to take a look at the dynamics in your relationship, how your husband felt very abandoned and excluded by you. I think this affair has brought to the fore some real issues like dependency, control, domination, victimization, and devaluation. You say your husband always tried to make you smile or laugh but would remain silent when you would ask him what he was feeling beyond the laughter. Obviously, there were some hidden messages.

What follows is an example of how listening to and analyzing the complaint both strengthens a marriage and helps a man get in contact with his long-lost passion.

Mr. Z, a very attractive, married patient was unsatisfied with his marriage and obsessed with the idea of having an affair. His wife was mortified each time he would bring it up in their sessions. As time went on, it came to my attention that he had composed numerous unfinished symphonies. I reminded him that unlike Franz Liszt, who is dead and no longer can compose, he does have the opportunity to work on his music. An affair doesn't last, but music stays for eternity. Gradually, he got so engrossed in his music that he never again brought up the desire for affairs. His wife then quipped, "I was better off before because now he is up all night long composing and completely neglects me. But I still prefer that he have this passion than his running around with other women!"

SUMMARY

This chapter examines various approaches to listening and discusses what to do after one has listened. Starting with common complaints rather than defense mechanisms, the chapter explores when a complaint is a complaint and when it is a legitimate need—and even when a complaint is not a complaint. This chapter draws from many different ways to listen to a complaint to distinguish those used for evacuation. Moving from the types and styles of listening techniques, which range from the objective to the subjective and the introsubjective, the therapist has an opportunity to listen beyond the words or to listen "with the third ear," as Theodor Reik states. The chapter also discusses the importance of the various forms of responding using the language of empathology and the language of dialectics.

Chapter 2

~~✕~~

The Psychodynamics of Complaints

Theoretical Contributions

Drawing from classical psychoanalysis, object relations, ego psychology, and attachment theory, and moving on to more contemporary methodologies encompassing behavioral therapy, dialectic behavioral therapy (DBT), and mentalization, this chapter discusses the methods and techniques available to deal with "common complaints" that bring individuals and couples to treatment. Just as each partner in the couple relationship has his/her own way of complaining, so do the various theorists have their own way of responding with their analytic ears. For example, the way a Kleinian responds to a complaint may be quite different than a Kohutian or a Bionian response. Klein might hear the complaint as a destructive form of projective identification, whereas Kohut would listen with an attuned empathic ear. Bion would distinguish a real complaint from a pseudo-complaint, a complainer without a complaint, or a beta element (unmentalized thought) to be transformed into a digestible form suitable for communication. Understanding Bion is similar to studying a musical composition, where one key can be transposed into another key. Using this paradigm, mentalization transformation could be transported from the reasonable mind to the reasonable complaint, the wise mind to the wise complaint, the emotional mind to the emotional complaint, or the invalidating mind to the validating complaint.

We will begin with Freud and move on to object relations, self-psychology, and then more contemporary methodologies (cognitive/behavioral, DBT, and mentalization approaches). Although I am most respectful of the theories and theorists mentioned, I pay particular homage to the works of Melanie Klein, mainly her offering one of the most invaluable tools applicable for couple therapy. This is the introjective/projective process (projective identification)—how one partner projects a negative part of him/herself onto the other and how the other then identifies or over-identifies with that which is being projected. Another valuable contribution is that of Fairbairn (1942), who helps us understand how and why the complainer will relentlessly bond with painful attachments to bad internal objects—or their "V-spots."

Although each framework embodies a different approach, they all offer the desire for psychological well-being and a positive pathway to find meaning out of the meaningless. Table 2.1 presents a brief outline of the various theoretical positions. We will now revisit some of our master founding fathers and mothers and offer a brief overview of their basic theoretical constructs.

SIGMUND FREUD

Can an unresolved Oedipus complex lend itself to an endless, lifelong deluge of battles, competitive struggles, the need to be right, and the inability to cope with those who have alternate views? Although Sigmund Freud (1909/1955, 1923) did not specifically focus on marital therapy or talk about complaints, he noted early on that there was a certain segment of women who suffered from hysteria, suggesting that there were root causes in childhood that lead to a variety of neuroses and mental conditions. He later acknowledged that women, like men, had sexual desires, but the repression of these urges made them go into fits of hysteria. Even though he embraced the subject, his emphasis was mainly on the intrapsychic, not the interpersonal. The interpersonal was intimated when he discovered transference, the relationship between patient and the analyst. His daughter, Anna Freud, construed different mechanisms of defense and their implication to the ego.

Freud also proposed the Oedipus complex, which attaches the child's love for the same-sex parent with feelings for the parent of the opposite sex, a psychodrama of pitting the son against the father in an uncompromising competitive position of jealousy, anger, revenge, and rivalry for mother's affection. According to Freud, if the conflict ensues and the child never masters the Oedipus complex, this will lead to endless battles and competition, especially with one's mate. On the other hand, if there is a successful resolution of the Oedipus complex, one eventually gives up competing and instead leans toward Eros, the quest for love and intimacy. In this case, a love partner, a spouse, or a family member may live happily and peacefully side by side in a harmonious love relationship.

TABLE 2.1

Theoretical Positions

Theory/Theorist	Position
Classical psychoanalysis	• Focus on the individual, not the relationship • Intrapsychic versus interpersonal approach • Oedipal rivalry • Drive/defense • Aggression • Id, ego, superego (impulses vs. reality vs. moral restrictions)
Object relations	• Focus more on the relationship than the individual • Splitting, projective identification • Distortions/delusions
Ego psychology	• Focus on the environment and adaptation to it; views the ego as an entity powered by its own devises; not in accordance with Freud's ego. Hartman claims that the ego is more environmentally driven than instinctually driven.
Self-psychology	• Need for mirroring self-objects • Empathic attunement • Intersubjectivity
O. Kernberg	• Aggression, drive/defense • Ego functioning • Four different kinds of relationships
W. R. Bion	• Thinking, containment (beta/alpha elements) • Detoxification • Without memory or desire • Finding meaning out of the meaninglessness
W. R. D. Fairbairn	• Attachments to internal/external/objects
D. W. Winnicott	• Different kinds of mothering experiences • Transitional objects • True and false self • Environmental/background/holding mother
J. Bowlby	• Attachment theory • Withdrawal/isolation
Behavioral/cognitive	• Focus on the partnership • Directive approach
M. M. Linehan	• Dialectic behavioral therapy (DBT) • Mindfulness/acceptance • Integrates transference and cognitive therapy (directive approach)
P. Fonagy and A. Bateman	• Mentalization • The reasonable mind • The thinking mind versus the emotional mind • The dialectic ambivalent mind

MELANIE KLEIN

Melanie Klein (1927, 1948, 1957, 1975, 1984), the mother of object relations, did not specifically deal with complaints. However, she does offer us the tools and techniques to understand the encounters that occur among individuals and couples in conflict. I find that Melanie Klein offers us the most valuable methods and insights into understanding the reason behind the battles in which couples engage.

Her main method entails the use and technique of the introjective/ projective process, how one partner projects some unwanted part of him/ herself onto someone like the borderline, and how the borderline will identify or over-identify with the negativity being projected. Her contributions are invaluable, especially in helping individuals face internal deficits, distortions, and projection. The introjective/projective process is a priceless construct that helps us sort out the tangled web that couples weave. It motivated me to coin the term "dual projective identification" (Lachkar, 2008a, 2011), or what I refer to as "the dance," that is, interactions that are circular, never-ending, and go round and round like a "rondo." In conjoint treatment, it often becomes a dance of shame and guilt. To be more specific, certain dynamic mechanisms of someone like the narcissist (grandiosity, entitlement, guilt, and withdrawal) can arouse and project states of unworthiness and a feeling of non-existence into someone like the borderline (shame, blame envy, abandonment, and persecutory anxieties).

I would like to get married!
What for? You have already been married.
You mean, I'm not supposed to have needs.
Not if they are unrealistic!

Although influenced by Freud, Klein broke new ground with her pioneering work on object relations, which marks the point of change away from the intrapsychic to the interpersonal. Her concept of splitting good and bad objects is known throughout the literature as the *good and bad breast*. Klein, more than any of her followers, understood the primary importance of the need for mother and the breast. Klein believed that the primary experience with the breast shapes how the child will perceive the world. If the infant has a good-breast mother, then the infant will grow up seeing the world as good. If the infant has a bad-breast mother, the infant will grow up thinking the world is all bad and destructive. What a suitable concept for the complainer!

Patient: Nothing I do is good enough. I cook, I take care of the kids, I entertain his family, his friends. I'm sexy! I'm passionate. I feel so devalued and unappreciated!

Therapist: So no matter how much you try to please him he coerces you into being bad-breast mommy.

THE CASE OF MRS. P: THE BAD-BREAST WORLD

The case that follows describes a bad-breast mother world and how taxing someone with a borderline personality can be on the therapist's capacity for empathy. Mrs. P. has been married five times. She has three daughters, who are estranged from her. She presents a history of sexual, physical, and emotional abuse. Her mother was a product of depression, who in her own life suffered from severe deprivation. Mrs. P's emotional backdrop is a tapestry of darkness, despair, and gloom.

Therapist: So you see the world as bleak and dark.

Mrs. P: What do you mean "see the world"? Are you doubting my perception? (The borderline patient seeking what Linehan refers to as the "validating environment")

Therapist: I am just trying to understand your perception because I don't see the world as all bad.

Mrs. P: Then you're blind. Just look around you. The world is going to pot and people are monsters.

Therapist: I see it as good and bad. (Addressing the splitting and enforcing "my reality")

Mrs. P: Don't you see all the crime, the terrorism, the tornadoes, and destruction around you?

Therapist: And yet people came from all over to offer help to survivors of the Boston Marathon and the devastating tornadoes in Oklahoma.

Mrs. P: But those are caused by those terrible humanoids, who destroy the environment with their computers, cars, electronics. They could care less about the environment. They only care about themselves.

Therapist: (Feeling despair and musing about projective identification: Is she putting her desolate self into me? My blood level is rising, and I need help. So I turn to Mrs. Klein.) I think you are letting me know what you were feeling as a child, that no matter what you did or said your mother always made you feel unworthy, empty, and undeserving of anything good.

Mrs. P: You are right. My mother was a horror, as was my father. All people are terrible. Look at my five husbands, and even my daughters, who turned out to be a mess because of them.

Therapist: (Caught in a trap of either colluding to blame the mother or making the attempt to bond; I choose the latter and, needing some soothing myself, I turn to dear Dr. Kohut for empathy, who reminds me to mirror and give up forcing my "reality" upon her.) Look, I know how you feel. You were an abused, terrorized child and had hardly any good people in your life to turn to or protect you. It is understandable how you see the world as all dark, and bad, as a "bad-breast place" that cannot feed or provide for you.

Mrs. P: My mother was awful.

With a wave of my therapeutic baton, we move into two major positions: the paranoid position and the schizoid position. The schizoid position versus the depressive position is basically a dynamic between wholeness and integration. "Everything is your fault" versus "I take responsibility for my wrongdoings!" The schizoid position is a fragmented position (not to be confused with schizophrenia). It is a psychic space in which thoughts and feelings are split off and projected because the psyche cannot tolerate feelings of pain, emptiness, loneliness, rejection, humiliation, or ambiguity. Words, listening, and empathy are not functional at this stage. Klein viewed this position as the earliest phase of development, part-object functioning, and the beginning of the primitive superego (undeveloped).

The paranoid position is exactly where the battling and complaining occur. Everything is the fault of the other, and one cannot take responsibility for any wrongdoings. In this initial phase of couple treatment (see Chapter Ten for more on treatment phases), complaints are non-stop, and the therapist must act more as referee than therapist. It is the earliest state of mind, where primitive defenses dominate. The latter phase, the schizoid position, is a whole and integrated position, with less blaming, shaming, and attacking. It marks the beginning of taking responsibility for one's own wrongdoings, a diminishment of envy, shame, blame, attack, revenge, and magical thinking. In this phase, the desire to make reparation and show remorse for the damage that has been done becomes more important than the baggage of the past.

Patient: Everything is her fault. I blame her for everything that goes wrong. She gets me so upset I don't know what to do. Should I stay married or should I divorce her?

Therapist: It's hard to know what to do when there is so much blaming and attacking going on; thus, it's best not to make any major decisions at this time.

Patient: I just want to divorce my wife, get rid of her. I am so bored and no longer feel the excitement I used to have!

Therapist: This is not about divorcing your wife; it's more about divorcing a part of yourself that you cannot tolerate.

The Depressive Position

This is a term devised by Melanie Klein to describe a state of mourning and sadness where integration and reparation take place in the last phase of treatment. There is more tolerance, guilt, remorse, self-doubt, frustration, pain, and confusion, and not everything is seen in terms of black and white (splitting). The couple begins to take more responsible for their actions, the way they listen, and the way they hear. In addition, there is a greater realization of what things are rather than the way they should be. As verbal expression increases, one may feel sadness, but also a newly regained sense of aliveness.

Patient: I feel so sad all the time. I go around crying, depressed.

Therapist: I know it is not a good feeling, but what you are feeling is normal. You are not depressed. You are dealing with normal states of sadness and taking more responsibility for your actions.

W. R. D. FAIRBAIRN

Fairbairn (1952) helps explain why people stay in painful, conflictual relationships. In some ways, Fairbairn has upgraded Klein. Fairbairn has expanded Klein's concept of the good and bad breast to the notion that the ego splits into multiple objects (the rejecting object, the painful object, the insatiable object, the betraying object, the enviable object, and the unavailable object). Certainly, the Kleinian "bad-breast complainers" will grumble no matter how much gratification is achieved, for they perceive the world a place of privation and deprivation. In many of my previous works, I have paid special tribute to W. R. D. Fairbairn for he has been a key contributor whose work has significance in understanding how and why people stay forever attached to painful bad internal objects. I am amazed at how easily his theories adapt to the topic of complaints and listening.

Object relations is a powerful theory that examines unconscious fantasies and motivations, reflecting how a person can distort reality by projecting and identifying with bad objects. There are those individuals who confuse love with pain and cannot feel a semblance of aliveness unless these concepts are fused in a dysfunctional, destructive attachment. They complain about the same thing again and again, without any awareness of how this can impact and provoke another person. Surprisingly, even after divorce or separation, one remains attached to the "bad object." "I'll sue the hell out of him." As Grotstein (1987) reminds us, any attachment is better than no attachment. Children who have had a history of physical and emotional abuse are targets for this kind of "traumatic bonding." Anything is better than the emptiness. "At least I feel alive! I know I exist!"

A narcissistic husband projects a feeling into his borderline wife that she is worthless and not entitled to anything, that she should not need or want anything. He complains, "All you do is nag, nag, nag." Not knowing how to legitimately express her real needs, the borderline wife continues to nag and demand with increasing intensity. The more she nags, the more he withdraws, and as he withdraws she attacks. As she attacks, she hooks into his harsh, punitive, internalized superego (guilt). So he ends up feeling guilty and she feels shame. Thus, it becomes a dance between guilt and shame.

In narcissistic conditions, the "entitled one" will complain because he or she never has enough (attachment to the insatiable object). In more severe pathology such as borderline conditions, this feeling of "never enough" equates with deprivation, where pain takes on a new dimension. Not only does the borderline bond with pain, he or she "becomes" the pain. "I am my depression and my depression is me." Pain is linked to the internal part of the self that one wants to destroy or get rid of. There are many factors in play: First, it is better to bond with pain than to face the void, the black hole, the emptiness. Second, pain stirs up an amalgam of unresolved infantile issues. Third, the pain becomes highly eroticized and sexualized. Fourth, pain is familiar (the familiar bad internal object). Fifth, pain is confusing and creates ambivalence. The lover who can be cruel and sadistic can also loving and kind.

Attachment to and Identification with Bad Internal/External Objects

I find that the concept of how couples identify or over-identify with their internal/external objects is one of the most valuable in conjoint treatment, especially when couples are in phase one, the shame/blame stage of complaints. Yes, there can always be an external abandoner, betrayer, or depriver that we identify or over-identify with, but there can also be an internal part of your- self that can deprive, betray, or mistreat. We have no control over the external demons, but we can control our inner abandoners, deprivers, or complainers, and this is where the power lies.

Rejecting Object: You complain your husband rejects you, but there is also a part of you that rejects yourself.

Depriving Object: I understand how you are trying to lose weight and how undeserving you feel about being attractive, and how you feel your husband deprives you, but there also is an internal depriver that deprives yourself.

Abandoning Object: You complain that your husband abandons you, but there is a part of you that doesn't listen to your feelings and abandons yourself.

Unavailable Object: You complain when your husband is unavailable, but there is also a part of you that is unavailable to yourself.

Withholding Object: You complain your husband is withholding, but there is also a part of you that is unavailable to yourself.

Painful Object (the Mother of Pain): You complain that your husband hurts you and abuses you, but there is also a part of you that bonds with the pain.

Idealized Object: You idealize your husband and see him as so great and powerful that you don't see the part of yourself that is successful and has good qualities.

Sadistic Object: You complain that your husband is sadistic, but you don't see how his sadism is a way of keeping you attached and offers you a sense of aliveness.

Disappearing Object: Yes, your husband does disappear a lot, and when he's gone it makes you feel like a nothing. This is the internal part of you that disappears and loses object constancy.

Insatiable Object: Whatever your husband gives you is never enough. There is an internal part of you that is like a black hole that feels empty and cannot be filled.

DISAPPEARING HOWARD

Howard, a screenwriter, came into treatment complaining of severe anxiety and panic attacks when he had to go to meetings or book-writing groups. "Most of the time I cancel because I get so anxious about presenting my material." He complains that when he enters the room, he feels he becomes invisible, as though he does not exist. In treatment he recounts that he cannot remember any of his childhood photos. "I see them but have no recollection of them being taken or where I was." He associates this with an absent father who was out gambling, drinking, or working, ignoring and neglecting him so that his attachment to his father was missing. He talks about how he feels when he goes to a social gathering or an interview, how suddenly he feels he does not exist or that he emotionally vanishes.

Although the session was a bit chaotic and the material did not flow smoothly, I was able to pick up on the main thematic motif of disappearance and non-existence in the patient's words: can't recall photos, father absent, and he emotionally vanishes. This little vignette embraces several different theoretical perspectives. First, we think of Kernberg's relationship of the ego to the mechanisms of defense, how the early trauma of an absent father syndrome can impact memory. Second, we think of Kohut and the feelings of non-existence that occur when the child does not receive the mirroring or self-object reflection from their caretakers. Third is Fairbairn's concept of how one identifies with a bad internal object, in this case the absent father with whom Howard identifies.

THE CASE OF MR. AND MRS. N

Mr. and Mrs. N reluctantly returned to treatment, feeling that nothing had changed after seeing many other therapists for conjoint as well as individual therapy.

Mrs. N: We're here, but I don't feel very optimistic; we still have the same old complaints. He continues to pull away from me, withdraw and harbors resentment over everything I say. And when I reach out for some contact with him, like even a hug, he pulls away and I feel rejected. This is when a battle begins and I start to complain.

Mr. N: I try to comfort my wife when she is upset, but then because she feels so hurt and rejected, I have to hold on to my hurt feelings and cannot talk to her while she is in this state. Meanwhile, it hurts so badly that I have no choice but to withdraw or pull away.

Therapist: So when you are hurt and feel attacked by your wife you pull away?

Mr. N: Well, she has said some very resentful things, like "I wish you'd drop dead" or "I wish I'd never married you."

Mrs. N: But I didn't mean those things; I was just pissed off at you. I said them because I felt rejected by you, especially when you shut down and don't talk to me.

Mr. N: I took it very hard.

Therapist: So when your wife throws these things at you when she's in a pissy mood, you take it personally?

Mrs. N: That's what he does; he distorts everything I say, takes it way over the top. This is when we get into our battles.

Therapist: It sounds like you don't know the difference between a complaint and an evacuation.

Mr. N: What is an evacuation?

Therapist: It is a term I use that basically reflects an act that has no meaning, something that just spills out without much thought.

Mrs. N: Right. Because if I meant for you to die or wish I never married you, why would I have made this appointment today to work on our marriage?

Therapist: Good point. But I can see how when you feel rejected by your husband you also personalize. And because you feel hurt you engage in a battle. So your choice is to argue or else not respond to your husband's issues.

Mrs. N: If I don't respond, then he shuts down and doesn't talk to me at all.

Therapist: What a dilemma! If you argue, then you feel engaged with him. But if you choose not to engage with him, then he shuts down. Mr. N, are you aware of how you are putting your wife on the spot?

Mr. N: Now that you say it that way, well, yeah, I guess I am.

Therapist: We have to stop now, but you certainly have given me a good under-
             standing as to why you both engage in these painful, never-ending
             battles. Better to be engaged and arguing than to face the emptiness
             or void.

Mr. and Mrs. N: Thank you. See you next week.

Therapist: Have a good week and take care.

Discussion

This brings up a highly sensitive issue in treatment: How to gradually wean the
patient away from the external bad object and get them to face the internal one
without undermining their reality. This case is a good example of why couples
stay in painful, conflictual relations. Mrs. N, who has remnants of early abandonment with an absent, "empty" mother, chooses to fight rather than to have
to face the black hole, the void, when her husband shuts down. Mr. N recognizes that when he tries to comfort his wife, he is left with the burden of his own
feelings of discomfort; not knowing how to process or contain these feelings, he
goes "into hiding." Thus, the dance goes on. In following sessions, we used the
metaphor of music to talk about the importance of timing. That when Mrs. N
is feeling hurt, abandoned, or rejected, it is not the time for Mr. N to talk to her
about his feelings. He need not "suck in his feelings," but it would be better
to wait for the right moment to share them with her. Although they were not
able to understand the music metaphor, Mr. N said he was able to get the point
because the same method occurs when one tells a joke. "Timing is everything!"

DONALD WINNICOTT

Winnicott (1965) is another prominent figure whose unique ideas and language
have enhanced and expanded the diversified field of object relations. His focus,
like Klein's, was on the importance of the early "mommy and me" relationship. He introduced us to varying kinds of mothering experiences—including
the environmental mother, the containing mother, the being mother, the doing
mother, the holding mother, and the background mother—that affect the infant's
capacity to be alone. Winnicott's concept of the "false self/true self," also makes
an important contribution to both individual and conjoint treatment.

In couple therapy, his concept of the transitional space provides a new
opportunity for partners to move from states of dependency and interdepen-
dency by making use of transitional objects. It is amazing how varied the
"mother roles" are in which I'm cast when dealing with the various complaints
that couples bring into treatment. At times I am the mirroring mother or
the containing mother, while at other times they regard me as the holding/

TABLE 2.2

Different Mothering and Bonding Experiences

The "good-breast"/"bad-breast" mother	The "listening" mother
The "empathic" mother	The "containing" mother
The "being and doing" mother	The "holding" mother
The "background" mother	The "rejecting," "absent" mother
The mother of "pain"	The "internal" mother
The "facilitating" mother	The "environmental" mother
The "mirroring" mother	The "self-object" mother
The "bonding/weaning" mother	The "idealized" mother
The "castrated" mother	The "introjected" mother
The "self-hatred" mother	The "internalized" mother
The average or "good enough" mother	The "thinking" (rather than reactive) mother

environmental mother, the listening mother, the mother of pain, or the bad-breast mother. The mothering roles of the therapist are many and varied, as Table 2.2 shows.

It is clear from Winnicott's work that without good enough mothering, the person cannot function as an adequate partner in intimate relationships. For example, a passive-aggressive person will constantly try to re-create the parent-child dyad by engaging in behaviors that essentially state, "I am the baby and you are the mommy/wife who is to take care of me!" Another clinical example demonstrating the utility of Winnicott's ideas centers around his concept of "good enough," which may have particular relevance for someone like a narcissist who imagines him/herself as being perfect when in reality he or she can be just good enough.

Another of Winnicott's contributions is the concept of the false self, a self in constant battle with the true self that lurks in the shadows and belies the true self. Bernie Madoff, who bilked investors of millions of dollars with his Ponzi scheme, had an exquisite false self. He is a prime example of someone who could fool some of the people most of the time. "He acted as though he was our best friend. He was family to us. We trusted him completely."

To the distraught woman who suffers from migraine headaches, a Winnicottian therapist might respond something like: "I can see you have been under an undue amount of stress" (the "being" mommy). To the woman who is genuinely seeking help, he might respond, "Take two Extra-Strength Tylenol" (the "doing" mommy).

HEINZ KOHUT

Heinz Kohut (1971), the pioneer of self-psychology, is another key figure relevant to the topic of intimacy. His innovative approach cultivated a new theory of self-psychology, mainly for those with narcissistic personalities. He believed the narcissist has more need of mirroring and responds best to empathy and interpretation. This is in contrast to object relations theorists, who believe narcissists respond more to confrontation. Kohut embraced the importance of mirroring, as well as the need for self-objects and empathic attunement. His approach included supportive interventions, empathy, validation, and understanding that the perceptions of others are not distortions or erroneous but that they come from an operating system empowered by a person's subjective experience or "truth." Kohut makes us aware that people with more severe personality disorders, particularly borderline personalities, are subject to fragmentation and susceptible not only to disruption in the therapeutic situation but in relationships as well.

Kohut's beliefs are often contrasted with those of Otto Kernberg. Kohut's theories invite closeness and intimacy. Kohut differs from Kernberg in that he believed in the subjective experience as "the truth," that the patient does not distort or misperceive reality. To the distraught patient who suddenly is "dumped," a Kohutian therapist with an empathic mirroring stance might say something like:

> This is not your fault. You are not a trained, highly skilled analyst that could diagnose his fragilities when you met. You had no idea that when he would go into fragmentation, that he could not sustain a close bond that an intimate relationship requires. You had no idea how he would just stomp off and leave you as he did the others. You don't have a crystal ball to predict the future. It is not your fault. Even though you saw the danger signs, you fell in love. So you must not blame yourself.

When all is said and done, whose "complaint" do we listen to? A Kernbergian complaint that is considered as having been altered or a Kohutian one that is believed to be the "real complaint?"

Defining the Ego (the Capacity to Think)

The ego is an amazing apparatus. However, often it is not user friendly and resists what it "knows." For Otto Kernberg, the ego is everything, a most powerful structure that is responsible for thinking, judgment, and reality testing. Kernberg loves reality and, in simple terms, is basically a "no-nonsense guy." The function of the ego is to see the world in reality by eliminating old memory traces left by unresolved early childhood conflicts or traumatic experiences. The ego has its own internal agent with the capacity to seek the real from the not real. It is like a computer with its own data bank and a spyware program to employ the capacity to think and learn from experience As painful as it is to face the unfaceable, the payoff is an inner aliveness. "Even though my conflicts are difficult, when I face them head on I suddenly feel alive!"

Kernberg is the master of the ego, which has great applicability to love relations and great value in addressing aggression to be channeled into creativity.
When we speak of complaints, we are also speaking about the ego's capacity
to organize the data of experience. Everyone knows what the ego is, but it is
also a slippery concept. Even well-seasoned mental health professionals lose
sight of the importance of the ego's function. It is astonishing how thinking,
judgment, perception, memory, functioning, and reality become distorted when
one's "V-spot," the crux of one's vulnerability that represents the archaic injury,
has been activated. It helps us understand why people fabricate all kinds of
preposterous complaints to the exclusion of reality and in the belief that their
complaints are legitimate. "Why did I get a ticket when I only parked in the red
zone to mail a letter?"

What makes a person who is anorexic think that he or she is fat? What
makes an abusive partner think that he or she has a right to lie and cheat?
What makes shopaholics think they can afford to buy the things they can't
afford? What makes a makes a person with no talent or a "wannabe" think
that becoming rich and famous is on the horizon? What makes a narcissist
feel entitled to anything and everything? What makes a borderline think that
acting the role of the victim will bring self-esteem? What makes the obsessive-
compulsive think that cleaning will assuage the desire for intimacy and feelings? What makes terrorists think their lies are the truth, or killers think they
can get away with murder? Of course, there are many psychological answers
and reasons, such as self-image, grandiosity, delusional thinking, and a plethora of defense mechanisms, including environmental and biological factors.
Let us not forget the observing superego, part of the psyche that is clueless
to one's own behaviors. Complaints can also cross boundaries that one would
dare not trespass. Here are some examples of a patient's sense of entitlement
overruling reason:

> A man who is a vegan and an animal activist walks into a restaurant. Sud-
> denly in walks a woman with a fur coat. To make matters worse, she orders a
> filet mignon, rare. In a flash he jumps out of his chair and bitterly scolds the
> woman for her transgression.
>   Mr. X blames his wife for withholding sex. Mrs. X blames Mr. X for with-
> holding empathy, presents, and vacations. Mr. X says he withholds these things
> because Mrs. X withholds sex. Mrs. X says she will look for another husband.
> Mr. X says, "Fine. I'm out of here! I'll go have an affair." Mrs. X says, "Fine.
> That's why I don't have sex with you, because you're always threatening me!"

We often hear couples say, "But I don't *feel* like doing this; I don't *feel* like
having sex." Or "Tell us what to do. Should we stay married or get a divorce?"
The ego has the answer. Often a feeling is often not a feeling but a defense, and
the complainer needs to be aware of this distinction. When these complainers
ask the therapist to help make important decisions, the therapist may respond

with a paraphrase of Goethe's advice, "It's difficult to know what to do, especially when so much complaining is going on."

Whose Ego?

When we refer to the ego, to which ego are we referring? A Freudian ego? A Kleinian ego? A Kernbergian ego? A Hartmann ego? A Kohutian self? Many authors offer detailed accounts of ego fragmentation or "ego weakness." Kernberg (1980) found Klein's and Fairbairn's theories of primitive defenses and object relations so confusing that it forced him to develop his own "operational definition" of ego organization. Freud was not an ego psychologist, but he was one of the first to describe the ego as a mediator between id and superego, an intrapsychic ego separate from environment. Heinz Hartmann (1958), the renowned innovator of modern psychology, was one of the first to redefine Freud's ego. Hartmann constructed an entire theory of ego psychology and adaptation, separating ego as an entity based on environment and adaptation, not on drives.

There are many conflicting theories about the ego, and what constitutes an ego is for many clinicians a very slippery concept. Kernberg and Hartmann recognize the power of the ego as it struggles against such primitive defenses as splitting, projection, and projective identification. Designed, ironically, to "protect" the patient, these defenses do so at the expense of weakening the ego's function, thereby minimizing its capacity to act as an adaptive tool.

OTTO KERNBERG

Can we diagnose a couple based on the kinds of complaints they present? Yes, I believe we can, to the extent of how much this behavior takes over the relationship. Kernberg provides us with four different types of relationships, along with some guidelines for evaluation. When couples begin conjoint treatment, they are often in phase one, "the shame/blame" stage, as outlined in Chapter Ten. In this stage, complaints are flying, and couples go to any length to find fault rather than face and take responsibility for their own shortcomings. Kernberg's relationships offer perfect venues not only for "diagnosing" the type of couple we are treating, but also for pointing out how to manage their "complaints."

In *Aggression in Personality Disorders and Perversions* (1992), Kernberg describes four kinds of love relationships: (1) normal, (2) pathological, (3) perverse, and (4) mature love. His premise is that in normal love the relationship overcomes the conflict. Internal strivings do not interfere with the capacity to maintain an intimate, loving connection. In pathological love, conflict overpowers the relationship, and internal conflicts do interfere with the capacity to maintain a loving relationship. It is love that goes in the wrong direction, implying that people who have been traumatized are like emotional cripples in relationships because they link idealization with eroticism.

Kernberg's Four Types of Love Relationships

- Normal: Relationship most important; love takes over conflict.
- Pathological: Conflict takes over the relationship; part-object functioning.
- Perverse: Search for excitement; partners reverse good and bad.
- Mature: Goal/task oriented; whole-object functioning.

In normal relationships couples can argue, banter, and fight, but because of normal/healthy object bonds nothing gets in the way of the capacity to maintain a love relationship. The couple pays attention to the needs of the other person, and when things get out of hand they are often overruled by issues that have more relevance and importance. Complaints, arguments, and outsiders do not interfere with the couple's love and the desire to maintain an intimate, loving connection.

> I know my wife gets upset when my mother comes over and starts to tell her what to do and how to run our house. But we just let her say her piece and then go on with our lives.
>   I know my wife gets upset when I watch porno sites, but she knows I love her and am more turned on to her than some artificial sex object.

In pathological love bonds, primitive defenses do get in the way of maintaining an intimate relationship. The primitive defenses operative are mainly envy, jealousy, control, domination, and victimization.

> When I first met him, I know he thought I was the sexiest, most beautiful woman he ever met. Now every time I see him look at another woman I go ballistic and become insanely jealous! (envy/jealousy dominate)
>   He'd rather look at pornography than have sex with me. When he withdraws and detaches, I get clingier and clingier. I know he is a loner and has difficulty with intimacy, but the more I cling, the more he turns to porno and perverse acts, which makes me become even more attacking.
>   He is very possessive of me. I knew all the time resentment was building up because he felt I paid more attention to my kids than to him. I love him and he loves me, but somehow the love got destroyed by his jealousy. He started to become more and more vengeful, doing cruel and sadistic things to hurt me. Where did the romance go?

A perverse relationship is dominated by excitement, of which there can never be enough. If there were to be any complaints about the relationship, it would be the desire for more excitement. In the end, one is left with an inordinate amount of shame unless he or she finds a partner who colludes with the need for constant external stimulation. What kills the perverse relationship ironically is love.

> He complains he is getting bored, and I cannot continue to feel comfortable with his three-way sexual encounters. He is insatiable, always wanting more and more! As I attack because I want more attention from him, he finds more justification for his preserve activities. In the end, he feels persecuted by the bizarre sexual fantasies and his need to find more external stimulation. With the excitement comes an inordinate amount of shame.

Mature love may be boring at times, but the couple finds deep satisfaction in maintaining a sense of peace, harmony, and intimacy, as well as the joy of knowing they both share common goals in raising a family and being good parents, good providers, and good citizens in the community. Perhaps my parents! "The most important thing is to make a living, put bread on the table and put our children through college."

JOHN BOWLBY

Bowlby is one of few theorists discussed in this book who does not have to deal with complaints. In fact, Bowlby's attachment theory, with its withdrawal and isolation, is at the opposite end of the spectrum from those who have detached from the maternal objects. A discussion of the early relationship to the mother and the separation process as they relate to intimacy would be incomplete without discussing Bowlby's (1969) work. He developed his theory of attachment from observations of severe disruptions in bonding among children. Bowlby's attachment denotes the child's tie to the mother. His work shows that a child's emotional attachment is a reflection of a child's confidence in the availability of attachment figures. A secure attachment creates a foundation for both intimacy and autonomy. When individuals have the confidence that attachment and intimacy are available, they can tolerate aloneness but feel longing and urges for the love object.

Bowlby stresses the difference between withdrawal and detachment. He sees withdrawal as healthier than detachment because when one withdraws one is still connected to the object emotionally. Children left alone for endless hours or babies crying in their cribs without anyone responding to them eventually become despondent and detach. The child's active protestation of screams, wails, and cries gradually ceases, and the child no longer "cares." Distraught women who complain about men that appeared loving and desirous at first cannot understand how all the love, good feelings, and closeness just went away. "Doesn't he even think about me? Doesn't he miss me? I can't believe

all the intimacy and experiences we had together just vanished in his mind."
To this Bowlby might respond with something like:

> The telltale signs were obvious from the beginning. At the start you com-
> plained how he hardly called you, did not returned your phone calls, did not
> invite you anywhere except at the last minute. And then you are surprised
> that he left the relationship abruptly and did not show any signs of missing
> you. From the onset, he had difficulties in bonding. For him you were only a
> momentary object that he could not bond with.

The Psychodynamics of Complaints

While writing *The Narcissistic/Borderline Couple* (2004a), I began to explore
a variety of dyadic configurations. For example, what happens when an
obsessive-compulsive hooks up with a histrionic, a passive-aggressive with a
perfectionist/caretaking personality, or a schizoid with a borderline/dependent/
histrionic? Subsequently, I went even further and described eight different kinds
of narcissists and eight different kinds of borderlines, including the "cultural
borderline" (*How to Talk to a Narcissist* and *How to Talk to a Borderline*). My
most recent work, *The Disappearing Male* (2013), was prompted by the plethora
of complaints I received from women who fall for men who appear to be madly
in love with them at first and then suddenly disappear. It provides a psychodynamic account of eight different kinds of men who vanish without warning or
explanation, leaving these women devastated and often traumatized.

Although these volumes primarily concentrated on diagnostic distinctions,
distinctive dynamics, symptomatology, and communication, I suddenly realized that these personality types were not only focused on their "complaints,"
but that their complaints all followed a similar pattern. The narcissist would
complain by withdrawing when not properly mirrored, whereas the borderline
would attack or go into revenge mode.

Having given this brief background, let me begin by briefly describing
a narcissistic/borderline relationship and its psychodynamics. I describe a
narcissistic/borderline couple as a beleaguered type of relationship between
two developmentally arrested people who consciously or unconsciously stir
up highly charged feelings of many early unresolved conflicts in the other.
Together, the partners enter into a psychological drama that I refer to as "the
dance." Interactions that are ongoing, circular, never-ending, and never reach
conflict resolution. The revelation that explains why couples stay in painful,
conflictual relationships is that each partner needs the other to play out his or
her own personal relational drama, embedded in old sentiments and archaic
injuries that get stirred up again and again (what I refer to as the "V-spot").

Just as there is a dance among the couples, there is also a dance between
their psychodynamics, between the introjective/projective process, between

guilt and shame, between envy and jealousy, between entitlement and deprivation, between grandiosity and victimization, and between dependency and omnipotence. Present are other interlocking dynamics such as abandonment anxiety, rejection, betrayal, and so forth. These dynamics can arouse feelings of unworthiness and non-existence.

There are those individuals who confuse love with pain and cannot feel a semblance of aliveness unless they are fused in a dysfunctional, destructive attachment. They repeat the same drama over and over again, without ever learning from experience. Thus, their dance becomes one of ongoing interactions between shame and guilt, envy and jealousy, control and submission, aggression and dependency, domination and victimization, and deprivation and entitlement. These dynamics keep them trapped, referred to as "traumatic bonding." Anything is better than the emptiness. "At least I feel alive! I know I exist!" For example,

> A deprived borderline wife tells her entitled, narcissistic husband that she would like to make plans to go out for her birthday. He tells her he will have to postpone her birthday celebration because an old friend is coming to visit. She attacks and accuses him of making his friend more important than she is. He tells her he has no time to listen to her nagging and her complaints and projects a feeling into his borderline wife that she is worthless and not entitled to anything, that she should not need or want anything. He complains, "All you do is nag, nag, nag." Not knowing how to legitimately express her real needs, the borderline wife continues to nag, demand, yell, and sob. This begins to make him feel guilty because she is attacking his perfectionistic self. He ends up feeling guilty and she feels ashamed. Thus, it becomes a dance between guilt and shame.

MARSHA LINEHAN

If Freud were alive today, he would be quite surprised to find that the analytic world has turned to short-term cognitive behavioral therapy, overpowering transference, oedipal conflicts, sexual impulses, and dream interpretation. Although many of Linehan's (1993a, 1993b) theories are tailored for the treatment of the borderline, I find her methodology also applicable for patients who suffer from intimacy and withdrawal issues. Her platform is also perfect for "complaints" as a two-dimensional phenomenon. Linehan's work on DBT inspired me to create the language of dialectics, which has proved invaluable in my work with borderline patients (Lachkar, 2011).

Although I see many psychological equivalents and parallels to the works of Wilfred Bion (1962, 1967, 1977) and Klein (1927, 1948, 1957, 1975, 1984), I find Linehan's concept of dialectics far more palatable. Dialectic thinking is part of a set of mindfulness skills that provides essential tools for balancing the emotional upheavals between acceptance and change and the validating and invalidating environments as important linkages to self-soothing and affect regulation.

Linehan's (1993a) techniques distinguish between the "wise mind," the "emotional mind," and the "reasonable mind." She incorporates into this methodology many variations of a state of mindlessness, disassociation, or the unmentalized experience. It is impressive how such a theory has revolutionized and taken over the treatment of the borderline personality. As innovative as it is, it is startling how closely Linehan's work on mentalization aligns itself with Bion's concept of projective identification and links on thinking, memory, and desire (Bion, 1967). This is also closely aligned to what I described in my book *The V-Spot* (2008c)—that when one hits a vulnerable chord, the V-spot explodes, and all capacity to think goes with it.

The poet Robert Frost may have stated it best in his poem "The Road Not Taken." The myriad decisions to be made in life can lead to inner conflict and turmoil. This parallels a psychoanalytic divergence. The mind splits into two "roads," with accompanying ambivalence. The language of dialectics that I abstracted from Linehan's concepts addresses the patient's ambivalence and splitting mechanisms and attempts to reconcile these oppositional dynamics.

The goal is to teach patients to differentiate emotional states so they do not relate each negative emotion they feel to every negative thing that has ever happened to them. For Bion, it is dialectic tension that occurs within the splitting mechanism. One might equate Linehan's emotional thinker to Bion's "thinker without a thought" (1967) or to a "complainer without a complaint." Linehan's "acceptance" motif is in close alignment with Kohut's empathy and mirroring of the patient's subjective experience. The idea of accepting the patient's subjective experience to be the truth is certainly compatible with her concept of the "validating environment" versus the "invalidating environment."

What follows is an example of how a DBT therapist might respond to a complaint via "acceptance" and how a Kleinian therapist might react.

Wife: I know he loves me. In fact, he is very possessive of me. But what also drives me crazy is that he likes to wear my underwear.

Husband: But that doesn't change who I am!

DBT Therapist (to wife): We have to accept your husband for who he is and not try to change him.

Kleinian Therapist (to husband): No, this is not who you are. This is a defense against abandonment and separation. You can't possess her so then you become her by wearing her underwear!

Integrating these concepts of how the cognitive and the analytic approach can "do the dance" is the recognition of the state of mindlessness known as dissociation and the unmentalized experience. Linehan says it all as she cites the example of a patient who refused to work on her workbook manual. Although Linehan "accepted" the patient's resistance, she also realized that the patient felt that if she did the work and improved, then she would no longer be in the group. To know this, Linehan must have stepped outside her DBT box to embrace Margaret Mahler's separation individuation concept, which has been around a long time (Mahler, Pine, and Bergman, 1975).

FANTASY INTERPRETATIONS: HOW EACH THEORIST MIGHT RESPOND TO COMPLAINTS

The following is a composite of how the analysts mentioned in this chapter might respond to a specific complaint from Mrs. O, who is mortified by her husband's actions. Obviously, these clinicians are not available for consultation, but hopefully you will leave room for imagination in these fantasy analyses.

Mrs. O: I know my husband loves me very much, but what drives me crazy is that he keeps looking at nude men's photos. When he does this I lose my mind. I yell, scream, and get totally out of control. I feel so betrayed as a woman.

Freud: Mrs. O, you are suffering from a case of hysteria, maybe penis envy. It is clear you are hysterical and overreacting to your husband's behavior. You have a very harsh, strict, prohibitive superego, a voice of your father in judgment of your husband. Because you get into these histrionic states, it inhibits you from standing up to your husband (unresolved oedipal strivings) and telling him how much this irritates you.

Klein: Mrs. O, apparently you don't understand the difference between the act and fantasy. Your husband is having fantasies about other men's bodies, perhaps a dissociated part of himself. You are projecting your own sexual inhibitions onto your husband because you are splitting from your own sexual needs, distorting and exaggerating your husband's actions. Your husband loves you, but you are seeing your husband as a part object and not one who is loving and kind to you. You are taking your husband's act way out of proportion and no longer see him as the good husband (splitting).

Kohut: Mrs. O, I totally empathize and understand how you must feel when you see your husband looking at men. I think you are telling us that you are not getting the mirroring and attention that you would like, a reminder of an old archaic injury when your father was giving more attention to your older brother.

Kernberg: Mrs. O, I believe Dr. Freud and Mrs. Klein are right. Because of your own sexual inhibitions and repressed thoughts, you are projecting onto your husband your own guilt. Not a good time to consider getting a divorce, for while these primitive defenses are operative you should not make major decisions (ego dysfunctionality).

Fairbairn: Yes, Mrs. O, there can always be an external husband who acts inappropriately, but there can also be an internal part of yourself that identifies with the inappropriateness—the part of you that yells, screams, gets hysterical, and momentarily loses her mind. By not getting in contact with your own impulsive acts, you are over-identifying with his behavior.

Winnicott: Your husband must feel very secure and safe with you, Mrs. O, because he is allowing himself to be his "true self," not a self that is shamed or must hide (safe holding environment). He knows he loves you and you love him. How about becoming more of the "being mommy" for him?

Bowlby: Mrs. O, perhaps this is a way of your husband detaching himself from you, even from his own body. Because his mother neglected him as a baby, now he is disconnecting from you. You must not take this personally.

Linehan: No, you cannot change him, Mrs. O. You have to accept him for who he is and get into a state of mindfulness and acceptance.

SUMMARY

We must listen with many ears to the complaints that couples bring into treatment, drawing from classical psychoanalysis, object relations, ego psychology, and attachment theory, and moving on to more contemporary platforms. Each theorist has his/her own unique way of listening and responding, just as each partner in the couple relationship has his/her own way of complaining. Analysts must devise their own ways of listening and responding along the lines of these corresponding psychodynamics.

Sometimes a complaint is just a complaint; at other times it can be so toxic that it can invade and destroy the intimate love relationship. The degree of toxicity is outlined briefly by Kernberg's four different kinds of love relationships, which I believe to be a credible diagnostic tool when evaluating a couple for conjoint treatment. Fairbairn reminds us how attachments to bad internal objects relentlessly fuel the complainer through what I refer to as their "V-spots." Although each theoretical framework embodies different approaches, they all offer the desire for healthier object relations through the search to find meaning out of the meaninglessness.

Chapter 3

≈⊂≈

It Takes One to Tango

Christopher Lasch (1979), in his groundbreaking work *The Culture of Narcissism*, touched a very sensitive social nerve. He brought to our awareness a society that has become increasingly self-centered and totally focused on self. The me-me American society is rife with excessive entitlement fantasies, with everyone seeking immediate gratification and recognition. Lasch strongly believes that such feelings of entitlement are the direct outcome of a preoccupation with wealth, fame, and materialism and are in part responsible for the decline of the family. With this booming culture of self-absorption comes a plethora of complaints when one's entitlement needs and fantasies are not in tandem with reality. "Even though I can't afford it, I must buy that new car!"

There are many disorders that exhibit excessive entitlement fantasies and are overly occupied with the self. Most commonly, though, it is the narcissist that springs to mind. Take, for example, the difference between how a narcissist and an obsessive-compulsive enact entitlement fantasies. The narcissist thinks that whatever he touches will turn to gold or thinks he is the gold, whereas the obsessive-compulsive fears that whatever he touches or touches him will be contaminated and turn toxic (see Chapter Five). The narcissist does not fear that his needs will contaminate him or anyone or anything else. In fact, the narcissist thinks that he and his needs are royalty. In contrast, the obsessive-compulsive views needs as infectious and dirty; to succumb to them is tantamount to becoming vulnerable, to be reduced to a Kafkaesque insect. Thus, although both the narcissist and the obsessive-compulsive may be accused of being selfish, there are distinct qualitative differences in the way they are selfish. "My husband the narcissist is selfish; he thinks only about himself" versus "My husband the obsessive-compulsive is selfish; he thinks only about his work."

In my book *How to Talk to a Narcissist* (Lachkar, 2008a), I describe eight different kinds of narcissists, mainly as a template for communication. In this chapter, I extend this template to address the common complaints that these entitled ones engender. Although Freud never specifically referred to "complaints," other than to describe patients suffering from symptoms such as hysteria, his discourse on aggression in *Civilization and Its Discontents* (1930) outlines how group members bond together as a solid unit to show their hatred of outsiders, who become the "scapegoat"—a target of the group's narcissism (Gay, 1988; Lachkar, 2004a, 2004b).

THE KINGDOM OF ENTITLEMENT

Today narcissism has become a household term. For example, in Woody Allen's 2006 film *Scoop,* when he is asked what religion he is, he responds that he was "Hebrew" but that he has converted to narcissism. These entitled persons wear many diagnostic faces. They live for the admiration of others. They feel they deserve special privileges and feel justified to complain about, criticize, and punish those who do not provide the expected respect, admiration, and attention that they are confident is due them.

From a broader perspective, the cardinal features of the narcissistic types described in this chapter consist mainly of a constant need for admiration and attention. They are wholeheartedly invested in their specialness and are dominated by such defenses as idealization and devaluation. The most common complaints of these entitled personages emanate from their selfishness and lack of empathy and compassion for others, along with their feelings of exaggerated accomplishments and talents. In addition, they have many unresolved preoedipal conflicts. They feel the world owes them something, and in the effort to get what they "deserve," these entitled ones may spend the rest of their lives trying to prove their sense of specialness. They find nothing particularly interesting aside from themselves and their needs. Their self-centeredness and self-love are all-consuming; there is no room for anything other than the most superficial thoughts of anyone else. Their boastful attitude and narcissistic preoccupation with self do not allow them to recognize legitimate complaints that others may have. It's all about them—all the time.

During their search for special mirroring/self-objects, narcissists can be most alluring, charming, and seductive. They are inclined to come on very strong and over-value the newly found love. However, as soon as the love object is captured and no longer performs the function of gratifying or glorifying the narcissist's magnified self, the object becomes a useless commodity and is no longer of interest. Because narcissists have the need to be perfect, one can imagine how they respond to a complaint—not as a request, a need, or someone's desire but as a direct assault on their bubble of perfection.

THE CASE OF MR. R: ROMANCING THE NARCISSIST

Mr. R, a 42-year-old well-known television director, came into treatment because his wife found out he was having affairs. They were on the brink of divorce and at the point where they had to decide either to work on their marriage or to separate. As the sessions unfolded, it became apparent that Mr. R was disengaging from his wife's requests for him to be "more romantic." Feeling she was making "unrealistic demands," he threw himself into the arms of women who were happy to be a one-night fling, with no strings attached and no expectations.

Therapist: Hi, please come in.

Mr. R: Well, nothing much has changed. I am trying to be more attentive to my wife's needs.

Therapist: Trying?

Mr. R: Yes, trying.

Therapist: Like how? Can you give me an example?

Mr. R: Well, like I try and talk to her more and find out how her day went.

Therapist: Do you carve out special time to talk?

Mr. R: No, it is just a spur-of-the-moment thing.

Therapist: In other words, you don't prepare anything, have a glass of wine together, and spend quiet or romantic time together? (therapist notices Mr. R squirming and making faces)

Mr. R: Oh, no, none of that. That is just not me.

Therapist: Maybe not. But what about your wife?

Mr. R: She loves all that stuff—flowers, diamonds, holidays. Me? I hate all that romantic trash. Holidays are just commercial things. The only ones who benefit are the jewelry stores and Hallmark Cards.

Therapist: But she likes them and enjoys tradition. You are in a relationship, and it is not all about what pleases you!

Mr. R: (pauses) This makes me think about an incident. After a one-night stand, the one my wife found out about, we went to a breakfast place. I get out of the car and start walking, then turn around and find the woman still sitting in my car. I went back to the car and asked her why she was still sitting there. She said, "I was waiting for you to open the door."

Therapist: So your wife is not the only one who would like a little chivalry.

Mr. R: I guess not, but I can't be bothered.

Therapist: Even if you hate it, your partner loves it. And you keep forgetting that you are not in this relationship alone.

Mr. R: I guess it takes two to tango, doesn't it?

Therapist: More than that. It takes sacrifice. Which means sometimes we have to give to the other to please them. So right now you are tangoing by yourself.

Mr. R: This reminds me of my mother. I once shared with her that I cheated on an exam. She was fine, acted like she understood. But the next day she blew up and was furious with me.

Therapist: Interesting that your mother couldn't contain or be sensitive to your needs. That instead of appreciating your honesty and willingness to share this with her she became very judgmental. Like you are.

Mr. R: That's what I'm doing? Judging?

Therapist: Indeed. You judge that romanticism is bad, that opening doors, buying gifts, giving flowers and birthday cards, and celebrating holidays are all stupid. Maybe you feel that when you do these things you are cheating (therapist holds her breath as she gauges his reaction to her throwing back to him his list of hates).

Mr. R: Well, I don't know how else to act. I can't change. I just can't do those things; it is not in my nature. I just know I want to be myself, and this seems phony to me because it's not the way I am.

Therapist: It is not in your wife's nature to have a husband who has affairs.

Mr. R: I know you're right, but at least with one-night stands we can just fuck and that's the end of it.

Therapist: Not really. What about the woman you forgot sitting in the car waiting for you to open the door for her.

Mr. R: (laughing) Okay I get your point.

Therapist: And I get yours as well. You feel that listening to this discussion somehow will force you to change or do something you resist. Earlier I saw you squirming and making faces at my suggestion about carving out special time with your wife.

Mr. R: Oh, you noticed that, huh?

Therapist: Of course. But what is more important than "changing" is opening up a new space in which to think about things and gain some understanding—how your resistance impacts your marriage and your relationship with your wife.

Mr. R:	Guess that's why I'm here. I don't want a divorce.
Therapist:	Meanwhile, I would like to see you again next week after our couple therapy session to continue exploring these issues.
Mr. R:	Thanks. I feel terrible that my wife caught me, and I really don't want to go on having these one-night stands.
Therapist:	Well, there does need to be some reparative work, which will require some sacrifice on your part, giving up part of your needs to take care of your wife's.
Mr. R:	Great. Barbara and I will see you next week.
Therapist:	Don't leave her in the car!
Mr. R:	(chuckles) Gotcha! Bye!

Discussion

Although Mr. R may have many traits and characteristics of a narcissistic personality, he also exhibits many borderline features. The inclination to rebel against materialism is not a typical trait for a narcissist. In contrast, narcissists often enjoy showing off their wealth, their fame, and their objects. What Mr. R shares with the narcissist brotherhood of disorders is an extraordinary sense of entitlement. In subsequent sessions, he expressed how his marriage vows were not as important as getting his sexual needs met. When asked why he devalues the marriage vows, he responded, "I have a vow to myself!" As treatment continued, Mr. R's rebellious and resentful side seemed to become more evident. At the same time, his narcissistic side was quite apparent. Everything was about him—what he needed, what he decided, along with repudiation for anything his wife desired that whiffed of romance. Narcissists, generally speaking, tend not to rebel or retaliate. They are more likely to withdraw or isolate themselves.

What both the narcissist and borderline share is fear of feeling vulnerable, giving, sharing with others, and sacrificing some of their desires to please their spouse. Such actions are seen as a threat to the grandiose or omnipotent self and result in behavior like having affairs to ward off feelings of vulnerability. On the surface, Mr. R's hate list made him sound like a man who simply doesn't like tradition, materialism, and celebrations. In actuality, these are enactments of aggression and rebellion against feelings of early deprivation and privation. "I got all the attention until my little brother was born, and suddenly I was no longer the favorite. Now I'm going to get my fair share!" The following case is an example of how the entitled ones allow others to intrude into their couple relationship by putting the needs of others before those of their partners and their family.

THE CASE OF MR. AND MRS. C

Mr. and Mrs. C have been married for eight years and have a five-year-old daughter. They both claim they want to have more intimacy and romance and to have fun together as they used to when they didn't have to deal with the stresses and strains of having a child and a mortgage. Both work full time and are always tired. They don't see how therapy can help them, nor do they see how their competitive natures get in the way of maintaining intimacy and romance.

Therapist: You've been coming here for a while now, so today I thought we would start by talking about treatment goals and what you would like to accomplish. Who would like to start?

Mrs. C: I would.

Mr. C: No, I would. You started first last time. I would like for Terry to be more of a partner to me and to appreciate the things I do.

Mrs. C: And I would like Ted to listen to me more and to make me more of a priority. He gives everyone more importance than me.

Mr. C: That's not true. When you got stuck in traffic, I went and picked up our daughter. I had to leave a very important meeting.

Mrs. C: That's not what I mean. I mean making me a priority. Like the other day we had plans and your friend called and said he was in town, and you cancelled plans with me to be with him.

Mr. C: That's an exception. Tom doesn't come in very often.

Mrs. C: If it's not Tom, it's something else. How about when the plumber was outside fixing the drain, and I had a quick question to ask you, and you couldn't stop for one minute to answer me.

Mr. C: That's because I was busy with the plumber.

Mrs. C: So the plumber couldn't wait one second while I quickly asked if you would drop off our daughter at her friend's house on your way to the poker game? See how everyone comes first—his mother, the plumber, his friends, the poker game, his iPhone?

Therapist: I am sure your husband loves you more than the plumber, but I can see how all this gets in the way of returning to the intimacy, the romance, the joy you used to have. It's not much fun when each of you is competing for attention.

Mrs. C: That's exactly it. He wants us to share everything and to have each of us do our equal part, but he doesn't share. Most of the responsibility falls on me.

Mr. C: Are you kidding me? I'm the one who keeps things going around our house.

Therapist: You want a partnership, but where is the love and caring? It seems to me that each of you is acting like it takes one to tango.

Mr. C: I don't think that's funny.

Mrs. C: I do!

Therapist: I tell you what we need to do. Let's get back to your goal to have fun. What can you do to bring back the good times you used to have?

Mrs. C: We can never have fun like that again. We used to party all night and have a blast.

Therapist: Of course not, but there is such a thing as adult fun.

Mr. C: Like what?

Therapist: Like plays, concerts, movies, dinners, planning romantic times just for the two of you, without your daughter.

Mrs. C: Oh, I would love that, but it's expensive.

Therapist: Actually, that's not true. There are many things going on in LA that are basically very inexpensive. I know you both like classical music, and every Sunday there are free concerts at the museum. There are free lectures—

Mr. C: Oh, didn't know that.

Therapist: What about having friends over to watch a rental movie with you or to play board games? Or taking long walks. Fun and romance don't have to be costly. It just takes a little planning.

Mrs. C: Okay, but who's going to plan these events?

Mr. C: Let's take turns. One week I will, the next week you will.

Mrs. C: (silent)

Therapist: Is something wrong?

Mrs. C: Look, I know he loves me, but I never feel he really cares enough about me to do something on his own to please me once in a while. Everything has to be shared. Why can't he just make the plans and allow me to feel that I am a priority to him?

Therapist: I think your wife is saying that she would like you to take charge, become the concierge, and make the plans. This could be a breakthrough and a way of getting back to the fun and romance.

Mrs. C: That would make me much happier. I would love for him for once to take charge without me having to do my fair share or have to nag him to do his.

Therapist: Right. This is not a tennis match, nor is it a political game of getting one's fair share. It is a relationship, where things are not always equal. The plumber can wait. You can let him know next time that your wife has an important question and that you'll be right with him. Yes, it will require a bit more work and time on your part to make plans, but think about the reward. Did you see how happy this would make your wife?

Mr. C: I will try to do it.

Therapist: Try?

Mr. C: Okay. I will do it!

Therapist: Great. Now we're all having fun! See you next week.

Mr. and Mrs. C: Bye!

Discussion

In this case, the therapist had to listen beyond the complaints that were voiced to get in contact with the couple's unresolved oedipal issues—namely, an ongoing rivalry. Mrs. C complained that she is not treated as a priority and everyone else comes first. Mr. C complained that his wife doesn't do her share in the relationship. As they banter back and forth, Mrs. C suddenly gets a rush of adrenalin and her heart starts to race, which I learn happens to her every so often. This is when I stopped listening to the complaints and paid attention to her racing heart, which I interpreted might have some relation to Mr. C's treatment of her, as well as to early childhood abandonment issues. She quickly retorted that I was wrong, that it had nothing to do with being abandoned but was the opposite. As the youngest of four children, she was treated as the favorite. I then realized that when Mrs. C's "rivals" seemed to come first in her husband's eyes, this constituted a narcissistic injury for Mrs. C and stirred up her V-spot. Realizing this was an unmentalized experience, I had to listen to her inner voice to open up a space for meeting and matching the goals they both desired. The simplest truth is sometimes the hardest to find. He will make the reservations!!

NARCISSISTS AND COMPLAINTS

The following brief descriptions reveal how each type of narcissist acts out entitlement fantasies and offer guidelines about the types of complaints that each type engenders. The entitled narcissists complain that they are not getting enough attention or admiration and that their talents haven't earned them enough success, fame, or money. One can imagine how this impacts the persons that live with them. "He shows no concern or interest in anything to do with my life. He doesn't even show up at his kid's graduation or open houses at school. It is as though no one else exists but him."

The Healthy Narcissist

In general, these entitled types are assertive, goal oriented, and overly confident. They are driven, have passion, and do not allow others to divert them. However, unlike the others narcissistic types listed in this section, they can also be considerate of the needs and concerns of others. Although they, too, are preoccupied with self and have a strong desire for achievement, they do not allow primitive defenses to destroy their capacity to maintain a loving, intimate bond.

The Pathological Narcissist

Unlike the healthy narcissist, the pathological narcissist allows primitive defenses (control, domination, envy, victimization, and oedipal rivalry) to impede and overpower the capacity to maintain the love bond. They are overly preoccupied with self; obsessed with power, fame, and achievement; and will do anything to achieve their goals, even if it is at the expense of others. They have an exaggerated sense of self, as well as a delusional sense of entitlement; they also exhibit such defense mechanisms as guilt, idealization, and grandiosity. When their grandiose sense of self is threatened or challenged, they withdraw or isolate themselves from the object. In love relations, they may begin with the desire to have a loving relationship, but eventually primitive defenses get in the way and destroy the capacity for intimacy because of issues like money, envy, oedipal rivals, and obsession with fame. Their endless search for perfection and specialness gets in the way of maintaining a loving and intimate bond with their partners.

Associated Complaints

- He used to tell me I was sexy and beautiful; now he is critical and picks on everything I do.
- He is always flirting with other women. When I confront him, he acts as though I am crazy and that I don't trust him.
- Money means more to him than caring about the needs of his wife and children.
- His friends, his family, his work, and even our dog are more important to him than our relationship.
- He always has to be right. He doesn't care about the truth or reality.
- Everything she does has to be perfect. She cannot tolerate any criticism or challenge.
- He wants everyone to stroke his ego and tell him he is the best. He can't stand to have any competition.
- He can criticize and judge others, but he can't stand even the slightest bit of criticism directed at himself.
- She knows we're on a tight budget, and yet she continues to shop for new clothes and things for the house. She has no regard for how much she spends, and it's putting us in debt.
- All she does is nag and complain. Whatever I give her or do for her is never enough.

- I got promoted at my job, but he would not celebrate with me because he did not get a promotion and was envious of mine.
- She always sabotages our good times. As soon as we get intimate, she complains about how she has a headache or a backache. There is always something.

The Malignant Narcissist

The influences and destructive nature of the malignant narcissist far exceed the bounds of most of the patients we see in our consultation rooms. They are the wife beaters, child abusers, molesters, murderers, stalkers, and the terrorists. They are ruthless, fearless, and aggressive and believe they are entitled to prey on innocent victims. They tend to be cruel, malicious, and sadistic, and their feelings of entitlement extend to the desire to have others reinforce their actions and beliefs. Sadism, paranoia, hatred, envy, and uncontrollable aggression are basic characteristics. Often they will do anything to get revenge or destroy those who betrayed or abused them in early childhood. Who knows what goes on the minds of someone like Ariel Castro, who kidnapped, abused, and kept three young girls captive for over ten years? In analytic terms, this may be interpreted as a form of projective identification. "Now I am doing to you what was done to me. Now you know what it feels like!"

Malignant narcissists are plotters and, under the guise of "a good cause," will act out their most cruel and sadistic impulses. They will get along fine with others until there is a disagreement, and then they will protest, punish, and try to destroy the object at any cost. The difference between someone like a sociopathic narcissist and a malignant narcissist is that the malignant narcissist answers to a higher power and is concerned about what others think, whereas the sociopath or antisocial could not care less. At the domestic level, they will form a group of supporters or forge collusive bonds to enforce their sadism (e.g., "The guys in the poker club all know what a bitch she is!") At the global level, the support team may be a cult or a group programmed to idealize the leader and his cause—someone like Saddam Hussein or Slobodan Milosevic, the Serbian war criminal who under the guise of the "good cause" killed thousands of Albanians in order to "save" his people (Lachkar, 1992, 1993a, 1998a, 1998b, 2004a, 2008a, 2008c, 2013).

Associated Complaints

- When he is angry with me, he takes it out on our son and punishes him without cause. He won't talk to us. Then he locks up the dog and takes the key.
- I tried to get my ex-husband to agree to allow our son to go out of the country to visit my parents, but he refused as revenge and punishment. He tells his buddies I am an unfit mother and can't be trusted.

- I work hard all day, come home exhausted, feed and attend to the baby. Yet, if I don't massage him or give him a blow job, he beats me.
- She gets her family to turn against me, and no matter how bad, conniving, and scheming she is, they always believe her.
- My ex-husband kidnapped our son, told everyone what a terrible mother I am. When I called the police, I got scared he would beat me.
- My ex-wife convinced the court that I was a child molester, to the point where my own daughter wanted nothing to do with me.
- He is so cruel and has no consideration for how I feel. The only time he shows remorse is when I am crying and black and blue.
- I caught him in bed with another woman and started divorce proceedings. He crippled me financially and convinced all the people in the court system that I was a crazy, overreacting, histrionic bitch.
- I am an A student and know the professor is giving me failing grades because I don't agree with her political views.
- My mother is an invalid, and my ex-husband will not allow my 17-year-old daughter to drive so she can help her grandmother. He does this to hurt me.

The Antisocial Narcissist

Of the narcissists listed here, the antisocial is one of the most difficult to treat. These entitled complainers are devoid of any sense of morality. They typically present more serious pathologies and are dominated by a lack of superego functioning and a heightened lack of guilt and remorse. Their sense of entitlement is so excessive that it overrides any capacity for self-reflection. They steal, lie, cajole, get caught, and even confess their crimes with no context of guilt, remorse, or concern. Their omnipotent entitlement fantasies delude them into thinking they can get away with anything.

Associated Complaints
- He took all the money out of our bank account and gambled it away. Even when he got caught, he never showed the least bit of remorse.
- My husband was arrested for drug peddling and sentenced to jail. He felt terrible about going to jail but not about the crime he committed.
- I really enjoyed the lavish lifestyle we had, and I never asked where the money was coming from. I discovered he was swindling money from elderly people, bankrupting them. When he got caught, he was remorseful only about having to go to jail. He didn't give a damn about the suffering he had caused his victims.
- My girlfriend was caught shoplifting. She justified stealing a $5,000 necklace by saying how deprived she was in childhood and felt that she was entitled to have nice things. There was no remorse, guilt, or sadness.

- I see right through her. She knows how to manipulate and fool people to get what she wants, and she doesn't care how dishonest and ruthless she has to be to get her way.

The Depressive Narcissist

Unlike the antisocial narcissist, the depressive narcissist is plagued by guilt and dominated by a harsh, punitive superego, as well as self-hatred. They are extreme perfectionists, and when life does not go their way, they blame themselves, a symptom of their self-hatred. They have a sadistic superego that runs amok and is self-denigrating and self-castigating. However, they are highly reliable, dependable, serious, and concerned about work, although they tend to judge themselves as harshly as they do others. They are often totally withdrawn and isolated from others. A depressed narcissist's grandiose self turns hatred inward to such an extent that it infects and invades all those around her. "I am no longer the beauty I used to be, and I cannot tolerate the thought of anyone seeing me."

When asked, the entitled depressive will say his girlfriend broke up with him because she got tired of his complaints. The depressive lacks awareness not only of how complaints can be draining on the relationship, but how they can destroy the love object. These types of complainers are always the victim and coerce others to show pity and sorrow. Typically, the complaints revolve around someone who is always whining, never happy, and never showing any signs of joy. Although it is imperative to keep in mind the need for a psychopharmacological workup for all disorders, it is particularly important for mood regulation of someone like a depressive.

Associated Complaints

- However much I reassure you, you are always depressed and unhappy.
- You feel the world is a terrible place, that it is going downhill, and you want me to go downhill with it and you.
- You always want reassurance. Yes, I do love and care about you, and, no, I don't have anyone else. But I wish you could find some joy in life.
- You know I am depressed. Why don't you care about my feelings?
- Why do you prefer to go out with your friends than with me? Don't you know I need you?
- You always see the world as a dismal place.

The Passive-Aggressive Narcissist

The passive-aggressive narcissist is childlike, is irresponsible, and has excessive dependency needs. They expect others to take over their responsibilities while they sleep, watch television, tweet, practice the guitar, play computer games, or feign job hunting. Unlike the other types of narcissists, they are not interested in fame, success, money, or power. They project their helpless states onto others by unconsciously working them up into a frenzy. Their passivity evokes rage in others while they are "innocently" busy doing their thing. "It wasn't my fault. I didn't know the store closed so early." They often hook up with caretaker-type partners whom they coerce into a parent/child relationship. "You are the mommy and I am the baby husband. I went to make a reservation, but lost the phone number." "I meant to take our son to his soccer game but forgot the location."

Associated Complaints

- He gets me so angry I could scream.
- I don't know why I get so angry with her. It is not my nature to feel so enraged, but nothing is ever her fault.
- I could kill him. He did it again. He forgot to get the tickets. He said he didn't have a credit card with him.
- He acts so infantile. When will he ever grow up? Meanwhile I have to do all the work.

The Obsessive-Compulsive Narcissist

Unlike the other narcissists who have excessive dependency needs (the pathological and the passive-aggressive), the obsessive-compulsive operates at the extreme end of the spectrum. They are obsessed with trying to avoid their "needy" selves, deluding themselves into thinking that their needs are dirty, messy, and toxic. To protect themselves, they will spend their days cleaning, filing, putting things in order, washing, and avoiding anything that hints of emotionality. Their repetitive acts, such as constantly washing their hands or checking lights and door locks, act as a shield against external contamination, as does their attachment to objects. Ironically, they often hook up with histrionic women, who are their complete opposites.

Associated Complaints

- She never says she loves me.
- When we make love, it is like making love to a tool.
- If he does say anything positive, it sounds robotic, as though he is not speaking from his heart.
- We are always late because by the time he's finished going back into the house to check and recheck the doors, the locks, the gas, and the windows, the event has already started.
- I can never talk to her about how I feel. When I do, she says, "Let's not start that now."

The Overly Entitled Artist

In many of my previous publications, I have discussed "the narcissist the artist," a category I created because very little had been written about the artistic psyche in the psychoanalytic literature (Lachkar, 2008a, 2008c, 2009, 2011, 2013). I also expanded the category of the narcissist the artist to make a distinction between the healthy artist, the pathological artist, the malignant artist, the wannabe artist, and the starving artist.

Many therapists do not understand that artists require a certain amount of narcissism to pursue their artistic endeavors. To stifle narcissism or severely wound the grandiose self can be detrimental to the artist. Many artists are accused of being too narcissistic, too entitled. However, are they? I have come to understand that within the performing arts, narcissism takes on a different connotation. Although clinical narcissism connotes pathology, there are also healthy aspects of narcissistic entitlement that one might call "aesthetic survival." Healthy narcissism allows room for grandiosity, pomposity, self-involvement, and an obsessive investment in perfectionism; yet there is realization of the "need" for the object. There is a sense that the artist requires some transitional space to experience his art.

Associated Complaints

- She is either always practicing, going to auditions, or performing and has no time for me.
- His writing is more important to him than I am.
- When she does not perform her best, she sulks and I get the sharp end of the stick.
- He lacks empathy and consideration for the needs of our family because he is totally absorbed with his art.
- He expects me to be the sole provider while he pursues his art. I'm the one who has to work full time to make the money to support our family. I also have to take care of the house and kids because he can't be bothered.
- It is impossible to live with her. She dresses weird, acts weird, and only talks about her career. When other people ask how she is, I have to hold my breath because I know she will only talk about herself. Socially, I feel humiliated and embarrassed. She is so transparent. Everyone except herself sees right through her.

TREATING THE ARTIST

There are extremely talented artists, and there are artists with much less talent. There are wannabe artists, with or without talent, who lack the drive and motivation to pursue and realize their artistic aims. Sometimes the most talented artists fail to realize their potential and never achieve recognition, whereas the so-so talents rise to the top because they work hard and, maybe more to the point, persevere and learn through their failures.

Who are we as therapists to decide who is a "real" artist and who is not? I may be able to tell if a singer is out of tune or if a musician is lacking in skill or technique, but who am I to judge who deserves to make it as an artist? If such well-known composers as John Adams or Philip Glass were my patients and played their electronic, dissonant-sounding scores and I were to cast judgment, they never would have reached the heights of the fame and success they enjoy today. We can only listen to our patients' complaints and encourage them to pursue the activities in which they long to excel. For those of us who live and practice in proximity to Hollywood, the hub of the entertainment world, it is not unusual to have in our clinical practice many artists, performers, actors, musicians, composers, and writers. Although the focus of this section is primarily on these artists, the material it contains has applicability to other professions as well, such as sports, law, medicine, education, science, and so forth. Many of these occupations encourage a sense of entitlement—and perhaps more than a soupçon of narcissistic showmanship.

The creative process, according to Freud (1908/1953), is an alternative to neurosis; it is a defense mechanism protecting against neurosis, a form of play away from momentary reality, a socially acceptable source of entertainment and pleasure. Freud also believed that the best way to unleash untamed aggression is to channel it into creative practice, that the artist has the ability to turn fantasies into artistic creations instead of into symptoms. Melanie Klein (1957) in *Envy and Gratitude* noted how envy can destroy the creative process. When such primitive defenses as envy, splitting, and projective identification are operative, the capacity for creativity becomes severely impaired. Kernberg (1976) discussed a form of creativity as a manic defense, a process whereby one rebels against a negative, resistant parent and becomes an artist out of spite. McDougall (1995) considered that no matter how strange, perverse, or even psychotic the process may be, as long as it fosters creativity it is healthy. Winnicott (1965) enhanced our understanding of creativity as a transitional space, an expression of the artist's soul at play and engaged in fantasy. Wolfgang Amadeus Mozart, more than anyone, knew the art of play. He was a prankster who could be whimsical and even outrageous.

Once an Artist . . . Always an Artist

One of my colleagues was treating a group of former artist retirees in group therapy and mentioned how sad and forlorn many of them felt because they were no longer who they "used to be." "I was a professional opera singer." "I was a concert pianist." "I was a costume designer for films." To my astonishment, I burst out, "Why do you say was? They're still those things; they're still artists! One must never lose one's identity, even with age." The artistic soul lives on beyond performance, as magnificently illustrated in the film *Quartet*, about a group of artists living in a retirement home reliving their memories as painters and musicians.

To inject a personal note, as a classically trained ballet dancer, I have experienced the artistic world my entire life and have treated many patients in the entertainment industry. I developed the category of the narcissist the artist to help therapists deal with the special needs and special treatment considerations that the artistic psyche requires. I may no longer perform, but I still take ballet lessons and still regard myself as an artist. When I walk down the street, I replay again and again in my head the familiar music and choreography. I transplanted this to the dance of the couple to explain why partners stay in painful, conflictual relationships. I remember going to see my analyst, sobbing nonstop. When asked what was the matter, I responded that I had had the worst ballet class and couldn't do anything right. His response was, "Well it really doesn't matter; you are not going to dance professionally." It was at this moment that I grasped the need for the therapist to understand the mind of the artist. What he could have addressed was my need for perfectionism: "I think you are being very hard on yourself. Some days are not great. Things aren't always perfect."

I recall studying with a great master teacher, Carmelita Maracci, who was so temperamental that if the pianist missed a trill or embellishment in a Bach piece, she would bang her cane on the floor and give out a yell. She would stomp out of the room when someone danced with no feeling or expression, saying, "You are nothing more than a robot I can't bear to look at you!" She would tell me to "bend your knees; you look like a piece of wood. Besides, I think you have gained weight." On the other hand, when she would explain how to do an arabesque, we all would forgive her moody outbursts. "You must think of your fingertips as branches; keep your fingers alive, moving through them, reaching as though longing for a lost lover." On one occasion, I came to class saying, "I am sorry, Carmelita, I can't dance today, I feel too depressed." To this she snapped back, "Oh, my dear, this is exactly the time you should dance and put your feelings into your dancing."

The narcissist the artist lives and breathes in a separate class from the other narcissistic types. Within this classification, I make the distinction between the healthy artist, the pathological artist, and the malignant artist.

The Healthy Artist

The healthy artist displays a certain amount of grandiosity, pomposity, self-involvement, self-absorption, and an obsessive investment in perfectionism. However, this preoccupation with self does not interfere with the creative process or ability to have healthy object relations ("aesthetic survival"). The healthy artist is able to take criticism and does not feel attacked or belittled but is able to apply the critique to their art form. A good example of the healthy artist is the renowned Argentinian conductor Gustavo Dudamel, who left his orchestra to ensure that he would be present for the birth of his first child.

The Wannabe/Blocked Artist: The Case of Mr. M

Therapist: Welcome: So what brings you here?

Mr. M: I know I am talented and a better musician than those you see performing today, but I am terrified to play in front of an audience.

Therapist: Then why not start small? Play at smaller venues like clubs?

Mr. M: What do you mean small? (therapist already getting the feeling that the word "small" was injurious to his nascent self)

Therapist: You can play in people's houses or in churches or synagogues, retirement homes.

Mr. M: No! I wouldn't waste my time. A fine musician like me should play in front of larger audiences.

Therapist: Why not think of it as an experience?

Mr. M: No way would I waste my time. I am either going to make it big or not at all.

Therapist: What a shame to waste your talent like that. An artist needs a place to practice and experience his work. Just think of Yitzhak Perlman, who played Klezmer music with people on the street in the Bronx, and he had never played that kind of music before.

Mr. M: Please don't compare me to others. I am me.

Therapist: I wasn't comparing you. I was giving you an example of how even great artists try new things and put their egos aside.

Mr. M: Well, that's not me. Besides, you are not a musician, and you don't have a clue.

Therapist: (frustrated) So why come here for help? Why not get treatment from another musician, someone who will understand you better?

Mr. M: Because I know you. Being an artist yourself, you would understand me better than other therapists.

Therapist: I do understand you and what you are going through. It is difficult for an artist with talent to undermine his principles, but there is something else holding you back.

Mr. M: Like?

Therapist: It is not your talent that holds you back. Rather, it is your grandiose, omnipotent self that feels you are overly entitled, that you're too good to go out and experience the world. But this is where you and I differ. I never felt that I had to be the best. Instead, I would perform for the love of dance. This is the place in which the artist must exist—the desire to express himself or herself, not just the desire to knock people's socks off.

Mr. M: My mother always made me feel I had to be the best, that unless I made it to the top I was a nothing.

Therapist: So glad you are sharing this. What a tragedy to have a talented and creative son and to make him believe that.

Mr. M: Maybe it's too late for me to start small. I am already 40 years old.

Therapist: The music world doesn't have an age. Never too late. See you next week.

Mr. M: Okay. Bye.

The Pathological Artist versus the Malignant Artist

The pathological artist functions at the extreme end of pathological narcissism and is dominated by such defenses as envy, control, competition, and domination—where winning becomes more pervasive than the joy of the creative process. They are driven by excessive entitlement fantasies and an overvalued sense of self, and they seek fame, no matter the cost or destruction to others. Unlike the healthy artist, the creative process of the pathological artist does interfere with the capacity to maintain healthy object relations. "Nothing else matters but me and my trombone."

Although the pathological artist and the malignant artist are equally competitive, envious, and self-absorbed and show little or no respect for the needs or feelings of others, the former is not intentionally cruel and sadistic. Such supercelebs as Lindsay Lohan and Lady Gaga, although transparently narcissistic and maybe viewed as "over the top," are not intentionally cruel. Other artistic types who lean more toward the malignant side of narcissistic entitlement are those like Charlie Sheen or flamboyant pianist Liberace, whose entitlement fantasies stretched way beyond the acceptable, as depicted in the HBO television film *Behind the Candelabra* (2013). Liberace cheated, lied, cajoled, and manipulated for his own self-serving purposes to feed a starved and desolate internal world, forming parasitic bonds as he whined and complained about his problems while moving his way through his object relational world from one "boy toy" to another.

I recall another example of a malignant artist, a ballet master who neglected, ignored, and criticized a gifted young dancer. Finally, the dancer's mother came to the studio to investigate why her daughter was not getting any recognition or any casting roles. He explained to the mother that her daughter had been taking classes at one of the rival studios and that he would not stand for that. Other examples abound in the ballet world, which is known to be a culture of cruelty, competition, and envy. One ballet master in a major ballet company tortured a dancer into losing weight to the extent that she became extremely anorexic and died. The artistic director and star dancer of the Bolshoi Ballet was attacked with acid outside his home in Moscow and suffered severe burns and damage to his eyes. Colleagues say it was because another dancer targeted him for professional unfairness.

The Myth of the Starving Artist

In my clinical practice, I have seen many couples where the wife complains that she's tired of supporting her artist husband. "He feels that the world should take care of him simply because he is an artist. I never know how to respond to his complaints that I am not being supportive of his career when I can hardly support myself. He tells me throughout history artists have been supported by governments, royalty, and wealthy patrons."

Many partners of artists get coerced into this myth when, in fact, the reality is different. Many artists have found jobs that allowed them to support themselves while indulging their artistry, such as teaching music, composition, and painting. Russian composer Alexander Borodin worked as a chemist. Even Mozart tried to find a job but had difficulty getting someone to hire him. So he went to Vienna and tried to make a living as a freelance musician. After struggling for many years, he finally performed at the Emperor's court, getting very little money until he started writing music for the dances at the court. The money wasn't much, and it wasn't like writing the symphonies, concertos, or operas that he was compelled to compose. He was technically under-employed, but he definitely needed steady work to support himself and his family. Author Anaïs Nin supplemented her income by writing pornography to survive difficult times. Even composers such as Bach and Vivaldi had had numerous other duties and made extra money on the side by publishing their music and giving music lessons.

> I actually confronted him about his bullshit—that great artists and composers throughout history were supported by royalty and did not have to work. It is a travesty that he expects me to take care of the house, the kids, and support him financially while he is free to pursue his art. I told him about how he had it so good. Anyway, I no longer will fall into the trap that I have to be his sole support because as an "artiste" he shouldn't have to worry about mundane things such as earning a living. Either he gets real, or I'm ready to pack it in.

SUMMARY

The types of narcissists delineated in this chapter provide guidelines for the therapist rather than hard-and-fast diagnostic/therapeutic categorizations. The delineations of the various types of narcissists do not remain constant; rather, they flow back and forth, one category spilling into the other. These qualitative distinctions serve to illustrate how each type elicits different kinds of complaints from their partners. Understanding these distinctions helps prepare the therapist to deal with the narcissistic variances outlined in this chapter.

As for the narcissist the artist, this entitled type exists in a different world with its own unique culture, and it is important for therapists to be careful as they deal with the problems of the couple not to destroy the creative process, no matter how bizarre it may appear. However, although therapists should overlook the eccentricities that allow the artistic talent to flourish, therapists also must guide artists into the realm of reality when they have overstepped the bounds of eccentricity and are endangering the loving and intimate bonds they have with their partners and their families.

Chapter 4

≫⪥

Promises, Promises

In *How to Talk to A Borderline* (Lachkar, 2011), I welcomed the reader to "Borderland," a world that knows no bounds and breeds a most complex and unique group of individuals. These are "the abandoned ones." Borderlines suffer from severe abandonment anxiety because they were emotionally abandoned in early life by parents who were absent, alcoholic, abusive, or physically or emotionally unavailable. They frequently perpetuate the cycle by staying in abusive, addictive, or obsessive relationships, enacting the role of the victim (bonding through pain that is either self-inflicted or other inflicted). They are the victims, the scapegoats. When betrayed, they will spend the rest of their lives getting back at the betrayer, even at the expense of self; they will do what it takes, sacrificing themselves and their families.

Although narcissists are always busy trying to prove a special sense of existence, borderlines are trying to prove that they exist as an entity in itself, sometimes destroying themselves or others in the process. "As bad as the pain and abuse is in my relationship at least I feel a semblance of aliveness" (Lachkar, 1992, 2008c, 2013). Their internal conflicts center primarily around shame, bonding, and attachment. Borderlines are often "as if" personalities, existing through an exquisitely formed false self. Their inability to deal with loss or face any internal deficits and their tendency to blame/shame keep them in an endless state of impoverishment. In an attempt to defend themselves against shame, they turn to substance abuse, addictive relationships, promiscuity, deviant and compulsive behaviors, addictions, suicide ideation, victimization, and sacrificial objects. These individuals are what I have described as follows: the Don Juan, the femme fatale, the abandoner-complainer, the promiser, the victim, the abuser, the addict, the insatiable one, and the saboteur.

Unlike the narcissist, the borderline is not a household term, but we intuitively know a borderline when in the presence of one, either by their over-zealousness to please, their dress, body language, eye contact, and so forth. They could not care less about fame, success, how they look, or how they dress. In fact, many are non-conformists and rebel against materialism and traditional societal values and often are guided by their own rules and standards. "Why should I dress up when I go to the symphony when I can be comfortable?" However, they require unconditional love. I am reminded of a borderline patient who refused to bathe and brush her teeth on a regular basis. When confronted by her partner, she responded, "Well it's just too bad; you'll just have to accept me for who I am!" Another borderline woman related, "I know I am 50 pounds overweight and he is no longer attracted to me, but that is just too bad. It is his problem not mine and if he loves me he will not try to change me."

We can almost say the emotionally anemic borderline is a reverse narcissist. Any hint of abandonment or betrayal can trigger an intense outburst of rage as their V-spot is exposed. Borderlines exhibit poor impulse control and lack a self-regulatory mechanism; thus, their feelings are often disproportionate to the reality of their environment. According to Marsha Linehan (1993a), they are tantamount to third-degree burn center patients, who are in agony at the slightest provocation—or what I refer to as "thin-skin" patients.

> Mrs. U came into session looking unkempt, as though she just rolled out of bed. She was wearing a puke-green tee shirt, a plaid red-and-blue shirt over it, un-ironed khaki pants, Earth shoes, and a carrying a large peasant-type tote bag. She said she was going on an interview for an assistant executive position at a corporation. The next thing I knew, the following words came tumbling out of my mouth: "You're going dressed like that!" To this she responded, "Who are you to judge and tell me what to wear? What do you want me to do, waste my money and time shopping so I can dress like you? You and they need to accept me for who and what I am! Looks aren't important."

Although Freud (1923) never referred to the term borderline, he did take note early on of the particular segment of patients who were self-destructive and formed a negative therapeutic alliance, would become deviant, and respond adversely to any praise or appreciation. In modern-day terms they are known as co-dependents, individuals who require excessive reassurance, are easily hurt by criticism or disapproval, and exist solely through the existence of the other. They feel uncomfortable and helpless, have a strong fear of rejection, and are devastated when a relationship ends. Their frantic efforts to avoid abandonment may include impulsive actions such as self-mutilating or suicidal behaviors.

In order to conduct a systematic study of complaints that aggregate around those exhibiting borderline tendencies, I took the liberty of expanding this syndrome to other personalities. The borderline condition is often co-diagnosed with other disorders that include major depressive, bipolar, and addictive characteristics and share the dynamic mood swings, bouts of depression, and lack of impulse control that are part of the borderline personality. The difference is that people with bipolar disorder can function relatively normally between episodes of depression (Lachkar, 2013), as opposed to other disorders that exhibit more consistency in their aberrant behaviors.

The psychodynamics of the borderline also cross over to other disorders. Their variances have significance regarding the kinds of complaints they arouse in their intimate partners and others who interact with them. For example, the narcissist abandons himself, deluding himself with grandiose schemes that relate non-realistically to his prowess or the importance of his nascent self; whereas the borderline will devalue and view himself as non-deserving and unworthy. The obsessive-compulsive, on the other hand, will unwittingly abandon feelings by replacing them with objects, time, and money that take on too much importance; whereas the passive-aggressive abandons responsibility as he forms a parasitic dependency bond with others that he needs to take care of him. The antisocial has abandoned a conscious moral guide, the superego, to help him stay on the moral path (or perhaps it is more accurate to say that he never had a functioning moral compass in the first place), and the slightest hint of real or imagined abandonment can trigger a most intense reaction.

THE KINGDOM OF MARTYRDOM

Typically, the abandoned, "orphaned" borderline babies grow into co-dependent adults who exist vicariously through their partners. In *The Narcissistic/Borderline Couple* (1992), I described how the borderline frequently hooks up with a narcissist and how the borderline's fabricated false self can for a short while play act at being the "perfect" mirroring object for the narcissist. "I will do anything, be anything you want me to be. Just don't leave me!" The following example illustrates this kind of drama.

> Abraham Lincoln's wife Mary was a good example of someone who used excessive shopping as a defense or replacement for her absent, neglectful husband (Berry, 2007). Historians agree that Mary and Abraham had a troubled and stormy marriage. Mary was considered self-centered and known to have a violent temper. She also exhibited eccentric behavior, had disturbing mood swings, and suffered from depression and exhaustion. Furthermore, she suffered from severe migraine headaches and had an irrational fear of dogs and storms. As the years passed, Abe grew more distant and withdrawn from Mary. She complained constantly that Abe was away for long periods and would perceive his travels as abandonment. As a defense, she compensated by engaging in uncontrollable shopping

sprees. The more she complained and the sicker she got, the more she shopped. It appeared that her only relief was to shop and spend way above their means. At one time she bought 300 pairs of gloves. Her abandonment issues got so out of control that on one occasion Lincoln actually had to send her back home.

Abe and Mary were two very different personalities. Abe was calm, quiet, and reserved while Mary yelled, screamed, wailed, and as a last resort would throw things, which resulted in Abe removing himself both emotionally and physically. Mary grew up in luxury while Abe was raised in poverty and hardship. Their relationship became even more burdened with the loss of their son Willy. The ongoing drama in their marriage was not only a product of Mary's inability to contain her role as wife and mother but of Mary and Abe's inability to find a way to relate to each other's personality and dynamics, which was further exacerbated by environmental and societal elements. They were reminiscent of a narcissistic/borderline couple. The more she would scream, yell, and complain in her histrionic state, the more he would withdraw.

THE CASE OF MR. AND MRS. K

Therapist: Hi! So! What brings you here?

Mrs. K: I am so angry and frustrated.

Therapist: Oh!

Mrs. K: I can't take it anymore. He is always late, forgetful, and comes with a bunch of excuses. Meanwhile, our bills aren't paid, and he still doesn't have a job.

Therapist: Like, for example?

Mrs. K: Last week he was supposed to meet me at a property that we were showing to clients, and he forgot the key!

Mr. K: I did not forget the key. You told me you were going to bring it.

Mrs. K: I did not. It was your responsibility, and your fault that the clients couldn't get into the house.

Mr. K: You are always blaming and picking on me.

Mrs. K: Of course I blame and pick on you. Why shouldn't I? You always pick up the kids late and forget to stop for food at the grocery store. So when I come home there is nothing to eat. When I ask you where you want to go, what you want to eat, or what movie you want to see, I always get the same response, "Whatever" or "I don't know."

Mr. K: See what I mean, how she blames and picks on me for everything? The reason I came late to pick up the kids was because I thought they had soccer practice.

Therapist: This is not about finding fault and blaming the other. This behavior becomes like a dance that goes round and round and never reaches any conflict resolution.

Mrs. K:	Then what do you suggest?
Therapist:	I suggest that we look at the couple dynamics. Mrs. K, you are not talking about a grown man, but a little-boy husband who sets you up to play the good mommy role. And you, Mr. K, are behaving in a way that is calculated to make your wife angry and force her to express the anger that you never learned how to express. It reminds me of what you said about your mother, how she never allowed you to express your emotions.
Mr. K:	What the hell are you talking about? Calling me a kid or a baby husband! What the fuck gives you the right? (Mr. K goes on a rampage. Mrs. K and the therapist remain silent until he finishes.)
Therapist:	I think this is wonderful!
Mrs. K:	Wonderful! What do you mean "wonderful?" The guy has lost his mind!
Therapist:	This is the only time in treatment when I actually encourage this kind of aggression. How great that the anger comes out directly rather than in an insidious or subversive way, by forgetting, feigning weakness, making excuses, etcetera.
Mrs. K:	I never would have thought about it in that way before—encouraging his rage.
Mr. K:	No one in my family ever allowed me to get angry or to express what I was feeling. I always had to be the good, obedient, quiet little boy.
Therapist:	I really don't like you swearing at me or your wife, but at this point it is preferable to expressing your rage silently and stirring up rage in your partner or me. I know this is not easy, but while you are here you have an opportunity to express yourself directly. This is the healthy part of you speaking, not the part with the pent-up rage against your mother.
Mr. K:	So you won't get mad at me if I tell you how I feel?
Therapist:	Of course not. We are just beginning to open up a new space, and it will take time for you to feel comfortable in it. You both did very well. See you next week.
Mr. K:	Can I pay you next week? I forgot my checkbook.
Therapist:	(with an amused smile) Yes, of course. See you both then.

Discussion

This case is a good example of how patients move through various stages of treatment (this will be discussed in more detail in Chapter Ten). Mr. and Mrs. K are clearly in the first phase of treatment (the paranoid-schizoid position). In this phase, it is important for the therapist to have empathic attunement with both partners (listening, authority, and timing), yet Mr. K, who is inclined toward borderline pathology, invites the therapist to be more confrontational. She intuitively knew what would incur his wrath. At the end of the session, when Mr. K said he forgot the check, the therapist made the judgment call to let it pass and not make an issue, even though she could easily have said, "Now you are forgetful with me!" Although it would have marked the beginning of opening up to the couple transference, the timing was not good and could have interfered with the main focus of the session—the insidious way he projected his rage. The therapist purposely held back getting into the couple transference and chose to wait until the couple moved further along. The therapist also chose not to push the boundaries too early—for example, "If your husband forgets to pay the bill, then the bills don't get paid." Or "If your husband is late to the theater, then go without him." To do so in the very early stage of treatment would have been precipitous. However, eventually the therapeutic challenge is to relieve the woman of her caretaking role. It is also noteworthy that the therapist purposely referred to the husband as Mr. K rather than by his first name to remind him of his adult/male status.

THE CASE OF MR. AND MRS. B

Therapist: Greetings! What brings you here?

Mr. B: Well, doctor, we have a very serious problem. My wife was raped and abused by her father starting when she was ten years old. When she refused to conform, he would beat her badly.

Therapist: (listening attentively, with deep compassion, already getting a sense their issues center around intimacy)

Mr. B: Now when we have intercourse, my wife often passes out. She actually faints.

Mrs. B: Last time that happened he got mad at me and pushed me off the bed.

Mr. B: I know that was wrong, but she gets me so frustrated. Sometimes when we start to have sex she arouses me, and then when I'm ready to go she stops and tell me she's tired and wants to go to sleep.

Therapist: How does this make you feel?

Mr. B: How do you think? Very angry.

Therapist: And before you feel angry?

Mr. B: Very frustrated and abandoned. I feel rejected and hurt.

Mrs. B: (sits in passive silence)

Therapist: You feel rejected, hurt, and abandoned, but you must have some sense that your wife's "rejection" has nothing to do with you.

Mr. B: Yes, I know that she was abused and molested and that this is the problem. But I still feel abandoned.

Therapist: Yes. You have compassion for your wife and understand that she is experiencing post-traumatic stress. But you need not be a victim as she brings this molester into the relationship.

Mrs. B: I know it isn't right. I just get scared at the sight of his penis, when it gets enlarged.

Therapist: So the sight of an aroused penis is associated with the bad daddy who violated you. Therefore, you can't see your husband's penis as something warm and loving, something to please you.

Mrs. B: I guess not, and yet I love my husband and feel so blessed to have a wonderful man like this in my life.

Therapist: (goes into the language of dialectics to deal with the splitting mechanism) So then, Mrs. B, what you're telling me is that there are two of you: one who sees your husband as warm and loving, and the other who sees him as the bad molester/penis, someone who violates you.

Mrs. B: I guess so.

Therapist: But now you have become the violator. You are violating the marriage vows and teasing your husband, almost doing to him what has been done to you.

Mrs. B: You are upsetting me.

Therapist: I am sorry. My intention is not to upset you. Besides, I am sure you are not doing this consciously. It's probably outside of your awareness.

Mr. B: Doctor, I so appreciate this because I also don't want to upset her and am always so cautious to say and do the right things.

Therapist: Maybe you are too cautious, and because you are so caring you may not be aware of how you are now being violated. I can understand how angry you get, but it still does not justify pushing your wife off the bed.

Mr. B: I know. What would you suggest I do?

Therapist: I suggest you stand up for yourself. Let your wife know how teasing you and getting you aroused is violating you, and that it is not acceptable.

Mrs. B: I would like him to be more assertive. My mother was weak and could not stand up for anything.

Therapist: Thank you, Mrs. B. I was wondering what role your mother played while all this abuse was going on. I would also suggest you get individual treatment to help you work out some of the trauma you went through and to help you understand how you are now projecting your pain into your current relationship. Mr. B, in terms of your feeling abandoned, any man would feel that way in your position. But you need to be aware of how you are abandoning yourself by not being more assertive—other than physically pushing your wife off the bed.

Mr. B: Yes, doctor. I think you are right. I will need more help with that.

Therapist: Great! See you both next week!

Discussion

It was obvious that Mrs. B's father was a malignant borderline. He maliciously violated his daughter, penetrating her from the age of 10 until she was 15. He had no bounds and no impulse control. Sometimes the "complaint" doesn't surface until years later in the form of post-traumatic stress disorder. The therapist was torn between being overly sympathetic with the wife and yet trying to show how she, the victim, is also the tormentor. It is not an easy task to keep both voices going. The therapist uses the language of empathology to empathize with Mrs. B's pain, while at the same time confronting her aggression by informing her that she may not be consciously aware of her covert "sadism" and "abuse" of her husband.

THE BORDERLINE'S MANY GUISES

A common dynamic inherent in all the "abandoned souls" described in this chapter is the notion of the unfulfilled promise, which encompasses many of the themes within the borderline matrix of abandonment and betrayal. The borderline promiser dons many facades, ranging from the womanizer and the femme fatale to the addict and the abuser. Whether the promise comes from the passive-aggressive, the wannabe artist, or the cultural borderline, somehow these promises never reach fruition. In my book *The Disappearing Male* (2013), I describe the Don Juan syndrome. The Don Juans woo, charm, and seduce women in order to conquer and dominate them. They promise their women the world and then disappear without warning or explanation, leaving the women feeling traumatized and devastated. These Don Juans know how to turn on the charm and make the woman they are currently courting feel as though she is the one and only. The dumped women end up with nothing but a string of empty promises and a broken heart.

To ward off abandonment anxiety, the promiser will say anything to maintain a bond. "I promise I'll do what you ask. Just don't leave me!" These individuals may promise the world, but their lack of impulse control does not allow them to follow through. Because of their carefully crafted false self, the

borderline knows to put on a persona that embellishes the virtues of their partners and makes them feel special, which is particularly enticing to the narcissist. The complaints that these bearers of empty promises ignite center around
the many roles they play. "I promise, baby, that I'll quit drinking (or taking
drugs/gambling, etc.) I swear I won't do it anymore." One of my supervisees
made a very astute interpretation about the philosophy of a "Don Juan" patient
that she was seeing: "A woman can disappoint or leave you, but a drug or a
bottle of alcohol never disappoints. It is always there when you need it."

The womanizer, the addict, the controller, the manipulator are not the lone
types of promisers in Borderland. They are very closely aligned to other promisers such as the passive-aggressive and the obsessive-compulsive. However, they
differ in the way they play out their drama. The passive-aggressive expresses
rage covertly by projecting it onto others, whereas the obsessive-compulsive
has the genuine desire to follow through on promises, but because of the fear
of intimacy withholds. "After I finish my work, I'll go to the movies with you."
However, for the obsessive-compulsive, "finishing" never happens. The passive-
aggressive promiser will respond with outrage at the slightest provocation as he
plays the "poor me, I'm the victim" card.

Many partners involved with borderlines complain that they are constantly
making promises but never follow through and will sabotage opportunities for
happiness even when things are going well. For example, in treatment a wife
complained that she and her husband had saved their money to go on a cruise,
but at the last minute her borderline husband went back to the bottle. To this
the therapist said, "Yes, because your husband cannot contain the good things
in life, he must sabotage and destroy. He fears happiness because it can be lost.
On the other hand, it is easier to depend on alcohol because there's always
another bottle available."

Lack of commitment is another trait inherent in the brotherhood of borderline disorders:

> My boyfriend keeps telling me how much he loves me and that eventually
> we will have a life together. So far there is no commitment, no ring, and no
> talk of engagement. I am 42 years old, and my biological clock is winding
> down. It's so frustrating. When I go to his house there is no privacy. He has
> all these roommates staying with him. He promises me it is only temporary,
> but they are always there. Sometimes I just want to run around in my under-
> wear, but I can't with them there. I had a dream. It was a rather stupid dream.
> In fact, I woke up laughing. I dreamt that I was in a house and someone left
> the door to the yard open. Suddenly out ran a pig, a goat, and a chicken.
> I tried to run after them but couldn't catch them. Then they all ran off the
> cliff. I was happy.

It was not hard to interpret that the animals represented her boyfriend's
three roommates, whom she wanted to get rid of. Feeling happy was a way of
justifying her feelings of resentment toward them.

What follows are brief description of the categories that fall into line with the types of borderline personality as outlined in my previous publications (Lachkar, 2008a, 2008c, 2011, 2013). These descriptions reveal how each type acts out their abandonment fantasies by projecting their paranoid, fragmented selves onto others and offers a segue into the kinds of complaints they arouse in others.

Different Kinds of Borderlines

Just as there are different kinds of narcissists, there are different types of borderlines. The grandiose self within the borderline structure functions under a unique operating system. The narcissist's grandiose self constantly searches for admiration, whereas the borderline's grandiose self is in search for someone to blame and onto whom they can project their victimized self. Typically, these borderline personalities exhibit a pervasive pattern of intense, unstable, and dysfunctional relationships. In addition, they have low self-esteem, are filled with shame, are insecure, and can resort to self-destructive acts such as addiction and self-mutilation. The borderline's aggression is linked to abandonment fantasies. Borderlines complain that they are being abandoned, attacked, and criticized, while at the same time they are bonded with "the mother of pain." One of the main criticisms is that they refuse to heed the good advice they receive and remain on a path of self-destruction. "He has such a distorted image of reality. He is always late, always finds someone to blame, and when he feels abandoned or betrayed will not let it go but does everything possible to retaliate or get revenge. I am tired of always being the one to be blamed."

Following are the various types of borderlines and examples of the kind of complaints they engender in others.

THE PATHOLOGICAL BORDERLINE

The pathological borderline resorts to such primitive defenses as splitting, projection, projective identification, omnipotent denial, and magical thinking. They are often delusional because of their distorted sense of reality, thinking disorders, thwarted sense of judgment, and frequently their severe or chronic paranoid anxiety. They exhibit a predominance of envy, shame, jealousy, blame, paranoia, co-dependency, and boundary confusion (what's yours is mine, what's your space is mine, and what's your time is mine). In order to ward off abandonment anxiety, they will form parasitic bonds with their objects (pity, victimization, and helplessness).

Associated Complaints

- She complains that I never make love to her. But how can I when she has put on so much weight and then expects me to love her for who she is and not what she looks like?

- I can't even look at or talk to another woman without my wife becoming insanely jealous.
- Everything that happens is my fault. He never can admit to being wrong.
- She always keeps me walking on eggshells. If I tell her how I really feel, I know she will freak out.
- She blows up at the least little thing. I told her she was driving too fast, so she pulls over, gets out of the car into oncoming traffic, and says, "Okay, then you drive."
- I have to lie to her when I go to visit my kids from my prior marriage. When she finds out she completely loses it.
- She's so paranoid that even when I tell her she looks good she thinks I have some ulterior motive.
- He always sabotages our good times. Whenever things are going well, he starts a battle or a conflict.
- He is so fake and full of shit. He doesn't fool me. I see how he uses his false personality to charm people.
- He's always the victim and gets everyone to feel sorry for him.

THE MALIGNANT BORDERLINE

The malignant borderline shares many qualities of the malignant narcissist with antisocial tendencies. Both tend to be malicious, cruel, and sadistic. They also are aggressive, ruthless, and insensitive and find victims on whom to inflict pain and punishment. However, although the malignant narcissist will inflict pain in order to feed his sense of superiority—"I inflict pain; therefore I am powerful, omnipotent, and almighty"—the malignant borderline inflicts pain in order to gain control—"Now you are the hopeless victim, and you will know what it feels like to have been abused." The malignant narcissist cannot be wrong and will do anything in his power to prove that he is right; to be wrong is felt to be an attack on the grandiose self that purports superiority over others. The malignant borderline exacts pain and revenge from his chosen victims through projective identification, sadism, hatred, uncontrollable rage, and revenge, with paranoia far outweighing any rational thought. The malignant borderline finds justification for his uncontrollable aggression by assuming the role of the controller, believing that it is his duty to protect himself from the projected external enemies.

At the domestic level, one would think of a malignant borderline in terms of O. J. Simpson, accused of murdering his wife after numerous attacks triggered by his bouts of uncontrollable jealousy. At the global level, the malignant borderline is personified by someone like Osama bin Laden, who with all his wealth was less concerned about fame, money, and success than about destroying and seeking revenge on the infidels in the West. "Now we are no longer victims. We are in control. Allah willed the September 11 attacks as a defense of his own people." On the political stage, sadism and paranoia drive the malignant borderline to protect those that align with him to commit the most heinous crimes against humanity under the guise of the "good cause." In relationships this causes confusion and ambivalence because the abuser who can be cruel and sadistic can also be loving and caring. "Oh, baby, I'm so sorry. Don't cry. Here, come to daddy. Let me hold you. I promise this won't happen again and I'll take care of you."

Associated Complaints

- He is abusive, a liar, and a manipulator.
- I had to call the police because he was abusing our daughter.
- To punish me he locked me in a room so I could not go to work or to my doctor's appointment.
- After he beats me and apologizes, I believe him and again fall into the role of his victim.
- He is sadistic and has no sympathy for anyone.
- To punish me he refused to let me use the bathroom, so I had to pee in the sink.

THE HISTRIONIC BORDERLINE

The histrionic exhibits an exaggerated expression of emotionality, cries easily, over-reacts to the slightest comment, and forms parasitic attachments. Histrionics may appear narcissistic, but their violent outbursts, excessive dependency needs, and volatile episodes put them closer to their borderline neighbors. They are notorious for having a history of eating disorders, alcohol and drug addiction, inappropriate anger, volatile mood swings, sexual confusion, and unstable relationships. Many share common childhood experiences of families where they were neglected or abandoned, or they are the product of broken homes. Some famous histrionics include celebrities like Marilyn Monroe, Robin Williams, Michael Jackson, Lindsey Lohan, and Anna Nicole Smith.

Marilyn Monroe is a classic example. Born to a mother who was diagnosed with paranoid schizophrenia, Monroe was left in a series of foster homes. She was the illegitimate child of a man who abandoned her mother before she was born and was killed in a motorcycle accident when Marilyn was three years old (Banner, 2012). One could speculate how Marilyn's search for a father figure and her excessive need for attention caused her to end up with powerful figures like John Kennedy, Arthur Miller, and Joe DiMaggio.

Associated Complaints

- She always plays the poor little victim and cries over the slightest thing I say to her.
- She asks me a hundred times a day how she looks.

- She exaggerates and makes a big deal out of everything.
- He has no control over his emotions.
- When I said, "The world is going to the dogs," she got mad at me and said, "How can you say that? You know I love dogs!"
- All she does is flirt with other men in order to get attention.
- I caught her in bed with my best friend.
- Whenever we go anywhere she is boisterous and silly. She needs to be the center of attention.
- She has promised a thousand times she would give up drugs and alcohol but never follows through.
- By acting like a victim, he coerces people to do all kinds of things for him, like getting doctors to prescribe painkillers, getting women to sleep with him by telling them I'm frigid or ill, and getting people at the office to do most of his work.

THE PASSIVE-AGGRESSIVE BORDERLINE

Although the passive-aggressive personality type no longer exists in the *Diagnostic and Statistical Manual of Mental Disorders* (*DSM-IV*), I have resurrected this category for the purposes of couple therapy. These are the couch-potato husbands and the forgetful wives. "I'll do it later; I'll do it tomorrow; I was going to get the cleaning today, but the car broke down." They forget, delay, avoid, cajole, and make an endless barrage of excuses—in short, anything it takes to protect the "good little child" from the screaming mommy. The passive-aggressive's primary aim is to unconsciously coerce a partner to behave in a way that recreates the parent–child dyad.

Associated Complaints
- He is so dependent. Everything revolves around him and his needs.
- While I am frantically busy with two jobs, as well as taking care of two kids and a sick mother, he lies on the couch napping or watching sports.
- He can never make a decision about anything, even a place to eat.
- He is always the nice guy, and I am always the angry bitch.
- He's such a baby. It's like having another child.
- What drives me crazy is that he acts like the victim and gets everyone to feel sorry for him. I keep our house and relationship going and get no credit for doing that.

THE OBSESSIVE-COMPULSIVE BORDERLINE

Compared to other borderline personalities, the obsessive-compulsive has a more developed and well-integrated ego, better tolerance for anxiety, better impulse control, and a harshly strict but well-integrated superego. At the lower level of functioning, obsessive-compulsives are devoid of feelings and are pre-occupied with orderliness, cleanliness, and perfectionism. These workaholics invariably put their partners down for having emotional needs and desires. They keep their partners on hold and never have enough time for them. Because obsessive-compulsives confuse needs and desires with dirt and disgust, they will find justification to work, work, work under the guise of efficiency or the "good cause." They will also do anything to avoid intimacy. These are the pack rats, the clutterers, who cannot throw anything away.

Associated Complaints

- She never has time for me. She's always working or doing household chores.
- We are always late because it takes us at least a half hour to leave our driveway. He has to check and recheck everything multiple times.
- He is a wonderful provider and makes a good living, but he will not give me any money for groceries, clothes, and other things I want to buy without conducting a thorough investigation about why I need them.
- When we make love, it is like making love to a stone.
- He is not romantic in the least. It's like talking to a robot.
- He thinks having feelings and emotions are bad. Whenever I try to talk to him about feelings he leaves the room or refuses to talk to me.

THE SCHIZOID

The schizoid is a proxy for the borderline. Although they display many characteristics, the schizoid might be described as a reverse borderline, one who moves in the other direction. Each personality has its own way of enacting abandonment dramas. Both the borderline and the schizoid crave intimacy. The borderline attempts to find it, however, and when he does will sabotage it or destroy it; whereas the schizoid will just shy away, disassociate, and become apathetic. Borderlines tend to be more extroverted, histrionic, and overly dramatic; whereas the schizoid tends to be more introverted, shy, and displays very few emotions. Both the borderline and the schizoid have difficulty with intimacy. The borderline bonds with intimacy through excitement or pain, whereas the schizoid feels repelled by even the prospect of intimacy, which ultimately leads to loneliness and depression. As a replacement for human contact, they turn to the Internet, iPods, boats, aerospace, rockets, and planes, which act as momentary supplies for schizoids. Unlike the borderline, the schizoid keeps a safe distance and tends not to regard sex as an intimate act, often choosing prostitutes, a short-term affair, or masturbation.

The schizoid personality's primary defense is a pervasive pattern of detachment. Schizoid types have few close relations and appear indifferent to the praise or criticism of others. Unlike the narcissist, who withdraws but remains highly sensitive to the opinions of others, the schizoid has retreated from his object world and has blocked involvement with external objects, which prevents new experiences from emerging. Continuation on this path can lead to schizophrenia and loss of linkage to the ego, leaving the schizoid borderline trapped and empty (Ogden, 1989). As one patient quipped, the only intimate conversation he has is with his own navigation system.

At the extreme end of the schizoid spectrum, we have the loners that turn into suicide bombers and terrorists who blow up planes and buildings. My friend and colleague Dr. Nancy Kobrin did a brilliant analysis of the 9/11 terrorist attacks, linking the acts of terrorism committed by pilots flying the planes to the "schizoid dilemma" (Kobrin, 2010). She describes these pilots as so far removed from their maternal objects that they plugged their instruments into the cockpit's "motherboard" to gain control and reconnect with the maternal figure.

Associated Complaints

- He never expresses any emotions. I don't think he feels anything.
- When I talk to him, he never looks me in the eye.
- He never goes down on me when we make love. He thinks vaginas are dangerous and suffocating.
- She doesn't seem to care what she does. Even when I ask her what movie she'd like to see or where she wants to go for a day trip or what kind of food she'd like to eat, I always get the same response: "Whatever."
- I can't believe the person next door, who was always so quiet, polite, and cordial, could have murdered his wife and child!

THE PARANOID BORDERLINE

Paranoia generally refers to intense beliefs or mistrust about the intentions of others. It is based on the feeling that the world is "out to get me." There is the classic form in which the paranoid personalities suspect that the government is spying on them and tapping their phones, or that their wife/husband is having an affair. At a lesser degree, there is persecutory and paranoid anxiety, which seeps into almost all the disorders described in this chapter. Paranoia is most prevalent in the borderline syndrome. It attacks their links to reality, so that borderlines see things only in terms of black and white, limiting them from seeing the "whole picture" and distorting their thinking. A man cut out of his father's will may feel everyone in the family is against him but may be unable to see the reason that he was cut out of the will—for example, that he avoided ever getting a job or refused help for alcoholism or substance abuse.

The paranoid borderline also fits perfectly with the abandoned orphan theme. Borderlines constantly accuse others of abandoning them but lack the observing ego to see how they abandon themselves. Many precipitously conjure up a negative story before anything happens: "I know if I ask my boss for a raise, he will reject me." Others will glom onto past traumatic experiences to get endless mileage. "My wife screwed me over in the past and I'll be damned if I ever date another woman again." I am reminded of a patient who would refuse to wait in the waiting room because she feared other patients would speak badly of her. Another patient was once bitten by a dog and transferred this fear to all dogs (including tiny puppies).

The paranoid borderline operates within the paranoid-schizoid position, a space of shame, blame, fear, and mistrust of others. In terms of projective identification, there is a tendency for the borderline to ruthlessly blame others in the absolute belief that they are guilty of the behavior that actually characterizes the borderline himself. "He is a liar!" "He is cheap and withholding!" (Although it is the borderline who lies and is cheap and withholding.) This position is most apparent in couple therapy. "My wife is paranoid. Just because I go out to lunch with my female work colleagues doesn't mean I am having an affair." Episodes of paranoid thinking can range from mild and short-lived to very severe and chronic. Some individuals with severe mental illness, such as psychosis or delusions, tend to have chronic paranoid episodes that have no relationship to reality.

Paranoid anxieties overshadow the capacity for a loving relationship. The most pervasive occurrence in love relations is the discontinuity between the self and the love object. As the paranoid desperately tries to hold onto his internal "good objects," they project their bad parts onto others, which keeps them always on the lookout for the "bad guys." Other characteristics are suspiciousness of people and objects, lack of trust, and the inability to believe they can be loved. "You don't really love me; you are just using me!" The attempt to sabotage is impulsive and precipitous; the paranoid borderline immediately jumps to the assumption before the ego has the ability to organize the data of experience.

One can imagine the kinds of complaints someone with this proclivity can ignite. "She always accuses me of being unfaithful. If I don't answer her text right away, she goes ballistic!" "I just know you are having an affair; you have been coming home later and later."

Associated Complaints

- When I tell her she looks nice or bring her flowers, she thinks I am covering up something.
- If he does say anything positive, it sounds robotic, as though he is not speaking from his heart.
- She's so paranoid I can't even give her a compliment. When I tell her she looks good, she either says I'm trying to "butter her up" or asks what was wrong with the way she looked before.
- When I come home late, she is suspicious and has already searched through my things, including my e-mails.

- She only sees things in black and white.
- She doesn't understand that she blames me for the very thing she feels guilty about.
- She complains that I am cheap and withholding when she is the one who is cheap and withholding. I haven't had sex with her for six months.
- Our kids want to have a dog, but because she was bitten once by a dog now she thinks all dogs are mean and dangerous. I'm not a therapist, but it seems to me she is projecting her own vicious self onto some innocent puppy.

THE BORDERLINE ARTIST

An amazing thing about borderlines is that in spite of all their pathology many are extraordinarily creative. The chaos of the senseless and primitive interior world in which they live is somehow defined by their art. Some of the most disturbed artists have produced magnificent art. Picasso and Van Gogh are good examples. One might venture to say that because they lived in a less inhibited world that allowed the freedom of fantasy and disorder, they felt less repressed, which allowed their artistry to flourish. On the other hand, there is also the victimized artist, who has long ago abandoned his art because of shame, feelings of inadequacy, a sense of being non-deserving, or fear of self-expression. I am reminded of a violinist who had such stage fright that right before scheduling a performance, she often would have to cancel it. "When I look out at the audience, I see face of my mother telling me to give up, that I would never amount to anything."

Associated Complaints
- I keep encouraging him to finish his manuscript, but he keeps putting it off. It drives me crazy. I wish he would finish it already.
- I have a contract with this jazz musician who promises me that when he finishes his album we will go on tour. I have done 30 tracks with him, and nothing has happened.
- Whenever someone expresses appreciation for the beauty of her artwork at a show, she immediately denigrates it and her ability. People start thinking their original judgment of her paintings might be wrong and walk off without purchasing anything.

THE CULTURAL BORDERLINE

The cultural borderline is outlined in detail in Chapter Eight, along with the cultural narcissist. They are similar in many ways, with the main difference being the level of aggression. The narcissist will wave his nationalistic flag, claiming that his country, traditions, and customs are superior; whereas the cultural borderline assumes a more violent and aggressive stance: "Anyone who pokes fun at our leaders or our God will be killed." They will retaliate, fight, resort to terrorism, betray the country in which they currently reside, and do anything else needed to maintain and support the group's collective national identity.

Associated Complaints

- If he wants to fight for his country to prove his nationalist alliance, why doesn't he go back to his country?
- Just because he wants to protest and fight for his beliefs doesn't mean I have to fuse with him, but that's what he wants me to do.
- In his country, women are mistreated, as if they are second-class citizens. I keep telling him that is not the way women are treated here.
- I cry every day for my son. My husband took him back to his country three years ago, and there is nothing I can do despite endless international court battles and government intervention.

SUMMARY

The many different kinds of borderlines delineated in this chapter can be described as the abandoned ones, the Don Juans, the femme fatales, the promisers, the controllers, the wannabes, the manipulators, the liars, the artists, and the nationalists. The primary theme of borderline pathology centers around abandonment anxiety, and each type of borderline has his/her own unique way of abandoning either self or others. For example, the obsessive-compulsives replace feelings and emotions with objects, whereas the passive-aggressives replace their responsible self with a co-dependent self.

When it comes to complaints, borderline patients are not only relentless but also very taxing on the therapist. Borderline pathology is unlike that of any other personality disorder. Borderlines are extraordinarily vulnerable, with V-spots exploding everywhere. They live in constant pain, which they try to rid themselves of by projecting onto others. They have a poorly developed ego structure, which makes them unpredictable, impulsive, and volatile. As mentally confused and chaotic as their lives are, many borderlines can be remarkably intuitive, sensitive, and perceptive to the body language and feelings of others. Many have been able to carve out of the chaos of their borderline existence some of the world's most magnificent art, music, and writing. When borderlines are able to unleash their creativity, they are unstoppable.

Chapter 5

⤬

The Robotic Relationship

Within the matrix of the obsessive-compulsive disorder (OCD) lives a group of personalities who play out certain roles that I describe as the robot, the pack rat, the withholder, the out to lunchers (i.e., the schizoid). Central casting could not have done a better job because all these variations on the theme are crossovers to this disorder.

These compulsive personalities are conscientious and have high levels of aspiration, strive for perfection, and are never satisfied with their achievements. They can never be perfect enough. People with this disorder take on more responsibilities than they can handle, to the point that they stifle and suffocate the people around them. They are reliable, dependable, orderly, and methodical, but their inflexibility often makes them incapable of adapting to changed circumstances. They are super rigid, and because they think they know everything, they feel they have a right to control others. People with obsessive-compulsive personality disorder are overly cautious, weigh all aspects of a problem, and pay attention to every detail, making it difficult for them to make decisions and complete tasks. When their feelings are not under strict control, their behavior is extremely unpredictable, and they frequently must depend on others to determine what to do. They often feel an intolerable sense of isolation and helplessness.

Those associated with obsessive-compulsive personality exhibit such symptoms as preoccupation with rules and order as well as excessive devotion to work, even at the expense of intimate or family relations. In relationships, partners often complain about the obsessive-compulsives "anal" tendencies, holding on to things that could give meaning and pleasure to others (money, time, attention, and emotions), which stems from their rigidity, need for control, excessive demands for orderliness, and lack of emotionality.

The complaints that center around the "robotic" personality generally involve the issue of withholding. Money problems are key. For example, money problems can include having too little or too much money, being stingy or overspending, fighting over spending priorities, compulsive gambling or compulsive shopping, lying about money, always trying to keep up with the Joneses, and the like.

In treatment, the dynamic of the withholder also plays itself out in the process of transference or the couple transference. In individual or conjoint sessions, the first concern is about money. "How much does this cost? How long will this take?" "Can you reduce the fee?" "Sorry my check was late. I've been busy doing my briefs." Often this puts the therapist in a very compromising position, where money and time become a more pervasive force than focusing on the needs of the treatment. Because of their perfectionist and controlling nature, these compulsive personalities can present a real challenge for the therapist, who often must confront these issues indirectly by finding another venue— namely, the emotional route—to help them deal with these issues by leading them to understand that they not only withhold money, help, and approval but also withhold themselves, which threatens the relationships they form. The therapist might say, "Aside from money, your wife is complaining that you don't express your feelings to her and withhold sex, and that doesn't cost anything!"

Some partners complain that the obsessive-compulsive will give thousands of dollars to charities and very little to them.

> I was absolutely shocked by my partner of ten years. He hardly ever bought me a gift. If he did, it was some cheapo thing. Then one day he took me to the Four Seasons Hotel for a special benefit. The chairperson called out the names of the donors who contributed the most to their cause. Lo and behold, my partner was called last and given a special tribute because he had contributed the greatest amount of money. I almost fell off my chair.

Henry Dicks's seminal book on *Marital Tensions* (1967) did not specifically focus on marital complaints, but they were inferred. He was one of the first to bring to our attention two oppositional individuals who join together in a marital bond from a psychodynamic perspective, the obsessive-compulsive husband and the histrionic wife—or the "lovesick" wife and the "cold sick" husband. Dicks wrote from a psychodynamic perspective, applying psychodynamic theory interwoven from many theorists on object relations (Klein, Bion, and Winnicott, among others) to describe what happens when these two oppositional types get together, which was my first inspiration for writing *The Narcissistic/Borderline Couple*. He masterfully described how each partner not only stirs up the other's unresolved developmental needs, but how they hold each other back from growth and development. Here is where complaints go flying. The histrionic wife complains that her OCD partner is cold, aloof, and void of emotion, while the OCD partner complains that his wife is too emotional and loses control at the least little incident.

Although I use the descriptive term "robot" to apply to those with an obsessive-compulsive personality, this term should not be limited to individuals with OCD, who share certain characteristics with their fellow neighbors in the *DSM-IV*. It also has applicability to those who withdraw, disassociate, or are split off from their feelings and emotions. Narcissists withhold empathy, but at least they maintain a connection to their objects. In contrast, someone like the schizoid personality does not deliberately withhold but instead detaches, whereas the OCD is very much attached (money, a cause, work, cleanliness, and orderliness). At the extreme end of this spectrum is the antisocial personality, who has total disregard for the rights, feelings, and concerns of others, and, while exuding the deceptive persona of a charming and alluring self, will commit criminal acts with no remorse or twinges of conscience. The robotic part of the antisocial is the disconnect from morality and conscience. Although disconnected from feelings, the OCD does have a conscience, a very harsh, critical and persecutory superego.

Following Henry Dicks's path, I would now like to say a few words about the overly emotional personality that is the most frequent partner of compulsive personalities, commonly known in the psychiatric literature as the histrionic. This type of personality disorder exhibits a pervasive pattern of intensely emotional, attention-seeking behavior. Individuals with this personality are excessively dramatic and are often viewed by the public as the "drama queen" type of individual. They are often sexually seductive and highly manipulative in relationships. One would think someone like an OCD personality would be inspired living with a histrionic, but, ironically, it has the opposite effect. "You see how she behaves, the disgusting outpouring of out-of-control emotions. Now you understand why I think emotions are bad."

THE OVERLY EMOTIONAL WIFE AND
THE ROBOTIC HUSBAND

Mrs. E initiated couple treatment because she was vastly frustrated by her husband's preoccupation with cleanliness and perfectionism (triggered after reading an article regarding NASA's new solar orbiter called MAVEN—Mars Atmosphere and Evolution Orbiter).

Therapist: Greetings! So who would like to start?

Mrs. E: I would. My husband is a scientist well known for space exploration. As much as I love and respect him, I am contemplating getting

	a divorce. He's terrible to live with. He never expresses any emotion. He accuses me of being too needy, being a nag, and being an emotional mess.
Therapist:	(Already getting the sense that her husband may be OCD but tries to listen without preconception.)
Mr. E:	Her emotions kill me. Why can't she just talk like a normal person? She whines, she weeps, she yells and complains constantly that I never listen to her.
Mrs. E:	When we have sex he just sticks it in, comes, and then in some perfunctory way plays with me. But I am always left frustrated.
Therapist:	Guess there is no perfect marriage, is there?
Mrs. E:	(annoyed with therapist's remark) What are you saying? My other therapist would never have said that, and she is the one who thinks I should get a divorce.
Therapist:	Guess there are no perfect therapists either, are there? Yet, you feel your husband has been a good provider and a good dad, and you respect his brilliance and accomplishment as a scientist and aerospace engineer.
Mrs. E:	That's the point. I do love and respect him, but I am completely frustrated.
Mr. E:	And complaining and bitching.
Therapist:	Actually, your wife is not really complaining, although it sounds that way. For so many years you have not listened to her. What you call complaints, I call needs!
Mr. E:	Needs! That's for people who are sick. Needy people make me sick!
Therapist:	Of course. That is why you are so obsessed with cleanliness. You feel needs are dirty and must be eradicated. Tell us more about the space mission.
Mr. E:	(suddenly comes to life) Oh yes! I am so impressed with how these men working on the project scrub and scrub. Cleanliness is crucial to avoid contaminating other worlds. Contamination from Earth could kill life-forms on other planets, which would ruin any discovery. This is a space project designed to search for life beyond Earth, which requires unadulterated robots to go into space. They must be scrupulously scrubbed to make sure there are no contaminates from the water and heat on Earth, if they are to explore another planet that is cold and dry.
Therapist:	(listening intently and thinking that Mr. E is referring to his own internal heat—passionate emotions that must be obliterated) So you are really telling us how you feel about emotions, feelings, and needs, something inside of you that you experience as dirt and must

be eliminated. You would like to have a perfect internal spaceship that is totally "germ free."

Mr. E: (squirming in obvious discomfort) This is a bunch of nonsense.

Therapist: But being the brilliant scientist you are I thought you would be open to new ideas. And, of course, it sounds like nonsense because these feelings are unconscious.

Mrs. E: See? Now he puts you down the same way he does with me.

Therapist: (noting the beginning of the couple transference) I am trying to explain how you might experience feelings as germs.

Mr. E: I like the fact that you value and appreciate me. I wish my wife would react like that.

Therapist: Sounds like you are already making progress. You just expressed a real need—how you would like your wife to express more appreciation for you.

Mrs. E: I can do that!

Therapist: Great! We have a lot of scrubbing and analytic cleaning up to do here, but in order to do it we have to stay on Earth. See you next week.

Both: We will be here.

Mrs. E: From Mars to Earth.

Therapist: Very good! See you both then.

Discussion

In the "dance," the therapist finds herself shifting back and forth from confrontation to empathy. When Mrs. E. critically compared her to the other therapist, the current therapist remarked, "There are no perfect therapists." This was a way of suggesting to Mrs. E that her other therapist was colluding with her to encourage a divorce. The therapist also addresses Mr. E's obsession with cleanliness. However, she senses he can only take so much and quickly goes back to clean rooms and space exploration: "Tell us more about the space mission" (mirroring and sharing his interest). The focus was not so much on confronting the robot husband as it was on the attempt to bond. The case that follows is another example of robotic behavior, but now we have the "tool husband."

THE CASE OF MR. AND MRS. T

Mrs. T came into conjoint treatment complaining that she was sexually frustrated. Her husband, an attorney, would stay up night after night working on briefs, interrogatories, and depositions, promising every night that when he finished he would come upstairs and make love to her.

Mrs. T: I love and respect my husband. Besides making a great living, he is always there, like a rock, unlike my own abusive father. Although our kids would like to have their dad be more emotionally available, they respect him, feel his strong presence, and accept him for who he is.

Therapist: So with all this, your main complaint it that you feel sexually frustrated. Mr. T, what are your thoughts?

Mr. T: She knows I'm busy, that I care about our family and work very hard to support them and pay all the bills. And, of course, there's her lavish lifestyle.

Mrs. T: That isn't the point. The point is you keep me on hold. You keep me waiting and waiting night after night, even when I walk downstairs practically nude to entice you. You give me, "Oh you look lovely; be right up!" But being right up never happens because you are so busy working. By the time you come upstairs, you are so sleep deprived that nothing ever does come up!

Therapist: (appreciating Mrs. T's quip) I hear your wife saying that you make promises, but somehow you don't follow through.

Mr. T: Well, I can't help it. When I am on a roll and writing a brief I just can't stop in the middle.

Mrs. T: And when you do have free time, you spend it in the garage working with your tools. All you think about are your briefs and your tools. So please don't make promises. Just be honest and say, "I will stay up for three nights, and my briefs are more important than you!!"

Mr. T: No, I am not saying that, and I wish you would stop complaining. All you do is nag!

Mrs. T: I will stop complaining when you stop making promises.

Therapist: Mr. T, your wife does have a point. You get her aroused and then she ends up feeling frustrated.

Mr. T: Feelings! This is all I hear about.

Mrs. T: And even when he does make "love" to me he is totally void of feelings. After he puts his penis into me, I ask him how it feels: "How do I feel to you? Do you love me?"

Therapist: And . . .

Mrs. T: You know what he says? His only comment is, "Don't talk to me. I am concentrating, and if you talk to me I will lose it."

Therapist: (in a very playful voice) It sounds like you use your penis like a tool instead of it being a means to feel love, warmth, and passion. Also, this is one thing that shouldn't be "brief."

Mr. T: I have always been that way. It's hard for me to feel emotions. Ever since I was little, my dad used to say that boys don't cry. My mother was a cold fish. So I guess I grew up feeling that emotions are bad things.

Therapist: And yet you put your wife down for having needs and feelings, doing to her what your parents did to you.

Mrs. T: Tell him, tell that is why he is always washing his hands, always careful not to get germs. He feels dirty inside.

Therapist: (again impressed with Mrs. T's insightfulness) Well, I don't know about the hand washing. We will have to discuss this next time. What I do know is that we have some "cleaning" up to do here. We need to stop now, so let me summarize. It sounds like you, Mrs. T, need to understand that your husband's promises are not real promises but to view them as wishes that get obstructed by his obsession with work. So do not make yourself sick and frustrated by waiting up night after night. You have every right to complain, and it is a legitimate complaint, but to your husband it comes across as a needy and messy or those things we call emotions. Mr. T, you have a distorted view of what feelings are about. You explained quite clearly that as a child you were taught not to express yourself emotionally. So instead of facing your real feelings you hide under your briefs. And in order to protect yourself you make promises you cannot fulfill. See you next week.

Discussion

This case is an illustration of a wife's legitimate complaint and how her complaint gets translated by her obsessive-compulsive husband as feelings that are messy, needy, naggy, and dirty. After confronting Mr. T about his coldness and aloofness toward making love to his wife, the therapist playfully uses his words to let him know about his lack of emotionality, which has been long ago abandoned or never connected in the first place. The therapist begins to make headway when she addresses feelings and how as a deprived child he was unable to express them, pointing out how these unresolved issues get enacted and replayed in the relationship with his wife.

Associated Complaints

- He's constantly cold and unemotional.
- He calls me a nag and says I am too emotional and overreact to things.
- He is always working and never has time for me or the kids.
- She is very critical and controlling.
- She complains about me, but I never can say one negative word about her. She is "Ms. Perfect."

THE PACK RAT

People with "pack rat" disorders are not only the most difficult to treat but also the most difficult to live with. They subvert their lives, as well as those of other people, by hoarding and collecting items, even though they are no longer useful. The hoarding usually starts in a closet, a garage, or an attic and slowly begins to take over the entire household. Pack rats go beyond simple "bad housekeeping." They form deep emotional attachments to their objects. One prominent professor could not put his car into the garage because it was filled with clutter, including journal articles, newspapers in every language, old photos, and collectibles from travels going back to 1959. When asked why he just simply didn't throw out these old dusty, smelly papers, his response was, "What if someone calls me and asks if I can help them find a reference? I need to keep them just in case."

In order to help someone with pack rat tendencies, remember that people who are hoarders develop emotional attachments to the stuff they hold on to. Do not underestimate the emotional connection that person has with the objects he's kept. Help the person get rid of things that have "sentimental" value by letting him photograph the object and start a journal detailing the importance of that object in his life. Pack rats need assistance and support for cleanup, along with psychotherapy. Cognitive behavioral therapy is generally recommended. Group therapy can also be useful as an adjunct treatment for the hoarder and the family to help them learn special techniques suitable for this infliction (Svoboda, 2009).

THE CASE OF MR. AND MRS. Y

Mr. and Mrs. Y, a married couple in their late fifties, have two teenage sons. Mrs. Y entered treatment complaining that she simply "could not take it anymore." Her husband's collectibles had expanded and were taking over almost the entire household.

Therapist:　Greetings!

Mrs. Y:　Hi, doctor. I really hope you can help us. I am so desperate I don't know what to do. My husband's hoarding is getting worse and worse, to the extent there is no room for us or our two sons.

Therapist:　Does his stuff take over your sons' space as well?

Mrs. Y:　Fortunately, he does not put anything upstairs where our sons' rooms are, but it is beginning to invade our bedroom, which was for me until now a safe haven. I can't stand his junk! I just want to get rid of it!

Mr. Y:	Please don't call my things junk! I have some very valuable collectibles, and they have special meaning.
Mrs. Y:	You keep promising you will throw these things away or put them in storage, but your promise doesn't seem to have an expiration date.
Mr. Y:	Look, I don't know why she complains. I am a successful lawyer with a busy practice. I make a good living. Our sons go to private schools. We have a housekeeper twice a week to clean the house.
Mrs. Y:	The housekeeper! She's ready to quit. She can hardly dust or vacuum anymore.
Therapist:	Mr. Y, what do these collectibles mean to you? (Therapist is very careful not to use the word "junk.")
Mr. Y:	(smiling because he's getting a chance to get in contact with his "objects d'art") Oh, I have a collection of blueprints back when I worked as an engineer. I have a collection of briefs I wrote when I was in law school. I have my medals and uniforms from when I was a boy scout. I have boxes and boxes of old photos that nobody else in the family was willing to store. And then there's the old telephones and typewriters that belonged to my father, who had a large office in LA. I have lots of artifacts from my activities and travels that have special meaning and memories for me.
Mrs. Y:	Who else takes a trip to Florida and brings back a suitcase full of old bottle tops and other stupid things he found in the sand? And what about the old hangers, light bulbs, broken pieces of I-don't-know-what, and rocks? Or the drawers full of old extension cords?
Mr. Y:	You never know when you will need an extra extension cord. And the rocks . . . those are from when I used to do mountain climbing. Wonderful memories. I love my quartz collection with all those different colors. They are as precious to me as gems. Just as beautiful but less expensive. A real bargain, if you ask me.
Therapist:	Sounds as though your memories are more important to you than making space and room for your current life and family. (Therapist surprised Mr. Y was not angered by the abrupt evaluation.)
Mr. Y:	Oh no, my family is very important to me. In fact I have promised my wife that I will start to make space.
Mrs. Y:	He has been promising me that for more than a year now and nothing has happened. In fact, the reason I made this appointment was because we had a bad incident. My women's group was supposed to meet at our house. I asked my husband to at least clean up the entry table so I could put some flowers and name

tags on it. He did not remove anything, so I took the liberty of getting a big box and throwing everything inside it. Suddenly he shows up, livid beyond belief. I thought he was going to hit me. His eyes became vicious, like some wild beast. I got so scared I put the stuff back.

Therapist: You have both given me a very good picture of the nature of the issues. Mr. Y, you are to be respected for being a good provider for your family and for your effort in at least making a promise to clear up the space. Obviously, this hoarding is beyond your control and may even be beyond mine to help you handle. I would like to meet again with you next week, but I will also make some referrals that will be helpful for you and your family in dealing with this type of condition. However, since you did make a promise to your wife, can you choose a small space in which to start removing the clutter? Maybe the housekeeper can help. It may not sound like much, but at least it will be a start.

Mr. and Mrs. Y: Sounds good. Thank you, doctor. See you next week.

Therapist: Bye now.

Discussion

Although the therapist had a firm grasp of the dynamics involved in this case—how objects became the replacement for love, intimacy, and commitment—she decided to move slowly by first using some cognitive techniques to help Mr. Y begin to think about how to "clean up." The therapist felt frustrated because it was hard in one initial session to address everything she would have liked to. In fact, it would have been precipitous to interpret how cluttered Mr. Y's internal world was—a world filled with lost objects to which he desperately clings, longing for memories, experiences, and people from his past to add substance and meaning to his life. Mr. Y exhibits a clear OCD personality, one that splits off from his emotions, feelings, and love objects and that he can only resurrect through his vast array of tools, wires, and photos. It is these objects that remain steadfast and supply him with the security for which he longs. The therapist will continue working with Mr. Y, using both a cognitive/behavioral and a psychodynamic approach.

Associated Complaints

- We can't even dust. There's not a square foot of space that doesn't have his stuff. We have to tiptoe around it.
- He acts as though his junk is gold.
- Sometimes I get really scared. If I try to organize the house so we can have friends over, he gets wild.

- He acts as though his objects are more important than his wife and his kids.
- It drives me nuts that he has no shame that we live in filth. To him the old pipes, bolts, bits of leftover tile and carpet, and piles of yellowed newspapers and magazines are like precious museum pieces.

THE WITHHOLDER

From my experience, there are two types of withholders. The first type not only withholds from the object but also withholds from the self. "I will drive my old car until it collapses." The second type is one who withholds from the love object but is generous with everyone else. This evokes anger, rage, and jealousy: "How come he gives to everyone else and is so stingy with me?"

> When I first met him, he was loving, romantic, and generous. He took me to the best restaurants, bought me gifts. Suddenly he tells me he has to watch his money. Yet he spends a fortune on cars, going out with his buddies, and donating to charities. I don't understand how he changed so much—from being the big time spender to Mr. Coupon Man!

Withholding is one of the most common complaints that occur in couple relationships. It is also prevalent in family relations, work relations, and on the dating scene. "Had a blind date, and would you believe the guy insisted we share a glass of wine? Too cheap to order me my own." Withholding is either about time, attention, space, compliments, money, or emotions. I could not help thinking about Kernberg's four types of love relationships, which provide us with a diagnostic tool to spot where pathology lies within the scope of the relationship. Of the four love relationships delineated by Kernberg—(1) normal, (2) pathological, (3) perverse, and (4) mature—I find most of the personalities described in this chapter fit within the category of pathological love, in which internal strivings interfere with the capacity to maintain an intimate, loving connection. It is where conflict overpowers the relationship, love that goes in the wrong direction.

Associated Complaints
- He drives me crazy. We can't go anywhere and do anything unless we have a coupon.
- At a restaurant, I feel embarrassed because he leaves a less than minimum tip, if he leaves one at all.
- He will never use valet parking. He would rather drive around the city for an hour looking for a parking space than have to tip anyone to park his car. He won't let anyone else drive it.
- She gives to everyone else but me.

- He not only withholds money; he withholds, time, attention, and even sex.
- He is stingy not only with me but also with himself. He wears old, worn-out, outdated clothes and insists that everything we buy should be washable so we don't have to pay a cleaning bill.

OUT TO LUNCH

In Chapters Three and Four, I described the schizoid within the context of eight different types of narcissists and borderlines. In this chapter, I mainly distinguish the schizoid from the more robotic obsessive-compulsive personality. Both share similar defenses of withdrawal, isolation, and splitting. Both are withholders, causing much pain and anguish to people who live and partner with them. Both the schizoid and the obsessive-compulsive are hardworking and obsessed with work. They often are very intelligent and have successful careers. They also share many complaints from their partners. "He never listens to me! He's always working. He never pays attention to how I feel." Ironically, they also withhold from themselves. Both share the psychic space of being out of touch with the feelings and needs of others. The difference is that the obsessive-compulsive feels needs are dirty and messy and will spend endless time defending himself against them by filing, cleaning, and organizing, whereas the schizoid merely is detached (the unmentalized experience).

The issue of intimacy is where the schizoid really parts ways with the borderline and the narcissist. The borderline clings; his relationship extends beyond normal attachment into the space of fusion, where there is no differentiation between self and other. "I am you and you are me. What I need you need, and what I like you like." The borderline is outgoing, loud, and sometimes boisterous and histrionic, whereas the schizoid is withdrawn, introverted, shy, and displays few emotions. The narcissist desires intimacy but only insofar as the self-objects to whom he/she is attached offer an ample supply of narcissistic gratification. The schizoid avoids intimacy and commitment of any kind. The schizoid rarely initiates a conversation and usually responds in a terse, simple "yes/ no/ maybe" manner.

In treatment the therapist needs to know that withdrawal is actually a healthier state because it maintains a certain libidinal attachment to the object. When one detaches, one splits off and goes into a state of despondency. Children who are left alone, ignored, or neglected for long periods of time enter into a phase of despair (Bowlby, 1969). Analectic depression results from a denial for attachment and bonding, turning one away from the world into a state of apathy. The child's active protest for the missing or absent mother gradually diminishes, and the child no longer makes demands. When this occurs, the child goes into detachment mode or pathological mourning. Apathy, lethargy, and listlessness become the replacement for feelings (anger, rage, betrayal, and abandonment). The schizoid personality's primary defense is a pervasive pattern of detachment. They have few close relations and appear indifferent to the praise or criticism of others. This is unlike the narcissist, who withdraws but remains highly sensitive to the opinions of others.

JANE'S BLIND DATE

I met this guy online. We met at a restaurant. I went over to the table where he was waiting for me. He was dressed nicely, almost perfectly. He wore a nice simple sport shirt, stylish shoes, and watch and had well-manicured nails. However, he was slouched over a bit. I also noticed his shoulders were hunched forward with his head in a slightly downward position. At first I thought he was kind of cute and shy. I liked him because unlike the other guys he seemed gentle and less aggressive. I said "Hi," and he said "Hi," and then I said it was nice to meet him. He nodded but did not respond. We sat quietly for a while, and then I realized I was going to be the one to do all the talking. So I interrogated him a bit, asking what he did for a living. He said he worked on high-end technology. I said, "Wow that is impressive!" To this he responded, "No big deal!" When the server asked what we wanted to order for lunch, he took some time to stare at the menu. I felt very uncomfortable. The restaurant was busy, and the server had other customers to attend to. I made a recommendation, which he agreed with, and we both felt an immediate relief. When I got up to leave, I asked if he would like my card. He said sure! I guess it was easier for me to take the initiative. I could tell he wanted the contact but was afraid to ask as he remained "out to lunch."

Associated Complaints

- It is embarrassing to go out with her socially; she does not connect with other people.
- He never looks at me when I talk.
- He never can express his needs; it is as though I have to implant them into him.
- He gives me a blank stare when I try to tell him what I need.
- He never initiates anything, but he does tag along when I make the plans.
- He is not romantic; in fact, he's rather stiff when we make love.

SUMMARY

This chapter highlights the characteristics most common to obsessive-compulsive personalities. The schizoid personality has been described as having similar features to the OCD, the main difference being the schizoid's withdrawal, isolation, and detachment. The cast of characters included the robot, the withholder (OCD), the pack rat (OCD), and the out to luncher (schizoid), whose distinctions were pointed out to show how their contrasting dynamics shape the kinds of complaints they arouse in others. Although the bonding and attachment elements in relational love bonds are seemingly missing in the OCD and the schizoid, many of these types are very high functioning and successful in fields that include medicine, science, education, business, and engineering. If I were to have surgery or go to the moon, my choice would be the robot rather than any other type of personality described in this book.

Chapter 6

The Self-Saboteurs

This chapter combines the passive-aggressive and the depressive, who at first glance seem quite oppositional. However, there is more commonality between these two personality types than meets the eye. Both play the role as victim and are linked by their inhibiting, self-defeating personas, which keep them from living up to their potential. The passive-aggressive and the depressive are also united by their ability to evoke anger, frustration, and exasperation in others. Both the passive-aggressive and the depressive persecute themselves for their failed selves, which they hide out of shame and then are baffled that others do not pity them. Furthermore, both subvert any attempts by others to help them because they believe that no matter what they do they will always be misunderstood and unappreciated. In addition, they cannot understand how their self-sabotaging behaviors cause others to be angry with them. "Why is everyone so upset with us? We are the victims!" The passive-aggressive expresses his anger with defiance, stubbornness, evasiveness, and procrastination, which many times proves to be a cover for depression—although not the pervasive depression that is the hallmark of the depressive personality.

RESURRECTING THE PASSIVE-AGGRESSIVE

The passive-aggressive has been "demoted" in the *DSM-IV*. No longer is this considered a mental disorder. The passive-aggressive has been termed the "Negativistic Personality" and defined as a person who resists taking orders, following rules, and cooperating with others. This resistance occurs through indirect means such as procrastinating and coercing others to do their work or

91

chores for them. They try to cover up their defiant, belligerent attitude with excessive, insincere excuses and apologies for their being constantly late, not doing what they have agreed to do, and missing important appointments and deadlines. I have reinstituted the category of the passive-aggressive (a term that I use interchangeably with "negativist") in this chapter because of its significance to the subject of marital complaints. The psychological structure that the passive-aggressive creates is based on a parent–child dyad, which coerces the other to be the constant complainer.

The negativist characteristically feigns incompetence and rattles off a litany of excuses for why he or she could not do what was promised. They are the wannabe people pleasers; however, when they realize they have subjugated themselves, they find an endless number of ways to escape their obligation. "I know I arrived late to the party but I really didn't want to go in the first place." Through their deception, they unconsciously set up the other person to get angry, translocating their repressed rage onto their significant others: "It is not me who is the angry one. It is you! You're always acting like a bitch! Me, I didn't do anything wrong." The negativist is one of the most frustrating personality types to live and work with. "My boss is threatening that if I keep coming to work late he will fire me. Doesn't he understand how far I live and how much traffic there is?" More than the other disorders that appear in these pages, negativists not only evoke the most complaints but also present the most excuses for their behavior in order to make others "the bad guys." They always have a story ready to explain why they didn't come through as expected.

Overall, I find the passive-aggressive to be quite closely aligned with the borderline, mainly because of the predominance of procrastination, victimization, and the tendency to form parasitic bonds with their objects. They differ, however, in that the negativist coerces his objects into a child/parent dyad—a specific type of dependency role: "I am the helpless baby husband and you are the all-encompassing mommy that must take care of me" (Lachkar, 1992, 2004b, 2008a, 2011, 2013). The negativist, like all the other personalities, displays his/her own unique ways of playing out entitlement fantasies to get others to perform special functions for them. It is the nature of these functions that constitutes and shapes the kinds of complaints they engender. For example, the narcissist will refuse to make child support payments, whereas the negativist will act as though he really is onboard with child support and insists "the check is in the mail." However, it never arrives. The negativist will show up late or not show up at all for appointments or scheduled child visits but will have a handy roster of excuses (lost the keys, forgot the address, the car wouldn't start, traffic was horrendous, etc.) and expect the other to show pity for their plight.

If you are divorcing a borderline (the "abandoned one"), he/she will do everything possible to exact revenge, no matter what it takes. You know you are victim of his or her wrath. If you are divorcing a narcissist (the "entitled one"), he/she will insist on the rights to everything—the house, the money, and custody of the children. There is no question that you are a victim of the narcissist's grandiose schemes and attitude of entitlement. If you are divorcing an obsessive-compulsive who insists on withholding money and child support, you are the victim of his anal, hoarding ways. If you are divorcing a passive-aggressive, he or she will play the helpless victim role and offer a barrage of excuses, setting you up to be the one blamed and to assume the parental/caretaking role.

The complaints swirling around the passive-aggressive take a subversive route. Typically, he will agree to take on a chore, but underneath lurks resentment. "Why the hell is she asking me to do this when she can do it herself?" This resentment begins to fester, leading to repressed, unconscious rage that is projected onto their partners. "I don't know why she's so irate. I told her my car broke down and I could not make it to the appointment." All the other personality types in this book share one common denominator: deprivation. The entitled narcissist arouses rage in others by only paying attention to his own self-serving needs; the borderline by feeling persecuted at having needs, which make him exact revenge on others when deprived; and the obsessive-compulsive by depriving self and others of needs that are felt to be dirty and messy. The passive-aggressive, unlike the others, offers to take care of needs but then procrastinates and keeps the other person waiting, often shaming their partners for being "needy."

Here is an example of how a stream-of-consciousness thought process might play out in the mind of the passive-aggressive:

I really want to follow through, but somehow things get in the way. If I can't do something right away, I'll try to do it later. I'm confused about why people make such a fuss, because I want to keep my promises. My therapist tells me I don't do what I promise I will do because no one ever gave to me, and this is my subversive way of letting others know what it feels like to be disappointed. He also complains that I do the same thing with him. I promise to mail him a check, to come on time, and not change appointments, but I just can't help myself and keep doing the same things. He calls it a form of projective identification, whatever the hell that means. I know I am a dependent personality, but, hey, I am a victim. I was abused as a child. So maybe sometimes I do make promises I can't keep. I'm told it's my way of staying connected and maintaining a bond. Maybe that's true. I know I irritate and annoy others, but at least I feel alive then and it's a kind of connection and, yes, I'm impulsive and can distort and misperceive the intentions of others. But it's not my fault. I cannot control these urges. They are unstoppable. My girlfriend complains I don't listen to her. I tell her that I do listen, that when she feels bad, I feel bad. This is when I push her buttons [V-spot] and she blows up! She says she doesn't want me to feel bad when she feels bad, but to take responsibility for what I have done. I'm not even sure what I've done most of the time. Guess she might be talking about the promises I make that she and others keep me from fulfilling. My therapist tells me I am fused with my mother and have never fully separated from my ex-wife. He talks to me about growing up and overcoming my oedipal issues. I get so disgusted when he tells me that I choose to keep being the baby-husband while I coerce my mommy wife to take on all the responsibilities. I don't think that's true. I just always have bad luck.

Narcissists will project shame onto someone like a borderline, who already has a thwarted self of self, whereas obsessive-compulsives will withhold and deprive. The passive-aggressive types take a different approach. Although they are withholding and deprive others, they do not refuse to give. Instead they unconsciously withhold, procrastinate, and make false promises. When they do not follow through and fail to gratify their partner's needs, they find ways to "piss" them off. Unlike other withholding personalities that are outwardly rejecting and refuse to give, the passive-aggressive hardly ever refuses. Rather, he will promise others what they want to hear but then will procrastinate or find other ways to withhold.

Both the narcissist and the borderline conjure up rage in their objects; however, the passive-aggressive choreographs his actions in a more subversive and covert way. As one colleague so succinctly stated, the other personality types are more "in your face," whereas the passive-aggressive agrees to everything but does nothing until "mañana"—which never comes.

I am reminded of a couple who were living together for more than three years. Their relationship came to a halt when the woman finally had enough of her passive-aggressive boyfriend's broken promises to take her on vacation, look for an engagement ring, find a new apartment—yada, yada, yada. The following brief vignette illustrates the kind of rage that these negativists, through their subversive betrayal and defiance, evoke in their intimate partners:

I don't get it. He always tells me he doesn't have enough money to take me traveling or to buy me gifts, yet he seems to have enough to pay for himself and everybody else. For example, he always picks up the check when we go to a restaurant with relatives or friends. I got so frustrated that I did something I know I was not supposed to do. I looked through the bank statements and found receipts that revealed he was spending a fortune at stores and restaurants. He even had bought opera tickets he never told me about. I looked through his e-mail and found that he was communicating with a woman named Jennifer. There were messages from her thanking him profusely for all the lovely evenings and the fine meals he treated her to and telling him how much she was enjoying the gorgeous Chanel purse he had bought her. I'm beside myself with anger!

Associated Complaints

- She really seems disconnected from reality. She agrees to everything I say, then does nothing and acts out her resentment at feeling coerced in sneaky ways.

- He gets me so angry. He is always late, always forgetful, and always expecting me to do everything.
- He misses deadlines, doesn't show up for appointments, and doesn't follow through on his work and personal commitments.
- He is so transparent. It infuriates me how he plays the victim, making me out to be the bitchy wife.
- He defies taking orders at work and resents when others make demands on him. He pretends he's not resentful and rebels in the most subversive ways.
- He procrastinates and somehow gets away with it.
- I do all this work, and he doesn't seem to have any appreciation for my efforts.

THE CASE OF JACK AND JILL

During the course of couple transference, a young couple was having bitter fights over responsibilities pertaining to money, children, and household chores. Actually, I shouldn't say "they" were having fights. Jill was the one fighting, whereas Jack remained calm and cool and looked innocent. He failed to show up at a conjoint sessions and later called to say he had another one of his misfortunes. He ran out of gas. Jill was exasperated. "He always keeps me on tenterhooks with his excuses. Right now I'm scared they are going to turn off our electricity because he still hasn't paid the bill he said he would almost two months ago."

I remind Jill how pleased I am that for once she did not enable him by paying the bill herself and allowing him to get angry at her. At first she was dumbfounded and appalled by my suggestion that she not rescue him: "Let the electric company turn off the lights to allow Jack to get in contact with his own anger as opposed to projecting his anger onto you." Jill stated that she thought therapists should avoid provoking this kind of rage. I told her that she was right, that the role of the therapist generally is to avoid encouraging aggression. However, in the case of deeply suppressed anger like Jack's, we actually encourage the person to begin to understand his anger by expressing it directly. To this, Jill said, "I know and hear what you are saying, but I'm terrified to live in a house without electricity." To which I responded that it is even more terrifying and frustrating to live with a man who causes so much pain and stress and projects his rage in the most insidious ways. "Frustrated?" cried Jill. "I am irate!" As treatment progressed, I let her know how the rage she experienced was not hers, but Jack's. It is like a foreign object, something alien projected into her as her passive-aggressive husband coerces her into enacting the parental role. "You mean I am not the angry bitch I feel like I'm turning out to be?" asks Jill. I respond, "Not at all, but we do need to take a look at the part of you that identifies with and goes along with Jack's behavior."

During conjoint therapy, Jack kept telling me his check was in the mail. Weeks would pass, and still there would be no check. Feeling shamed and humiliated, Jill would write the check for him, even though he was the one responsible for the finances. I decided to ask him to write a check and promised I would not cash it until I got his okay. A few weeks went by without his okay to cash the check. I decided this was the perfect time to get into the couple transference and told him, "Now you are doing with me what you do with your wife, keeping me on hold and forcing me to become the caretaker, treating you week after week, saying very little about your coming late to sessions, and listening to your excuses such as the car broke down, you couldn't find the directions, there was an accident on the freeway. I find this unacceptable, degrading, and dismissive of the work I am trying to do."

I held my breath, waiting for an outpouring of rage. Yes, there it was! "Who the hell are you to attack me and tell me I make excuses every time I come here? I have a legitimate reason. All you care about is your goddamn money!" Jill was sitting on pins and needles. Although I was not exactly comfortable, I knew I was on the right course. If I as therapist could not contain Jack's rage, how could I expect Jill to be able to handle it? After Jack's rage subsided, we all sat quietly, somewhat stunned. No one moved. There was utter silence. Finally, in a very soft voice I said, "Jack this is great! This is excellent! I so much prefer that you express your anger to me directly as you just did as opposed to expressing it by withholding your checks and making mañana promises." Then Jill piped up and expressed her concern about the bills getting paid. To this I responded, "If your husband doesn't pay the electric bill, then there will be no electricity. If he doesn't pay the telephone bill, then the telephone will be turned off. If he doesn't pay for the session, then there will be no more sessions." Jack was flabbergasted. "Hey, doctor, have you lost your mind?" My response: "Maybe it is kind of crazy to encourage someone like you—a creative, intelligent man who comes across like a baby-husband and doesn't follow through on his promises—to act in a more responsible manner. If you will okay the check you gave me a while ago and write another check for the sessions to date, I can assure you I will feel less crazy." To my and Jill's surprise, Jack (looking quite irritated) took a pen from my desk and wrote out a check. "Now we're up to date." To this I responded, "This is terrific. Now the baby check is a grown-up one."

Discussion

Many women come into treatment claiming they do not have a responsible husband but rather a "baby husband" who acts out his most primitive fantasies. In psychological terms, these individuals have not overcome their oedipal conflicts, nor can they stand up to their oedipal rivals. To directly refuse, negate, or say no is tantamount to taking a stand or a firm position, which they are unable to do. Passive-aggressives do not feel safe in their father's "big shoes." Instead they opt to maintain a dependent parasitic attachment with the maternal figure, including the wife that now becomes mother. In treatment, the therapist takes a different approach as she actually encourages the patient to channel his anger directly. Working within the couple transference provides the opportunity for the partner to begin to separate from the victimized husband and for the couple to learn to tolerate the pain that the reality of life presents to them.

Even though my final words in the session were cutting, somehow they both knew I was playing out their drama within the couple transference. For Jill it was very reassuring to know that the anger Jack projected was not targeted toward her but toward himself. She also came to the realization that the rage she was feeling was alien to her; she was merely acting as a perfect container for Jack's covert furor. Jill's history revealed that as the eldest of four sisters and three brothers she was placed in the role of caretaker for her siblings at an early age because of her ill mother. As treatment progressed, Jill came to understand how her role as caretaker—particularly for her infant brother, whom she had to feed, care for, and nurture—was being replayed in the present by a baby brother/ husband. As an elder sister, she could not tolerate seeing her little brother cry, and as soon as he felt any discomfort, she would quickly try to relieve him. It is not an easy task to tell someone not to help out his/her partner, not to pay the bills and risk having their utilities turned off. However, until someone comes along with a better treatment plan for the mañana syndrome that characterizes the passive-aggressive, this is the way things will be.

THE DEPRESSIVE

What distinguishes this personality type from the other complainers is that the depressive's complaints are leveled against the self—hatred turned inward, resulting in self-loathing and self-blame. They are the victimized, "poor-me" personalities. The slightest sense of defeat sets these complainers on a down-ward path. They are plagued by self-blame and dominated by a harsh, punitive superego, as well as by guilt and self-hatred. They are perfectionists, and when life does not go their way, they blame themselves (self-hatred). They have a sadistic superego that runs amok and are self-denigrating and self-castigating. However, they are highly reliable, dependable, serious, and concerned about work. They tend to judge themselves as harshly as they do others, causing them to withdraw and isolate themselves from the rest of the world. Their depression and negative attitude affects everyone around them.

In all my years working with couples, I have never noted complaints that are more glaringly apparent than those associated with the depressive personality. These are complainers wrapped in complaints. Not only do these self-haters complain about themselves, others, and life in general, but the people who interact with them complain about their complaining.

The borderline shares many similarities with the depressive, as well as with the passive-aggressive. Both are victims. Both experience self-hatred and bouts of aloneness, isolation, and depression. The major distinction between the borderline and the depressive is that for the depressive self-hatred is turned inward, whereas for the borderline self-hatred is turned outward and targeted toward others. The borderline projects unwanted parts of the self externally: "I didn't do anything wrong; it's all her/his/their fault!"

CLINICAL DEPRESSION VERSUS STATES OF MOURNING AND LOSS

The exact cause of depression is not known. Moreover, there are many different kinds of depression: normal depression due to loss and mourning, major depression, clinical depression, unipolar depression, bipolar depression, borderline depression, and psychotic depression (Lachkar 2013). Many researchers believe that depression results from chemical changes in the brain that stem from genetics in conjunction with the environment and stressful events. Clinicians often confuse clinical depression with normal states of loss, grief, and mourning. Treating major depression with antidepressant medication merely ameliorates the symptoms. Medication should be an adjunct to psychodynamic psychotherapy that addresses the root cause of the depression, as well as the delusion and distortion regarding one's self-image. Other forms of treatment can include a combination of behavioral, supportive, and dialectical behavior therapy. In more severe cases where there is a serious threat of suicide, hospitalization may be required. In Chapter Two, I refer to Klein's (1957) two positions: the paranoid and the depressive positions. The latter inextricably relates to loss and sadness. If not addressed or recognized in the early stages of mourning, it can become a more severe depression. Diagnosing depression and dealing with the kinds of complaints the "self-hater" triggers in others must be understood within the context of these dynamics.

> I am my depression and my depression is me!
> Mary not only feels depressed, she becomes the depression.
> She not only feels despair, she becomes the despair.
> She not only feels the alienation, she becomes the alienated one.
> She not only feels the victimization, she becomes the victim.

THE GROUP AND THE SELF-HATER

Bob was obviously depressed and showed it outwardly as he attended my group therapy sessions. He frustrated the other group members by repudiating whatever suggestions they offered in terms of making his life more satisfying and more meaningful. I will never forget the looks of frustration on their faces as members of this caring group tried desperately to help this sad and forlorn man. Bob did not have a family history of depression or show any signs of suicidal ideation. His depression appeared to be more a product of social pressures and strains. He is a prime example of someone who has experienced numerous losses but has never mourned or come to terms with his sadness.

Therapist: Bob, you look very sad still. What's going on?

Bob: Nothing!

Group: (Members of the group eye one another, as if to say, "Here we go again.")

Therapist: The group has been trying to give you support and helpful suggestions, but whatever they say you reject. They are getting a bit frustrated with you.

Bob: I know. Everything is my fault.

Steve: Hey, man, that's what you always say, and we are getting sick of you constantly blaming yourself.

Alice: I feel the same way. Last week we suggested you send your résumé out to get some work and keep yourself occupied, and all you could say was you already did that and nobody contacted you. And even if they did contact you, they wouldn't hire you.

Avi: And when you said you were lonely, we suggested that you join an online dating group, only to hear you say that you didn't feel like doing that because you wouldn't get any responses.

Bob: I just feel like I'm a loser and nothing I do is right.

Therapist: The group has a different view of you than you have of yourself. Last week Marge was saying that you are an attractive guy—until you start complaining.

Veronica: When you refused to go online, when you said you felt lonely and hated going back to your apartment, I suggested you get a little dog or cat. You rejected that idea, too. I agree with our therapist. We are not only getting frustrated with you, but you take up all our time. We have other issues to discuss besides you.

Richard: Yes, I agree. Let's move on. There are things I would like to bring up.

Therapist: Veronica, thank you for bringing our group back on track. I think we can all agree we have done everything we can to help Bob.

Alice: Now we are going to spend all our time listening to Richard talk about himself and all his great accomplishments.

Therapist: Wouldn't it be nice if Bob could have a little of Richard's self-confidence, and Richard could have a little bit of Bob's humility?

Steve: What about me! Me! Me!

Group: (Everyone chuckles, knowing that Steve is a closet narcissist.)

Therapist: What I love about this group is how we play off one another's dynamics and how we play out some unconscious role we see in the others.

Alice: I like our group and enjoy everyone in it.

Therapist: Bob, before we stop. I want you to know that in spite of our frustration we all care about you. But in order for us to help you, you have to show that you care about yourself and have respect for those in the group who offer you help.

Steve: Hey, man, yeah, we all do like you. But do us a favor and get a dog!

Therapist: On that note, we will stop now. See you all next week.

Discussion

In the interplay of the group's dynamics, we can readily observe how Bob becomes the group's victim, the self-hater who refutes whatever the group offers. Bob is unaware that the very thing he craves, human contact, is the very thing he defends against. He is almost a deflated narcissist. Like the narcissist, he requires a great deal of attention, but in the opposite direction. However, unlike the narcissist, Bob could care less about self-mirroring objects. Basically, he is unaware of his own needs, let alone the needs and concerns of others (Lachkar, 2008a, 2008c). The self-hater is more invested in masochistic bonding via pain, victimization, self-flagellation, and self-blame. Bob is a good example of this kind of masochistic bonding. He not only feels the despair and isolation, he becomes it. It is one thing to describe an affective state of mind and another to "become it." This is not a far cry from the psychotic who cannot describe, for example, how he feels when he is cold. Instead of describing the feeling, he becomes the cold and freezes up like an iceberg.

In the session described previously, I felt as though I was Winnicott's "being mother" rather than the "doing mother." The "being mother" is the one who is just there to listen, understand, and empathize with the depressive's feelings of isolation and despair. At the onset, the group was empathic with Bob's pain, but after a while they got frustrated and angry and started to complain about how he took up all the group's time.

Taking into consideration the overlap between various forms of depression that are caused by genetics, a chemical imbalance, or early trauma or societal influences, it is important to address the feelings of loss and grief that occur in the depressive position as outlined by Melanie Klein. Most common among those who suffer from this disorder is a predilection for avoidance and isolation. Despite his/her depression and self-hatred, the depressive has a sense of inverse omnipotence. This sense of entitlement and superiority serves to keep others at arm's length. It is frustrating and often very hurtful for people, especially for caretaker types involved with a self-hater, to feel cutoff and useless.

In treatment, the therapist can effectively deploy the introjective process to help partners involved with self-haters disidentify with the negativity the self-hater projects. The most effective treatment is dual projective identification. In this process, the therapist joins in the patient's affective state of mind to ward off aloneness and feelings of alienation. Through their mutual projection, the patient becomes the therapist, and the therapist becomes the patient as they work toward the shared goal of alleviating the depressive's self-loathing and depression.

THE CASE OF KAREN

Karen, a 59-year-old nurse, was referred to treatment for clinical depression by a sibling who noticed she was not eating, avoided social events, and would not return phone calls to people who attempted to check up on her. Karen had recently undergone a double mastectomy and was feeling hopeless and desperate. She indicated she felt paralyzed, couldn't work, couldn't sleep, and could hardly get up in the morning to get dressed, let alone summon the energy to come to her therapy appointments.

Therapist: Hi Karen!

Karen: (silent)

Therapist: (silent)

Karen: Well, I'm here!

Therapist: Yes, you are here!

Karen: Okay, so what are you going to do with me?

Therapist: (feels a bit stunned and gives Karen a quizzical look)

Karen: Look, I'm a lost cause. Everyone is trying to help me, offering advice right and left. And it doesn't do any good.

Therapist: Well, I hope I can help you in a different way than friends or family can.

Karen: Okay. And what would that way be?

Therapist: I would start by letting you know that things are not as hopeless as you think they are. Otherwise you would not be here.

Karen: But I am depressed. My last therapist said I had a clinical depression and needed to go on medication. I hate medication. So how can *you* help me?

Therapist: Okay, let's begin. First of all, Karen, I am not convinced you have a clinical depression. You have just experienced some huge losses—your breasts, the passing of your brother, and the loss of your beloved ten-year-old cat.

Karen: Okay? So?

Therapist: (feeling very frustrated that Karen is acting like a revengeful borderline patient but determined to keep an open mind and continue to stay on the mourning trail) You know there is a difference between a clinical depression and mourning.

Karen: What's the difference?

Therapist: Mourning is not a mental illness; it is a perfectly normal state that people go through when they have experienced major losses.

Karen: (becoming more intrigued and seeming to like that I implied she probably did not have a mental illness)

Therapist: (struggling not to fuse with Karen's loathing and self-hatred) You may have other issues, but this is the healthy and normal part of you. There is no need to turn against yourself.

Karen: I've done that my whole life. My mother was very hard on me. She was always very critical, as if I could never do anything right.

Therapist: So now you have internalized this critical, attacking mother and attack yourself, even when there is no need to.

Karen: Okay, so I'm not depressed. I am in mourning. So what?

Therapist: Now you're letting me know how helpless and worthless you feel.

Karen: Well, you are worthless if you can't help yourself.

Therapist: I think I have already helped you to help yourself.

Karen: How?

Th: By allowing you to understand the normal parts of you so that you do not have to turn against yourself and be so harsh. This is what paralyzes you and prevents you from getting up in the morning.

Karen: I feel such a heavy weight. Yes, I had a mother who did nothing but criticize and demean me, and that can be quite heavy. But it is not just my mother; this is me and my feelings.

Therapist: You see, Karen, you not only feel hopelessness and despair; you actually become them. It would be as if instead of telling you I'm cold I would sit here like an iceberg and refuse to acknowledge you or talk to you.

Karen: Interesting.

Therapist: This is what you were doing with me. You were not just telling me about the loss of your breasts, your brother, and your precious cat; you actually sat here showing me your despair and state of paralysis. For a moment I started to feel paralyzed myself, but luckily got myself out of it.

Karen: Then I hope you can help me get out of it and regain my self-esteem. I feel awful with the way I look—having no breasts.

Therapist: Of course, I will help you. You are not alone. Many women have gone through the same experience. But for me to help you, you have to allow me to be the breast that can feed you and not cut me off.

Discussion

Karen's revelation allowed her to understand that her depression was a defense against intimacy, dependency, and vulnerability. As bad as she felt, she was not going to let me in, so I had to enter through another path. Projective identification was the route I took after realizing how I became the worthless therapist and she the critical mother, letting me know what it feels to be helpless. As therapy continued, I was able to open the window of transference, sharing the feelings of isolation, loneliness, sadness, and guilt she was projecting into me. However, mostly I felt and shared her pain. I let her know that although she and I differed, I could "feel" her feelings and her pain, but I don't become the pain.

There was a fine line between Karen having a clinical depression and suffering from trauma over the loss of her breasts. I used the metaphor of the breast as an object that can feed and nourish or a breast that is biting, attacking, and cutting. At first I thought Karen would reject these Kleinian interpretations, which I felt were important to address her primitive mental state. However, surprisingly, she actually was emotionally awakened by them. She admitted she never mourned her losses. Instead she was quick to blame, attack, and berate herself. Although Karen refused to take any medication, she did see a psychopharmacologist. Her refusal to take medication became part of the therapeutic issues. Karen presents many of the common symptoms of a depressive, a self-hater.

Someone in the depressive position experiencing mourning and loss definitely needs to be distinguished from those suffering from other types of depression (e.g., a major clinical depression). These distinctions are often not clear, but although the diagnosis is unfolding, it is important for the therapist to take these other types of depression into consideration.

Self-haters obviously have a great deal of difficulty with intimate relations. They are irritable, lethargic, desolate, and feel forsaken. Depressives are extremely critical of themselves and equally critical of others. Unlike the borderlines, who will spend the rest of their lives blaming others, the self-haters blame themselves. "If I hadn't asked my brother to meet me at the restaurant, he would still be alive today." They often see the world as dark, bleak, and destined to end or at least experience a major disaster. Depressives, particularly depressive men, often hook up with borderlines—dependent, caretaker types that frequently lack self-esteem and fuse with the pain of others (Lachkar, 2013). As much as borderlines want to be needed and appreciated, they internalize and personalize the self-hater's rejection: "I want to help him but he doesn't let me in. Every time I ask him if he needs or wants anything he merely replies, 'No, I don't your help. I don't need anybody's help!'" Many self-haters are withdrawn, isolated, and cannot communicate or express their feelings. They frequently feel too ashamed and too undeserving to allow others to comfort or console them.

Common Characteristics of Depressives

- Concrete thinking
- Low self-esteem, accompanied by a distorted view of self and reality
- Restlessness and irritability
- Devaluation of those who try to help
- Constant state of despair, isolation, and withdrawal
- Chronic sense of hopelessness, worthlessness, and self-persecution
- Lack of drive or motivation to seek pleasure
- Behavior that makes everyone around them feel miserable and guilty
- Thoughts of death or suicide, loss of appetite, and too little sleep or too much sleep (more chronic cases)

Associated Complaints

- He's always blue, always grumbling about something.
- I've never known her to be happy or even fairly satisfied with anything.
- He makes not only himself unhappy but also everyone around him.
- She always thinks the worst, that some shattering event will occur like a recession, an earthquake, or an accident.
- She is always putting herself down.
- He is impossible to live with. He says no to every suggestion I make.

SUMMARY

Both the depressive and the passive-aggressive are like reverse narcissists, with a grandiose, omnipotent self that goes in the opposite direction. Although the depressive turns against the self in obedience to the inner voice of a punitive and critical superego, ready to attack at the least semblance of wrongdoing, the passive-aggressive projects his/her victimized self onto others. Somehow the borderline seems to seep his way into every chapter, and this chapter was no exception. The borderline has many similarities with the passive-aggressive and the depressive. If I were a casting director, I would cast the borderline for all parts!

In the next chapter, we revisit the antisocial and the psychopath. If the self-hater has a severe guilty conscience, which in effect turns all the doom of the world against the self, the sociopath has no conscience at all.

Chapter 7

≍⫟≍

A Life of Lies

Otto Kernberg (2013) pointed out that the antisocial personality was funda-mentally a narcissist without morality. He called the antisocial a malignant narcissist, in the belief that the antisocial was a sadistic psychopath who was unable to distinguish between right or wrong and lacked the capacity to empa-thize with the feelings of suffering and abuse he engendered in others. The antisocial personality is usually regarded as being mentally ill, although some regard these individuals as having a medical condition that influences a per-son's thought mechanism.

On the milder end of the antisocial spectrum are the sociopaths. These personalities are outwardly very charming and will make every effort to woo others to do their bidding. They are masters at duping others, including even the most seasoned therapist! They feel that they are entitled to everything they want and can be extremely manipulative in order to ensure that they achieve their ends, including lying continuously. Sociopaths offer grandiose schemes and promises that often end up to be a sham.

A salient characteristic of the antisocial/sociopathic personality is a lack of remorse, shame, or guilt. Even when they are caught in lies or deceptive acts, their lack of empathy doesn't allow them to feel remorseful for the harm and suffering they have caused others. They do not take responsibility for their deceitful and hateful actions except in the most perfunctory way. Sociopaths have difficulty with love, bonding, and attachment; however, they can put on a great show when it satisfies their own self-serving purposes. They tend to have many sexual partners because they can easily charm women to get their needs met. But they cannot love. They are often deadbeat dads, who show no evidence of caring for their family and think they are above the law.

Characteristics of a sociopath include the following:
- Failure to conform to social norms with respect to lawful behaviors, as indicated by repeatedly performing acts that are grounds for arrest
- Deception, as indicated by repeatedly lying, deceiving, and conning others for personal gain, profit, or pleasure
- Controlling, manipulative use of others solely for their own self-serving purposes
- Reckless disregard for safety of self or others
- Lack of remorse and empathy; indifferent to the hurt or mistreatment of others, even of the ones that they have severely harmed
- Greedy, ambitious misconduct that often flies in the face of societal norms
- Prone to isolating, often schizoid, avoidance tendencies
- Malevolent, cruel, and sadistic

THE ANTISOCIAL VERSUS THE BORDERLINE

Borderline pathology, which was described in a preceding chapter, is often confused with the sociopathic personality, and the crossover between the two presents many challenges for the therapist. Both borderlines and antisocials exhibit a false self, are manipulative liars, and have a distorted view of reality. The major difference is that the borderline personality disorder is a character-logical disorder in which people experience reckless and impulsive behavior. The borderline is dominated by abandonment anxiety, uncontrollable rage, and unstable moods and relationships. Antisocial disorder is thought to be a medi-cal condition that affects a person's way of thinking, relating, and dealing with injustices. The lack of superego functioning as it links to morality and guilt makes it difficult for the antisocial to distinguish between right and wrong. In contrast, borderlines definitely do have a superego, although it is a persecutory rather than a mature one, which is still powered by a sense of morality. "I knew what she said to me was wrong so I just let her have it."

Borderlines are dominated by a profound sense of abandonment anxiety and feelings of emptiness. They are characterized by stormy and unstable rela-tions, uncontrollable rage, reckless behavior, suicidal ideation, paranoia, and loss of impulse control. Because of their defenses, such as splitting, they have a warped sense of reality. They overreact to the statements and actions of others, often distorting or misinterpreting their intentions. Borderlines are the addicts and children of addicts, who have been severely traumatized and abandoned in early childhood. They are driven by persecutory anxiety, including self-destructive behaviors and the tendency to bond with pain. "Anything is better than the emptiness!" The borderline may have the distorted idea that a woman is in love with him when she is not, whereas the sociopath will convince the woman that she is absolutely in love. Sociopaths have more impulse control than their borderline counterparts, and as long as they stay connected to a cause, they will remain in control.

> The borderline: "You are the most beautiful woman I have ever met. I have waited my whole life for you."
> The sociopath: "Stick with me, baby! I'll show you the world and buy you whatever you want."

The sociopaths and the psychopaths are the charmers, the manipulators, the liars who can convince others to trust them. These con artists will do anything necessary to satisfy their desires and exhibit a pervasive pattern of disregard for the rights of others. They are emotionally abusive and use others as pawns for their schemes. They are often cruel and are entirely devoid of feelings and empathy not only for their partners but also for their work colleagues and those with whom they deal on a frequent basis. They lack superego functioning, the moral guide that accesses the ability to distinguish right from wrong.

I am reminded of a patient whose husband was arrested by the FBI for illegally laundering money. His only regret was that he would have to go to jail. He felt nothing for the hundreds of people whose lives were harmed by his illegal activities. As far has he was concerned, if they were stupid enough to be duped, they deserved what they got. However, he was incensed that he was caught and would be punished.

Sociopaths can be anyone from a close relative, best friend, neighbor, or coworker, someone you would never realize is dealing with this disorder that affects everything in their daily life. Sociopaths go above and beyond to make sure that other people around them have no idea that their life is something other than what it appears to be from the outside looking in. More than likely you have met one or two sociopaths in your life and were not even aware of it. I often refer to Bernie Madoff as the icon of sociopaths. With his Ponzi scheme, which was the largest in history, Madoff duped trusting investors, who later were aghast to find that their beloved "Uncle Bernie" was the culprit responsible for their losing millions of dollars.

The Case of Mrs. F

The sociopath is a mixed breed. Mrs. F kept insisting that her sociopath husband was a narcissist, claiming that she had read all the books on narcissism and he fit the description perfectly. What she didn't factor into her layperson's diagnosis was the lack of a conscience and a sense of morality, or his acts of sadism and cruelty. When her dog died and Mrs. F was distraught, he told her, "It was only a dog." She described how self-centered he was and how much he

craved appreciation and recognition for his work in the music industry. She
mentioned how they started a couples' group together and that he convinced
everyone she was the bitch, the nag, the complainer and didn't appreciate him
and all of his accomplishments. Mrs. F also expressed how frustrated she felt
in the group because of his charm, social skills, and ability to woo and seduce
others into believing what a good guy he is and how his bitchy wife does nothing but complain. "All he has to do is give everyone his doe-eyed, poor-me-the-
victim look, and I seem like a terrorist compared to him."

Complaints associated with the sociopath:
- I feel so humiliated when I hear him convince people to trust him and
  invest their time and money in his stupid schemes when I know they will
  get screwed.
- I feel so out of control. I know that behind his facade of friendliness and
  caring lurks a monster who only wants to use his "victims" for his own
  selfish purposes.
- He is so mean and cruel to me. It makes me sick to watch him turn on his
  charm. Everyone thinks he's a great guy. He is so transparent; I see right
  through him. It makes me furious that others don't see him for who he is.
- I feel stuck. I can't report him because if I do I could also go to jail when
  they discover the kinds of scams he has been involved in. Someone has
  to think about the kids.
- If the FBI comes to arrest him, then I don't know how I will be able to pay
  the bills.
- He lives way above our means. He puts on a splashy show of wealth and
  success when really he is a con man.

DEADBEAT DADS

Sociopaths also are often likely to be deadbeat dads. These master manipulators
feel they are above the law, refuse to pay child support, abandon their children,
and totally disregard their parental roles. In many of my previous publications,
I have referred to the borderline as being the prototypical deadbeat dad. But
borderlines differ from their sociopath counterparts in that they will refuse
to pay child support purely out of revenge. They are retaliating against the
partner that presumably has betrayed or abandoned them and whom they will
spend the rest of their lives plotting to get back at, even at the expense of their
children, their money, or themselves (Lachkar, 1986). The sociopath deadbeat
dad will refuse to pay child support out of the desire to control and manipulate
the system for his benefit and will use any means necessary to avoid payments.
Even though it is unconscionable to disregard the feelings of their own children
and bring them into custody battles and disputes, sociopaths will show no
compassion or concern. They feel they are above the law above and the system

and will go to great lengths to best the jurisdictional authorities: "She has more money than I do" or "I gave her money and she spent it on drugs." The socio-path has no compunction about fabricating all kinds of stories to stall or avoid alimony or child support payments. In many case, the "good" parent is so emo-tionally victimized that he or she cannot move past the disastrous situation and lacks the emotional stamina to fight the sociopathic manipulator to the finish. Deadbeat dads are cunning enough to find ways to work the system. Often they make the children the target of their disputes and hold them accountable.

THE PSYCHOPATH: A SOCIOPATH ON STEROIDS

Both the sociopath and the psychopath lack the normal functions of the super-ego. They also lack conscience, morality, and concern for others. They rarely anticipate or even think about the risks they take in their premeditated actions. They are devoid of guilt and rarely show remorse for the impact their transgres-sions have on others. However, the sociopath is more companionable than the psychopath and enjoys interaction with others as long as something is in it for them. Psychopaths are often, but not always, recluses. But because they have difficulty maintaining emotional bonds, they are usually loners, with no or few emotional connections.

When people hear the words "psychopath" or "sociopath," they automati-cally think of some hideously deranged serial killer. In the case of the psycho-path, this is often true. The sociopath relies on a facade to manipulate society in order to get away with some kind of criminal scam. Psychopaths are the killers, the murderers, the terrorists—very organized, systematic, and cunning. They are the closet monsters, the perpetrators of unimaginable violence, the abusers, the molesters, the terrorists at the domestic and global level. Notorious psycho-paths include David Berkowitz, Son of Sam, who shot and killed 13 people in cold blood; James Holmes, who shot 14 people at a Colorado movie theatre; and Adam Lanza, who shot his mother to death in their home and then slaugh-tered 20 children and 6 staff members in an elementary school before killing himself. Other infamous psychopaths are Charles Manson, Richard Ramirez, and Nidal Hasan, who killed 13 and wounded 30 others when he went on a shooting spree at the Fort Hood army base in Texas.

Today we have more nuanced research and a deeper understanding of sociopath and psychopath personalities because of neuroscience. Adrian Raine's book *The Biology of Violence* (2001) stresses that although much is known about brain scans and genetics in sociopaths and psychopaths, the importance of maternal attachment cannot be overlooked. In Kleinian terms, if the infant's need for the breast is thwarted, this deprivation creates unconscious envy; therefore, "the mother/breast" must be destroyed. This is the nature of envy. Envy, unlike jealousy, is destructive by nature. Raine addresses psychopathy that cannot be understood in terms of social or environment factors, indicating that brain scans show there are important inherent predispositions that contribute to the proclivity toward violence. Other researchers agree that psychopathy is a product of many complex and intertwining biological forces, along with social and environmental conditions. Hare (1999) notes in *The Disturbing World of the Psychopath among Us* that psychopaths are not born criminals but experience the world in a way that they cannot make sense of, which causes them to react suddenly and violently.

Martha Stout (2006) presents a broader view of the psychopathic personality in *The Psychopath Next Door,* claiming he could be the devil you know— your cheating/lying ex-husband, your sadistic teacher, or the boss who betrays or humiliates you and others. Stout reveals that a shocking amount of ordinary people walk around with an undetected mental disorder, people with no conscience or ability to show guilt or remorse. She urges us to take precautionary, self-protective measures and to question authority, suspect flattery, and beware of those who exhibit self-pity, which can lead us to collude in acts of victimization.

Crime writer Ann Rule, author of *The Stranger Beside Me* (2000), a book about serial killers, was working at a counseling clinic for suicide prevention, unaware that the "stranger" working beside her at the clinic was Ted Bundy. Rule shared many long nights with Bundy but never imagined he was a cold-blooded serial murderer until the news came out.

A more recent case shows how hard it is to distinguish the psychopath. James DiMaggio, who kidnapped 16-year-old Hannah Anderson after he killed her mother and brother and set fire to their home, was a long-term friend of Hannah's parents. DiMaggio was someone who would be among the least suspected by the family to commit such a crime because of his close ties to them.

Characteristics of a Psychopath

- Psychopaths put on a false self to lure their victims.
- Psychopaths are extremely selfish and self-absorbed. Psychopaths are very deceptive and constantly lie, cheat, and manipulate.
- Psychopaths show no empathy, remorse, or guilt toward the people they have harmed.
- Psychopaths get a thrill killing, murdering, and even mutilating their victims.
- Psychopaths are very controlled and plan heinous crimes carefully and meticulously.
- Psychopaths are often loners and frequently live isolated, detached lives.
- Psychopaths have strange body language, and their eyes are often schizoid-looking, detached turned inward.
- Psychopaths derive excitement and sexual gratification from their heinous acts.

- Psychopaths are often very intelligent and frequently are high-tech types that are good with computers; they relate better to hard objects than to people.
- For psychopaths, killing becomes a mere sport and engenders a perverse, pervasive excitement that is more important to them than life itself. (Psychopaths often risk and take their own lives.)

Associated Complaints

- I complained to others that I didn't like to be around him. I wish I had been more aware and paid more attention to the danger signs.
- I always knew there was something off about him.
- I told my boss this guy was a bully, but when nothing was done I stopped complaining, fearing he would hurt me.
- I noticed that he kept staring oddly at the young girls at our high school and wanted to tell the authorities. But I was afraid my complaint would get me in trouble.
- I told everybody he was such a phony. On the outside, he seemed so cordial, polite, and nice. However, it was also kind of annoying that he always made over-the-top flattering comments to me and everyone else. Yet never did I suspect he was a predator.

SUMMARY

Sociopaths and psychopaths populate the antisocial disorder spectrum. The terms liars, manipulators, users, and con artists are commonly used to describe them. There are many compelling portraits of hustlers, rapists, and other predators who charm, lie, and manipulate their way through life. The sociopath is not a violent predator or killer, but exploits and lures others with a false sense of charm, manipulating them for his own self-serving purposes. This chapter also distinguished between the borderline and the sociopath, two personality types that are often confused. At the extreme end of the antisocial continuum, the psychopath suffers from chronic mental illness characterized by abnormally violent and manic psychotic tendencies and thrives on killing, raping, and mutilating innocent victims. Perhaps the sociopath and the psychopath can be differentiated most vividly by the following description: The sociopath will blow other people's money; the psychopath will blow up buildings. Chapter Eight on cross-cultural complaints also touches on the psychopath within the context of terror and terrorism fueled by extreme cultural ideologies.

Chapter 8

≫≪

When East Meets West

Complaints at the cultural level take on a unique form. As a marital therapist, I find that many couples bring with them to this country their nationalistic pride and nationalistic flag, to which they relentlessly cling. Often the refusal to adapt involves the desire to maintain one's sense of identity, which is tied to the culture in which one was born. What a complaint is to a Westerner may not be a complaint to someone from another culture, which presents the therapist with an additional challenge.

Today's consultation rooms are filled with individuals and couples with disparate backgrounds—multicultural couples, cross-cultural couples, interracial couples, interethnic couples, same-sex marriages, blended family marriages, and step-family marriages. Many people do not realize that when they tie the knot with someone from another country, they are also marrying an entire culture, with its unique customs and outlook on every aspect of society. "Marry me, marry my country. Marry me, marry my family!" This includes religion, ideology, childrearing practices, gender, and political heritage (Lachkar, 1992, 1993a, 1993b, 1998a, 1998b, 2004b, 2008a, 2008b, 2013).

Those who come to the United States from other countries often have trouble integrating their nationalistic upbringing with their new surroundings. The cultural narcissist, whom I have described in many of my previous publications, clings to his/her nationalist or religious identity and refuses to adapt to the societal norms in this country. Just as couples think their battles are over money, sex, children, and custody but really are about control, domination, victimization, rivalry, and unresolved oedipal issues, the same holds true for problems in the political arena. Countries think battles are over territory, economics, and

113

ideologies, but the real issues are over betrayal, entitlement, control, and domination. To effectively treat the emotional vulnerabilities within the context of
the "complaints" among cross-cultural couples, it is imperative to take into
account these qualitative differences.

My first real insight into cross-cultural complaints was at a sushi bar with
my daughter. When I received my meal, I complained to the manager that the
server had misunderstood my order and that it wasn't what I wanted. A few
moments later the manager appeared with a young man who bowed low, then
got on his knees and begged for forgiveness. He was newly arrived from Japan,
and by sending the meal back I had unknowingly shamed him.

A second influence was my interest in psychohistory, starting with a psychoanalytic study of the Arab-Israeli conflict (Lachkar, 1992, 2008a, 2008c,
2011). I began to view Arabs and Jews as a mythological narcissistic/borderline
"couple" whose dance of accusation and retaliation goes on and on without
reaching conflict resolution. I saw Jews as the "narcissistic/chosen ones" and
Arabs as the "borderline/abandoned orphans" and their "political dance" as
having its origins in narcissistic injuries rooted in demons of the past, age-old
sentiments of unresolved oedipal rivalry. I saw a parallel to couples in clinical
practice, which made me wonder why couples stay in painful relations and
refuse to heed the good advice that is given to them.

As I began to study cultures that are vastly different than ours—where
feelings, emotions, and protest take on a subordinate role—I learned how the
psychodynamics in one culture can take on a completely different shape in
another. Middle East and Asian countries are vastly different than countries
such as France, Germany, Spain, and England, which, although diverse in many
aspects, share many of our values and Judeo-Christian beliefs. Although Israel
is a democratic country and its values and standards are akin to ours, there are
definite cultural differences. In the West we value individuality and separation
between self and object, whereas among Israelis the group takes precedence
over the individual. Group bonding and fusion remain central to the building
of the Jewish state, in which the Holocaust definitely played a role.

An American patient now living in Israel complained about having to stay
out too long when she goes out with friends at night. Although she is Jewish,
she is the only one of the group not born in Israel and did not understand that
their reluctance to separate at the end of the night had to do with the past history of the Israeli Jews and the need to bond. Even after people announce that
they are leaving a gathering, it takes them at least another 20 minutes to actually leave. "I have to be really careful not to act as though I am anxious to go,"
she relates. An early or abrupt departure is regarded as offending the host and
"abandoning" the group.

Group psychology honed my interest in understanding the dynamics of
cross-cultural couples and those of countries and even corporations (described
in Chapter Nine). The seminal works of Wilfred Bion (1959) explain why

people in regressed groups form idealized bonds/attachments with destructive leaders/bosses/managers who collude with the group's collective fantasies. "We know our leader is destructive, but he is our father and our savior and we worship him."

In one of my early papers, "Psychopathology of Terrorism" (2008b), I raised the issue of nations, countries, and societies having a cultural V-spot, whereby an entire culture adheres to certain group fantasies based on painful archaic injuries, myths, and sentiments handed down from generation to generation. Transposed to the cultural level, the V-spot might sound like: "How dare you dare insult our prophet!" "You shook hands with a woman!" "You didn't bow the right way!" "I'd rather die than give up allegiance to my country!"

As a psychohistorian specializing in the Middle East and Asia, I explored how we distinguish a "normal" complaint from a pathological one. Just as each personality type has its unique way of complaining, so do cultures. One culture's mental health is another culture's pathology. Some say terrorists or jihadists are normal people who merely have been brainwashed to fight for a cause. Others have referred to this as a culture of intimidation, where repressed behavior is rewarded and individual rights are demonized. One of the most comprehensive studies about the differences between cultures is by Robert Endleman (1989), whose research indicates that people are culturally diverse but psychologically share basic instinctual relationship drives. He claims that the bonding and development stages of a child are fundamental to every culture. One needs to master and overcome oedipal rivals and incest taboos within the family matrix. He further argues that the healthy aggression and self-expression encouraged in the West is stifled and enacted masochistically in Middle Eastern cultures (self-punishment turned inward or outward).

The work of Professor Emeritus Peter Berton (1995, 2001) of the University of Southern California's School of International Relations, which received an honorary award from the Emperor of Japan, was immensely valuable to my exploration of cross-cultural dynamics and provided background for my book *The Disappearing Male* (Lachkar, 2013). His in-depth analysis of Japanese behaviors shows how men from various cultures "disappear" from their women. Professor Berton gives the example of the Japanese male who is rarely present, likening him to a 7-Eleven store because he leaves home at 7 a.m. and returns at 11 p.m. At the more extreme level, Islamic suicide bombers literally disappear as they blow themselves up to "honor" their country and families. Not only do these men disappear, so do major historical episodes. The Japanese still deny their World War II war crimes, and Ahmadinejad insists the Holocaust never took place.

Some scholars question the very concept of defining national character, believing that we are stereotyping and arbitrarily labeling people. I argue that what they call labeling I call examining the role of culture and its historical significance. One of the broadest generalizations would be to classify Middle Eastern and Asian societies as shame–honor cultures, as opposed to countries like Germany or France, which can be characterized as guilt cultures (Berton and Lachkar, 2001). It is obvious that not all members of a given group behave in a manner consistent with the overwhelming majority, and some behavior might actually oppose the societal "norm." Still, one must grapple with some generalizations while remaining aware of their limitations. Many view the French as having an attitude of superiority, the Italians as overly emotional, the Germans as stoic and reserved, and the Russians as paranoid. Whatever the nationality, it is difficult enough to deal with complaints in general, let alone those layered with nationalistic shame, envy, and rivalry, which turn a simple question or complaint into a traumatic event.

PSYCHODYNAMICS AND CULTURAL COMPLAINTS

One cannot fully understand the complaints of couples from different cultures without understanding such contrasting dynamic variances as dependency, entitlement, shame, honor, peace, promises, and sense of self. It is not enough to understand shame without comprehending the need to "save face." In the Middle East, shame is inextricably linked to honor and saving face at any cost, even to the destruction of self and/or others.

Even words like *promise* can be poles apart. In the Muslim world, a promise or commitment is tantamount to a wish or a whim, depending on *Inshallah*, the "Will of Allah." One Muslim patient phoned at the last minute to cancel an appointment because he was called to prayer. I later learned that prayer overruled everything for him. Another patient confronted a Muslim friend about being "stood up" for a lunch appointment and was told "it was the will of Allah." Her anger abated when she understood that his response was cultural and that she should not take it personally.

Cultural differences also extend to the meaning of the concept of justice implemented through Sharia law. The word *Taqiyya* literally means deception or dissimulation, to disguise the truth, especially for "the greater cause." This is in contrast to the Japanese form of "deception," where the intention is not to deliberately derail the other person but rather is a form of politeness. In international negotiations and in therapy, these cultural nuances become a real challenge. Muslims will say one thing and in the next moment say another, based on the will of Allah. The Japanese have more than 16 ways of saying "yes" when they mean "no," which they employ to avoid confrontation. A Western psychoanalyst will encourage the patient to express his/her needs as directly and openly as possible, but a Japanese patient will remain silent, waiting for the analyst to offer what he or she needs (*amae*).

Another important dynamic to consider is the difference between an individual self and a group self. In many societies, particularly those in Asian and Middle Eastern countries, the individual self is virtually non-existent. Where American culture emphasizes uniqueness and self-expression, Asian societies stress the group self. If the individual defies the group, he/she can be subject to humiliation and ridicule and may even become an outcast. Then there is the true self and false self, terms originated by Donald Winnicott (1965). Most Western psychotherapists help struggling couples become more attuned to the true self, which is belied by the false self. The Japanese adhere to two selves: *Honne* represents the home self or private self, whereas *tatameo* is the public self, which does not display emotion. This can cause a great deal of confusion when treating a Japanese person, who would be unlikely to free associate in a therapist's office. For Korean patients, it is not enough to understand their "complaints"; one must also understand the concept of *han* (Lachkar, 2008a, 2008b, 2008c, 2013), the relentless rage that Korean women hold onto that has deep historical significance—the loss of many of their men through wars and their having to learn to fend for themselves.

In Japan, shame is a major component of the culture, as many scholars affirm. Shame constitutes a major sanction, whereby people are humiliated and made fun of. The most common threat that a Japanese mother uses to discourage behavior of which she disapproves in her children is to tell them that people will laugh at them. In Japan people are encouraged to hide their feelings in order to save face.

This cultural reticence partially explains the relative unpopularity of psychotherapy in Japan. In a shame society, individuals cannot admit their wrongdoings. This is supported by the complicity of a government that continues to deny the crimes committed in the World War II era, such as the killing of 300,000 Chinese during the Rape of Nanjing (Berton, 2001; Lachkar, 1998a, 1998b). The Japanese have since laid down their swords and become financial warriors. One might speculate that after losing the war Japan more than ever felt alienated and isolated and responded to the urge to become part of the global economy.

The Germans, on the other hand, have attempted to make enormous reparation for the "sins of their fathers." One criterion of a guilt society is the capacity to mourn and come to terms with wrongdoings, the paranoid-schizoid position. Shame cultures rely on external sanctions to encourage good behavior, whereas guilt cultures rely on an internalized conviction of sin. Shame operates between the person and the group; guilt has a conscience and operates between the person and his superego. Shame is the need to hide one's true feelings; guilt is the recognition of one's wrongdoings and eventually mourning, repenting, and making reparation. Without admitting guilt, one cannot atone. Guilt can be relieved by confession, whereas shame is not so readily resolved. A person in the West who has sinned can get relief by confessing to a priest or a therapist. By contrast, in a shame society reprehensible acts remain repressed and masked.

LISTENING TO COMPLAINTS
AT THE CULTURAL LEVEL

The material that follows is in no way intended to undermine the abuse, violence, and terrorism taking place on a global level. We cannot regard as "complaints" the violation of human rights and injustices to women under tyrannical regimes. In no way can we compare a wife complaining about her husband forgetting to put down the toilet seat to Burmese brides being burned over the coals. The intent here is to offer therapists a background for listening with a "cultural ear" to enhance their understanding and their ability to treat couples.

In many cultures, people are not encouraged to express their basic needs and desires, let alone voice their complaints. In Japan, people are encouraged to conform and be in harmony with others. In the Middle East, people are also repressed but suffer far graver consequences should they violate the rules of their society. It is only when they come to our country that we begin to hear the "real" cross-cultural relationship complaints, which often revolve around the following:

- A spouse needs to be more communicative.
- A spouse wants more respect.
- A husband is more loyal to his boss than to his wife.
- A husband is more loyal to his mother and to his family than to his wife.
- A person is more loyal to his or her country than to his or her spouse.
- A husband treats his wife like an object.
- A spouse shows little emotion and or feelings.
- A spouse is too controlling or too submissive.
- A husband does not spend enough time with his wife and children.
- A spouse is too rigid, needs to be more flexible.
- A spouse expects magical thinking, as if his/her needs should be evident without the need to voice them.

My concept of the cross-cultural hook (Lachkar, 2008a) is a means to find pathology within each partner's own culture and construct a platform for "negotiating" by pinpointing cultural contradictions and hypocrisy. For example, a Japanese wife finds solace in nursing her baby while sleeping with the baby in another room, giving the therapist an opportunity to point out the conflict with Western childrearing. Or an American wife complains that her Japanese husband is cheap and cannot accept our materialistic society. In reality, Japan is a hub of materialism. Objects, in fact, often become the replacement for human contact.

The Case of Mr. S: The Good Daddy

Mr. S, a politician and diplomat, came into treatment complaining that Yoko, whom he met at a massage parlor in Japan, was unlike his previous wives. As his masseuse, Yoko was always patient, soothing, nurturing, and attentive to his every need. He had divorced his demanding, hostile wife and was thrilled to be in the presence of an Asian woman who made no demands. It was not until they married that everything changed.

Therapist: Hi, Mr. S. Are you all right? Please come in and have a seat!

Mr. S: No, I am not all right. I thought that marrying an Asian woman would mean she would be subservient, easygoing, and make fewer demands of me. She is worse than my ex.

Therapist: (listening attentively) Like?

Mr. S: Oh, you have no clue what this woman has done to me. First of all, I found out she gets money with our credit card and mails it to her family in Japan. She has four sisters, two brothers, and a mother.

Therapist: She does it without asking?

Mr. S: If she asked, of course I would help her family. But when I need to give money to my sons, she has a fit. She goes into a non-stop tirade.

Therapist: Isn't it true, though, that in Japan the women don't usually ask for what they need and are in charge of the finances?

Mr. S: Yes, that is true. But we are not in Japan. We are here in America.

Therapist: Even so, as a Japanese woman she feels she is in charge of the finances.

Mr. S: But in her country everything is supposed to be fair. So why is it okay for her to give money to her family and not to mine?

Therapist: That is an excellent point. A Japanese woman does not distinguish her family from others; they are treated the same. In Japan, this is known as *wa* (harmony).

Mr. S: Then we can't blame it on culture. This gives me an advantage because the next time she points out it is her job to handle the finances, I can say only if we distribute the wealth evenly. Tell me more about what's behind Yoko's thinking.

Therapist: In Japan, unlike here in the West, there is no such thing as an individual self, only a collective group self. So if one person is greedy or selfish, it dishonors the group.

Mr. S: Wow! Why didn't anyone tell me this before? This stuff is powerful.

Therapist: Be careful. You don't want to attack or shame your wife. But you need to take charge of the accounts because she truly believes she can do anything she wants with the money.

Mr. S: She spends money like a drunken sailor.

Therapist: In Japan, even though the wife is in control of the money, she shows respect, and her husband has the upmost respect for her judgment.

Mr. S: Yes, respect is exactly what's missing. She tells me that in Japan the husband is away long hours. So to occupy themselves the women become obsessed with shopping, shopping, and shopping!

Therapist: (listening and thinking)

Mr. S: I am away a lot, working late hours and leaving her alone many evenings and weekends.

Therapist: But you are not Japanese. In our culture, men take better care of their women, don't neglect them, and try to spend quality time with them. It is nice for families to do things together. In Japan, a man is rewarded for making his work come first. In our country, working all the time and not seeing your family is considered neglect.

Mr. S: I feel guilty.

Therapist: There is a solution to your guilt.

Mr. S: Like what?

Therapist: Fix it! Look, it is not just about your wife and her culture. It is also about you as a couple. If you can understand the part you play, then this relationship is workable.

Mr. S: Okay, I'm just going to tell her straight out what I think and what I expect.

Therapist: Won't work!

Mr. S: Why?

Therapist: Japanese people don't respond to confrontation. You will shame and dishonor her.

Mr. S: I don't give a shit!

Therapist: It should not be hard for you to find a way to negotiate this with your wife. After all, you are an international scholar and diplomat. If you can handle Asia, you can find a way to handle your wife.

Mr. S: Got it! See you next week!

Discussion

This case illustrates the dance between shame and guilt. For Yoko, it is the shame of having to ask for something, and for Mr. S it is guilt for leaving Yoko alone for long periods of time. Mr. S has to be careful not to shame his wife, and the therapist must help Mr. S come to terms with his guilt. The major therapeutic challenge with cross-cultural couples is to go beyond the emotional borders to find pathology within each partner's own culture. The therapist uses the cross-cultural hook to show how Yoko's behavior would not be accepted even in Japanese culture and that Mr. S was acting outside his culture by working long hours like a Japanese man.

A GROUP MIND-SET

Generally speaking, one of the fundamental differences between the West and other cultures is the importance and identification placed on the group as opposed to the individual. The group can be thought of as a big family, with the members all enmeshed and fused with one another. For example, Japan is xenophobic, unlike America where we invite everyone into our smorgasbord of ethnic groups and cultures. In Japanese society, children are encouraged not to think or act individually but to think within the ideology of the collective group self. Conformity is prized. Rote learning, as opposed to creative and analytic thinking, is encouraged in the young. The purpose is to create a sense of oneness, so that one child does not stand out in any way or create envy in others. In the West, the socialization of young children begins with teaching them to "speak up," think for themselves, be creative, and consider themselves unique beings.

I am reminded of a young Japanese medical student who came for treatment looking very forlorn. After sitting quietly for a few moments, he disclosed that he hated medical school and never wanted to become a doctor but had acceded to his parents' wishes. He was an artist with dreams of enrolling in an art academy but feared his parents would scorn him. Being unfamiliar with Japanese culture and its group mentality, I naively suggested that he develop his sense of self and decide what would be best for him. At this he looked at me as though I were some creature from another world and asked, "What do you mean by a sense of self?"

The Western notion is that the infant is born dependent, then goes through stages of separation individuation and eventually develops autonomous ego functioning. In Asian societies, the process of individuation is not encouraged. This keeps children, particularly boys, forever dependent on the mother and even suffocated by her neediness for them to need her. *Amae* is a form of dependency relating to the mother's intense internalization and identification with her child's needs, especially her male child. Under the guise of "closeness," the mother will co-sleep, co-bathe, and in some instances engage in incest by masturbating baby boys to relieve their erections (Adams and Hill, 1997).

The Japanese view the concept of *amae* as the desire to depend and presume upon another's benevolence. The eminent Japanese psychoanalyst Takeo Doi (1973) called *amae* a key concept for understanding Japanese personality structure and said that this longing for dependency can be fulfilled in infancy but cannot be easily satisfied as one grows up. This complex concept has been the subject of debate among Japanese and American scholars. Some have argued that the search for *amae* beyond infancy is unique to Japan and have intimated that it is a sign of pathology in Japanese society (Iga, 1986).

The Case of the Controlling Mother

Sam met Sakura at a sushi bar when they sat next to each other. She methodically showed Sam the different kinds of sushi and how to handle chopsticks. Sam had never dated anyone other than Jewish women and was immediately intrigued with Sakura's quiet demeanor and soft elegance. After they married, everything seemed fine until their first son was born.

Therapist: Greetings! So what brings you here?

Sam: My wife will not allow my son to express himself. She is very controlling and domineering and wants him to do everything her way.

Sakura: In my country, we have order. Children must be sensitive to the behaviors of others.

Sam: I can't stand it anymore. As soon as he cries or shows any discomfort, she grabs him and picks him up as if there is an earthquake.

Therapist: And why is that?

Sam: Sakura says it is customary in Japan not to allow children to cry but to soothe them. Not only that, but she still nurses him, and he's not a baby anymore.

Sakura: Sam is complaining because he wants to have sex, and I can't if I am nursing.

Therapist: Why would it interfere with your ability to be intimate?

Sam: Because they are like glue. He's five years old. Give me a break!

Therapist: Way beyond the weaning years.

Sakura: Not in my country. It is common for mothers to nurse until their sons are least five.

Sam: I can't stand it! Every time I go into the bedroom there is our son just sucking away.

Therapist: You sound very angry.

Sam: I am. I'm also beginning to resent our son.

Sakura: (softly) Sam doesn't understand. Japanese mothers form a special relationship with their sons. It is called *amae*. Also in Japan we don't show anger. We try to be in harmony or *wa*.

Sam: *Amae!* I am sick of her amae! *Wa!* Bah! I'm sick of *wa*, too. We're not in Japan! Let the kid grow up! Let him become his own person!

Sakura: In Japan there is no such thing as becoming "my own person." The group is the person!

Therapist: Thank you, Sakura; that was beautifully stated and very helpful to me in understanding our differences. In our country, we respect individuality and encourage children and the mother to separate much earlier. So I can understand how confusing this must be to have to adapt to a completely different way of life.

Sakura: (weeping) So sorry. I don't mean to show my emotions.

Therapist: In our country, we encourage it.

Sakura: I understand. But this custom has existed for centuries.

Sam: See what I'm talking about?

Therapist: But you did break away from your culture when you chose to marry a Westerner, Sakura.

Sakura: Yes, but I am a Japanese woman, and I need respect for my ways.

Therapist: Actually, that really isn't so because in your culture the woman acquiesces to the man's desires (the cross-cultural hook) as a way of keeping harmony—*wa*.

Sakura: But I really feel shame when I have sex. I try to hide my feelings.

Therapist: So you hide behind your son's need for *amae*? Here women are free to express themselves, and men treat their feelings with respect. What do you think Sam?

Sam: Of course, I treat her with respect. I would love for her to show her feelings when we have sex.

Therapist: Sakura, just think, you have the best of worlds here: the freedom to express yourself and help your son grow up adjusting to our country. But in trying to be the good mommy and using your son to hide your feelings, you are being insensitive to your husband's needs.

Sakura: In my country, we give each other *amae* without using words to tell others what we really need.

Therapist: I respect and appreciate that, and I have to show *amae* to both of you. Sam, your needs are important, but these adjustments will take some time. In a way, Sakura is right. You did marry a Japanese woman, and understanding her traditions goes beyond eating sushi. Sakura, you are also stepping beyond the borders of your culture by not taking care of your husband's needs. In no way do I mean to shame or humiliate you. In fact, I very much appreciate the beauty and wonderful traditions your country brings us. I am trying to help you both find a way to get your needs met.

Sakura: I guess I am hiding my true feelings because I am really afraid if I let
             go of my son I will have nothing because my husband will run off.

Therapist: You mean as the men in Japan do: work long hours, go to Geisha
             houses, and abandon their wife and children?

Sakura: (begins to cry)

Sam: Not to worry. There's no chance that will happen. I love you. In fact,
             it is the opposite. I want to be with you, not some Geisha girl!

Sakura: (sobbing, while Sam caresses her)

Therapist: What a blessing and joining of two cultures right before my very
             eyes.

Sam: Thank you, doctor. (They walk out, Sam with an arm around
             Sakura. At the door, Sakura bows slightly.)

Therapist: Bye, see you next week. Sayonara!

Sam: Sayonara and Shabat Sholom!

Discussion

Although Sakura appears to be attached to her culture, under the guise of the
Japanese banner she hides behind nursing her son to avoid expressing her sexual feelings. Her attachment to her son is not so much cultural as a defense
against her own fear that her husband would abandon her like a neglectful
Japanese husband. Much to Sakura's surprise, it was quite the contrary. Sam
was asking for more intimacy. Issues around shame, the role of women, and the
true self were an integral part of this case. The cross-cultural hook was used to
show Sakura how the very person who expects *amae* is the one who refrains
from giving it.

EAST/WEST CULTURAL DISTINCTIONS

If we compare the cultural differences between Japan and the United States, we
find that a Japanese person is careful not to show emotions and has a tendency
to pretend not to see them in others. This is diametrically opposed to what
occurs in the United States, which encourages individuality, expression, and
perception of feelings and emotions. In Japan, emotion is considered a threat to
the group's harmony. One can imagine how this can shake up a therapist whose
entire treatment focus is based on self-identity and self-expression. By contrast,
Muslims under the shield of jihad (holy war) have no problem showing emotion, as exhibited by their frequent rages and outbursts of violence.

Another factor to consider is hierarchical positions. Who comes first in
the culture? In China, deference is given to country, elders, big brother, and
boss; whereas wives and children are last on the list. For example, Zhou Yan,

a Chinese Olympic gold medal skater in 2000, was criticized for thanking her parents first and not her country. The same holds true for other Chinese athletes, such as basketball sensation Jeremy Lin, whose skill at basketball is not considered his own personal accomplishment but as giving honor to his country (Kaiman, 2012). In Middle Eastern societies, deference is given to religion, prayer, and loyalty to prophets.

One could generalize that Japan tends to be a more male/masochistic society and Islam a sadistic one. Based on the commands in the Qur'an, Muslims are indoctrinated to slay all Christians, Jews, and Buddhists, any group of "intruders" and "infidels" that defies Islamic doctrine. According to Sam Vaknin (2007), masochistic love renders a person prone to self-destructive, punishing, and self-defeating behaviors. Although capable of pleasure and possessed of social skills, the masochist avoids or undermines pleasurable experiences. Masai Miyamoto (1994) notes that Japan's culture vacillates between narcissism and masochism. He refers to this as selfless devotion to the group that involves denial of pleasure. The Japanese male avoids or undermines pleasurable experiences and instead sacrifices his life for his boss and company, and even to some extent for his wife and children.

As the common wisdom of Japanese housewives goes, "a good husband is healthy and absent." The Japanese male fits my "Disappearing Male syndrome," an entire culture of men that adheres to the same collective group fantasy: loyalty to the group or workplace. Even though Japanese men wear a suit, a different kind of armor, they are still hardwired to be warriors. On the surface, it appears as though they have relinquished their undying loyalty to the master and have abandoned their "sword" mentality, but basically the slavish devotion, self-sacrifice, and masochism still exist.

Miyamoto states that Japan is a "closed society," a bureaucracy coated with institutional self-masochism. I refer to this as "reverse narcissism," domination by the needs of the group and the culture rather than the pull of the omnipotent, grandiose self. Although masochism is still a primary element in Japanese culture, an American therapist could easily assess Japanese childrearing practices as abusive by Western standards because children are raised as scapegoats and helpless victims of the absent father and the suffocating mother.

Hiroshi and Elanna

Hiroshi never wanted to leave Japan, his work, boss, or family. He met his wife in Israel while working there as an engineer. He succumbed to her pleas and moved to America (where most of her family resides). Elanna had no problem adapting to life in the United States. She joined a temple and found an Americanized Israeli community. She had difficulty understanding and accepting her husband's inability to adapt to an American lifestyle. Hiroshi now had more time and freedom, which Elanna believed he should be spending at home with family.

Elanna:	It's horrible. The children and I hardly ever see Hiroshi.
Therapist:	Oh, why is that?
Elanna:	Because Hiroshi is always away at night, while I am home with the kids.
Therapist:	This must make you feel very alone, especially when you desire to be intimate with your husband.
Elanna:	It isn't only that. In Israel families are everything. We enjoy spending time with our kids and our friends. Besides who wouldn't want their husband home at night instead of out drinking sake with the guys?
Hiroshi:	(in a very soft-spoken tone) You see, in Tokyo it is quite common for the woman to stay home and take care of the home and the children. We men work long hours, and at the end of the day we need to relax.
Elanna:	But this is not Tokyo! Why can't you relax with me? Why do you need to get hot baths and massages?
Hiroshi:	(again in a soft-spoken voice) Elanna doesn't understand. Japanese men are devoted to their work. We form a very special relationship with our boss and our work.
Elanna:	And in Israel we form a very special bond with our kids, our families, our community.
Therapist:	In your country, wives and children are proud to have a father hard at work. (therapist mirroring the cultural difference and throwing in a cross-cultural hook) In this country, the children feel abandoned if their father is not present. You are making your wife and children feel ousted from society because they are unlike other wives and children whose husbands and fathers are present.
Hiroshi:	I understand that, but it is hard to get over a custom that has existed for thousands of years.
Therapist:	Yes, it is hard. Nevertheless, Hiroshi, it must have been hard for you to break away from your country and even go so far as to marry a Westerner.
Hiroshi:	But she also married me, a Japanese man, and should have known we are different than American men. We work long hours.
Therapist:	Actually, it really isn't true. I know that in your country men work long hours even on weekends and hardly ever take vacations. Here we have certain hours, and companies are also closed for weekends

and holidays, so you do have time to spend with your wife and family. So now you need to give her some *amae* (the cross-cultural hook).

Elanna: I need my husband to recognize my needs, not only as an Israeli woman but also as an American. I came here because of family but also because I am proud to be in America.

Therapist: Elanna, there is a difference. You came here because you wanted to. Hiroshi came here under a threat. You must have known that it would be a difficult transition.

Elanna: Yes, but he also came not because he loved me but because he wanted to save face and not shame his family by getting a divorce.

Therapist: Hiroshi, the reality is that no matter the reason you did come here (therapist responding to "the reality" as opposed to the subjective), in a way this is really a blessing. You have the freedom to work and time to play.

Elanna: In our country, he would be shamed for ignoring his wife and family.

Therapist: Elanna is making a good point. In your country, you would be shamed for staying home, but in our country you would be shamed for abandoning your wife and child. It would be as if I went to Japan and shamed the waiter by returning my food because I didn't think it was cooked enough.

Elanna: That's what happens with Hiroshi when I tell him how I feel. He becomes like that waiter who feels shame.

Therapist: Elanna, with all due respect, you need to be a little patient. It does take time to adjust. But if you attack and criticize Hiroshi instead of helping him learn to adapt, you are pushing him farther away—the very opposite of what you want. (language of dialectics) Yet, I can tell you really love your wife, Hiroshi. (he blushes)

Elanna: He has a very hard time admitting that he loves me and the kids.

Therapist: As you know Elanna, feelings in Japan are not always expressed directly. Hiroshi, when you work you can hide your feelings behind your engineering drawings, but in this country we are engineered differently and are very open and direct.

Hiroshi: In my country, that is considered confrontation, and we seek peace and harmony.

Therapist: We find peace through direct communication, but we can deal with this another time. Meanwhile, it will take time to get accustomed to having the freedom for pleasure and happiness that this country offers you. Shall we meet again next week?

Hiroshi: I can't. I have to work.

Therapist: Now you are withdrawing from me, treating me like you do your wife. Yet, I am very impressed that you are here because in Japan this would be frowned upon. A Japanese analyst would help you comply with the group. Here you need to comply with us!

Hiroshi: (laughs) You shamed me into it.

Therapist: Sayonara and Shalom!

Hiroshi: Sayonara and Shalom!

Discussion

Hiroshi appears to be genuinely attached to his culture but is unaware how work also is a veneer that hides his true feelings and his dependency needs. As the case unfolds, we begin to see how preprogrammed he is to be the loyal, dutiful employee. The therapist applies the cross-cultural hook and mirroring techniques by first empathizing how difficult it is to adapt to a drastically different culture and then showing him how he is refusing his wife *amae* by neglecting her needs. The therapist is careful not to shame him and attempts to help him understand that by ignoring his wife he is shaming her in front of her American friends. She also shows him (going into the "reality" listening mode) that his work does not warrant obsessively long hours. The therapist uses empathy and mirroring to show sensitivity to each partner, while highlighting the dynamics operative within their diverse worlds.

TREATMENT OF WOMEN

Not all shame-honor cultures handle aggression, rage, violence, and trauma in the same way (Kobrin and Lachkar, 2011). As therapists we need to be aware of how various cultures deal with women. In the West, men are programmed to show deference to the female. When a woman in the West complains of domestic, physical, or emotional abuse, she receives support from a society that guarantees her human rights. On the surface, one could say that both Japanese and Arabs legitimatize the neglect and abandonment of their women. Although worlds apart, both Japanese and Muslim women are prescribed to be compliant and submissive to men. However, women in Japan do have a say in decisions and are in charge of the finances. They are also free to get an education, hold a job, and have a career. They have become obsessed with objects of modernity—materialistic transitional objects symbolic of their self-image. The oppression of women in Islamic regimes is well documented. If the Muslim male feels a woman has shamed or dishonored him, he will physically abuse her. The Japanese male will withdraw or work even longer hours to avoid the female whom he believes has brought dishonor to him. To divorce, all a Muslim man has to do is say "I divorce you" three times! In more simplistic terms, it comes down to tolerance versus intolerance—the Louis Vuitton purse versus the burka.

The chaos and violence we see in a large sector of the Arab population stand in sharp contrast to the stoicism of the Japanese and their ability to cope. The Japanese go to great lengths to maintain harmony or *wa*—the desire to be devoid of conflict and envy. This is apparent in the regard for orderliness and tranquility in their houses, gardens, and shrines. The group seeks to maintain synchronicity by avoiding conflict even under the most dire circumstances. The Japanese are able to keep their cool after major disasters and are masters at containing their envy. Moreover, they believe that one should not show that he has more than the other.

In Islam, women are relegated to secondary status, as mandated by Islamic doctrine. According to the standards of the West, these laws are abusive and violate human rights. Shari Goodman (2012), chapter leader of Calabasas-West Valley ACT for America, cites two cases of "honor killings." One involved a Muslim man who was convicted by a Canadian court for killing his three daughters and former wife. He not only did not express remorse but said that if they came back to life 100 times, he would kill them again. In the second case, the husband strangled his wife for having borne him a third child that was not a son.

Another dynamic that takes precedence in Arab society is female conformity. Arab women are restricted from taking on any position of authority or to have an opinion, let alone a "complaint." If they try to escape the bonds of male authority, they are beaten, publicly humiliated, or worse. If the woman disobeys or is viewed as having dishonored her husband in some way, he can beat, stone, or even murder her under the rubric of an honor killing. The film *The Stoning of Soraya M.* (2008) depicts this kind of atrocity. There is no shame for such abuse; it is accepted in the culture. Muslims are not attuned to a woman's complaints because she virtually does not exist for them.

Women from other countries who have been politically exploited and violated often consider it normal that their role is to be subservient to men and to please them at any cost. On a more positive note, Afghan businesswomen are beginning to seek their rights in the business world dominated by men.

The Case of Nancy and Sharof

While visiting his family in the United States, Sharof, a computer specialist from Iran, met his wife, Nancy, at a restaurant where she was a cocktail waitress. This case represents the conflicts that ensue as the couple presents the issue of hierarchy in their relationship and the intrusions of his family. The therapist attempts to open up the therapeutic space through couple transference.

Therapist: Salam. (therapist greets the couple in Arabic and starts to shake hands but notices that Sharof pulls his hand away and makes no eye contact)

Sharof: Salam.

Therapist: Please have a seat, and we shall begin. I would like to hear from each of you. Who would like to start?

Nancy: I will start.

Sharof: No, I will start.

Therapist: Very well.

Sharof: My wife does not understand that in our culture women must show obedience to their husband and respect to their family. Family is of most importance. She must learn that when my mother needs me I must go, but she gets upset when she remains at home.

Nancy: Upset isn't the word. I go ballistic! He's not telling the whole story. We decided to go to Paris and Morocco for a vacation, and he insists on bringing his mother and his aunt.

Sharof: My first allegiance is to my mother, and in my country the wife understands this. I have been trying to explain this to her, but she doesn't get it.

Therapist: But things are different in our country. Here men treat their women with respect and as equals.

Sharof: I understand that. But Nancy knew how it is with my mother when she married me.

Nancy: No, I certainly did not! And how did I know that when I did not "obey" your commands you would beat me?

Therapist: Is this true?

Sharof: Yes, that is my right. And you know what she did? She called the police.

Therapist: And what did they do?

Sharof: They put me on probation and said if this happens again they will send me to anger management. What they don't understand is it is not anger. It is our right as men. (starts to recite the Qur'an) Allah says admonish them first, and then beat them.

Therapist: So you feel it is your right to beat your wife?

Sharof: Not only is it my right, it is my duty.

Therapist: Your "duty" can put you in prison.

Nancy: See what I have to live with? And now he wants to drag his mother and aunt with us on our vacation.

Sharof:	My mother and aunt have no one. I am like a protector for them. They are alone.
Therapist:	Sharof, have you ever considered finding them a support group or helping them expand their social life?
Sharof:	Support group! You got to be joking. In our country, family is the support group. You just don't understand. You are an American and have no clue where I come from.
Therapist:	I am impressed that you are here, Sharof, and that you would choose an American therapist, and a Jewish one at that! There must be some part of you that does want to adapt to our way of life. (opening up the couple transference and the cross-cultural hook)
Nancy:	Good point. Why would he choose you or me?
Therapist:	Yes, Sharof, you could have married a Muslim woman and chosen a Muslim therapist.
Sharof:	I happen to like American women. I find them very attractive and sexy.
Nancy:	You should see his porno sites. (laughs a bit to break the tension)
Therapist:	As much as you find American women attractive and lust after us, you must destroy us because you cannot allow yourself to need us or be dependent.
Sharof:	(looking toward Nancy) What is she talking about?
Nancy:	She is right. You cannot allow yourself to depend upon any woman except your mother! Tradition? Baloney! He acts like a believer, a true and faithful Muslim, but he steps out of his tradition when it suits him. Even in his own country he would drink, not pray, eat pork. Yet when it comes to me, he suddenly becomes a devout Muslim. (therapist didn't have to find the cross-cultural hook; Nancy did it for her)
Therapist:	Nancy, you are finding contradictions in Sharof's behavior?
Sharof:	Hold on! I did not come here for you to shame or dishonor me.
Therapist:	What you call shame, I find very helpful because it allows us to understand that behind your "traditional" flag is a very healthy, normal man who would like to be freer to express himself, to love, to be vulnerable. I think you both did an excellent job in helping me understand not only your cultural differences but how underneath all this you are two people with real and legitimate needs. Can we meet next week at this time?
Sharof:	I guess so. As long as you wear a burka.
Therapist:	(laughs) I see you have not lost your sense of humor.

Nancy: Great! See you then.

Sharof: (looking therapist in the eye) Salam!

Therapist: Salam!

Discussion

In this case the therapist uses the language of dialectics to show the conflict between the couple's real needs. Under the guise of religion, Sharof hides his dependency needs and vulnerabilities. His choosing an American wife and an American therapist shows the split part of himself: one part that desires, loves, and needs us, and the other part that he rejects. In psychodynamic terms, one could say the good breast that is needed is also the breast that must be destroyed (Kleinian envy). The therapist didn't have to work very hard to find the cross-cultural hook as Nancy confronted head on the contradiction in Sharof's devotion to "tradition." The therapist then used the cross-cultural hook to show empathy with the difficulty of adapting and adjusting to another culture.

However, the therapist had to curtail her own countertransference issues—her rage toward Sharof when he said it was okay to be abusive to his wife and his nonchalant attitude about his imposing his mother and aunt on their vacation. In terms of the domestic violence, she had an obligation to inform him that in our country it is a criminal offense and he could go to jail, even though in his country it was acceptable. Mirroring the conflicts and using the language of empathology and dialectics were most effective in this case. The therapist cautiously offered empathy around the struggles of adaptation as well as the splitting parts of him, while also advising Sharof that cultural traditions and religious laws can never be used as a rationale for abuse, violence, and the mistreatment of women.

JAPANESE WOMEN REBELLING

Many Japanese women today are marrying American men because they are frustrated with having to stay home and take care of finances and children while their Japanese husbands work long and tedious hours, even when they're not in Japan. In treatment, the therapist must be very cautious not to shame or humiliate the Japanese man but rather to bond with him and embrace his culture by mirroring his experience. According to Kenneth Adams (2012), little has changed in Japanese society. Despite its productivity and economic growth, it still remains an institutionalized, masochistic, and sacrificial society. Men are programmed to sacrifice themselves to the workplace and women to the home and children. Adams refers to this as the "salaryman" mentality, an archetype of the *Nihonjin* warrior, which translocated the historical Japanese to a new generation. Economically, there has been a financial boom. Women are more active in the workplace, and the desire for home and marriage is of less importance.

One might suggest that the current rage among young Japanese females is a rebellion against *amae* and against societal inhibitions that require a person to conform or be ostracized from the group. The girls of this pop cultural revolution, known as "Japanese Kickboxers," do not show any restraint. "Here we are in your face! See Mom! Look between my legs; no underwear!" From a psychohistorical perspective, one might interpret that these young girls have moved away from the image of the peaceful, harmonious chrysanthemum to that of the vagina/sword—no longer objects to compel men but to repel them. They have relinquished old roles to join the increasing ranks of women who no longer want to stay home and raise children. In fact, the prime minister of Japan was brutally criticized when he referred to Japanese women as "birth machines."

I would interpret the extreme behavior of the Kickboxers as a manic defense of girls who envy Hollywood starlets and not only mimic them but "become" them, caricaturing them by wearing ten-inch high heels and short miniskirts and sporting huge red lips. Some even sew their lips to resemble Japan's iconic Hello Kitty. Have these girls become the sword, a society of plastic women acting as robots in the attempt to escape a repressed, pacifistic society? What a paradox that the Japanese male, who depends on marriage and family for status, is confronted with a segment of women who forgo marriage and children to avoid the subservient life of their ancestors. Could this be a cry for help? "Wake up, dad, we need you!"

KVETCHING: THE JEWISH "V-SPOT"

Jewish humor, food, and thought have become part of the fabric of American life, and one could not think of writing a book about complaints without discussing the art of *kvetching*—a Yiddish word that means to complain relentlessly, to continually find fault. Who better than a Jewish analyst to understand the comfort one gets from kvetching? Much to my amazement, kvetching is not confined to my Jewish patients. Clinical practice has shown this to be a common and universal phenomenon. Narcissistic, borderline, obsessive-compulsive, passive-aggressive, and depressive patients all engage in it, albeit with their own qualitative distinctions.

I first learned about kvetching from my mother, who would feign sickness and portend imminent death if I did not eat all my food. I was further initiated into the art of kvetching when I started to take ballet lessons at the age of seven, and my mother would complain each time I attended ballet class. "What is this ballet? Ballet is for shiksas! Nice Jewish girls don't spread their legs; they either study piano or violin."

Throughout time, Jews have gone through a painful and sometimes humorously delightful sojourn to take the art of complaining to new heights, voicing their continual suffering and losses and questioning, "Why us? If we are the Chosen Ones, why has God chosen us?" The Yiddish language has endured for thousands of years and become a part of our everyday expressions. Jews and non-Jews alike understand rich, colorful terms such as *chutzpah, schmuck, schlepp, putz,* and *maven.* Some of these enduring expressions were designed to reflect the mind-set of the Eastern European Jews, who endured years of persecution, suppression, and anti-Semitism yet maintained their ability to laugh at and mock themselves and, of course, kvetch about life—like the Jewish wife who cooks too much, spends too much, always comes to bed with a headache, and so forth.

Freud (1905) was one of the first to psychoanalyze Jewish humor, recognizing the meaning behind the acerbic Jewish wit, which is as hard on themselves as it is on others. He recognized that Jewish people used humor to transcend the oppressive social conditions that had been imposed on them. Theodor Reik (1948), a follower of Freud, noted that Jews realized that by laughing at themselves, others would accept and forgive them for their "strangeness," including a total commitment to success and intellectual achievement. Reik views Jewish humor as a kind of vacillation between masochism and self-inflicted humiliation, which sends a message of paranoid superiority. Furthermore, he claims there are two sides of "the joke." The high degree of resiliency and courage displayed in Jewish humor also serves as a defense mechanism, enabling Jews to confront and rise above adversity.

Woody Allen is a case in point. He may be ambivalent about his Jewishness, but he has certainly not rejected the Jewish tradition of humor, of which his movies are a prime example. He has been quoted as saying, "I have frequently been accused of being a self-hating Jew, and while it's true I hate myself, it's not because I am Jewish." Of course, we cannot neglect to mention the mother of all complainers—the Jewish mother. Many jokes depict the ambivalence of the Jewish mother who on one hand has high expectations for her son's success and on the other hand knows to prepare herself if he disappoints. One joke, which has many variations on the theme, goes like this: A Jewish mother buys her son two shirts for his birthday. Wishing to please her, he goes to his room and puts on one of the shirts. When he returns, his mother immediately says, "So you didn't like the other shirt?"

TREATMENT POINTS AND TECHNIQUES

Treating individuals or couples from another culture can be overwhelming and cause much frustration, not only because therapists may not have an understanding of the languages, traditions, childrearing practices, or identities involved, but also because resistance and rigidity to adapt to their current environment is often so embedded in these patients. The following is an example of an American woman who was married to a Muslim man:

> He always left me behind, as if I didn't exist. I never knew where he went.
> He never invited me to family events, parties, celebrations; he took our son

and daughter, but not me. He had numerous affairs, and when I threatened to divorce him he told me he would leave me with no money and take our children away from me. And that's what happened when I finally did divorce him. The judge in his homeland granted sole custody to my husband. He accused me of being an unfit mother, and the judge supported him. He said my duty was to obey!

Following are the main elements that the therapist should keep in mind when dealing with cross-cultural complaints:

- Understand the fundamental differences in the dynamics of the cultures involved.
- Empathize with the resistances and the differences, but *not* with the aggression.
- Self-psychology and mirroring techniques are most effective in reflecting the aggression.
- When stuck or in doubt, "mirror" the conflict.
- Locate the cross-cultural hook to find hypocrisy within the respective cultures.
- Remind the couple why they came to you in the first place.
- Set treatment goals.
- Be familiar with the basics of the culture—music, foods, a few expressions, greetings, traditions, and holidays.
- Make use of the language of empathology and the language of dialectics.
- Be aware of body language and position (sitting too close, shaking hands, etc.).
- Focus less on the cure and more on acceptance and tolerance of cultural differences.
- Remember that all therapists are mandated reporters, and abuse and violations must be reported regardless of what another culture dictates.
- Use humor to avoid sounding punitive or hooking into shame or guilt.

SUMMARY

Our increasingly global therapy practices challenge us to reach new levels of understanding. It is difficult enough to listen to and analyze complaints from patients from our own country, let alone the complaints of those from other countries, who bring with them their own nationalistic beliefs and grievances. Although psychoanalysis does not provide us with all the answers, it does offer us tools from a broad spectrum of theoretical perspectives. This can help distinguish when a cultural complaint is legitimate and when it is a form of defense.

As a psychohistorian who has treated cross-cultural couples for many years, I have found three techniques to be invaluable: (1) use the cross-cultural hook to find pathology within the cultures involved; (2) when frustrated and feeling stuck, move into Kohutian mode to mirror and reflect what you hear; and (3) bond with the patient by becoming familiar with a few words in the patient's language and a few customs from his/her country. Rather than getting into a battle of the superegos as to whose culture is more psychologically correct, recognize that beneath the surface differences we all speak a universal language based on the desire to be heard, respected, and loved.

We now turn to corporate America, whose culture is replete with operative primitive defenses not far removed from those of the cult-like societies we have just discussed.

Chapter 9

$\asymp$

Taking Complaints to the Professional Level

Over the years, I have treated numerous patients working in large corporations who complain of abuse, mistreatment, humiliation, and degradation. One wonders how an entire group, institution, university, or corporation joins together in collusive bonds and mistreats employees who do good work. In the previous chapter, we saw how people in various cultures bond together to act out in unison their unconscious collective group fantasies and how these group myths are passed on generationally. The same thing, unfortunately, can happen at the corporate level.

Collectively speaking, people who work in corporations and institutions use the workplace as a platform to act out regressed primitive defenses, targeting scapegoats on which to project their defective selves. The area of employee complaints still has not been clearly defined in the legal system or in the business world itself. There is little consensus on the rights of employees, how they can best present their complaints, and the consequences of their complaining. Some employees can even get fired for voicing their complaints, despite their legitimacy.

Unfortunately, as it now stands, emotional abuse in the workplace does not constitute grounds for legal action. Even if it did, it would be hard to prove. Many patients who experience "corporate abuse" come into treatment puzzled and baffled that a person with their pristine record and long-term commitment to their employer can be mistreated or terminated. Many have recognized the danger signs of abuse or at least had an inkling that something was amiss, but the behaviors were too covert and subtle to justify their filing a formal complaint.

THE CASE OF MELISSA

Melissa is an attractive woman in her mid-fifties, who worked for a female head nurse in a large hospital. Her feeling that something was wrong grew steadily. She entered treatment very distraught, complaining of being abused by the head nurse. At meetings her boss would dismiss her ideas without giving them any consideration and even would cut her off in mid-sentence. Melissa started to hear about meetings and social events to which she was not invited.

Although she felt it coming, the hospital management never came straight out and said it opposed her being a lesbian; rather, it enacted its dismay in the most insidious ways.

> Sure enough, they fired me when I announced that my lesbian partner and I were going to have a baby. I knew this was a Catholic hospital and management was morally opposed to gay marriages and partnerships, but I never would have imagined in this day and age that there would be such discrimination. Even worse, the staff—including the doctors, nurses, and administrators—all gave me "the look," the cold shoulder. At first I thought I was imagining it, but after a while I realized that I was being ostracized increasingly, shut out of staff meetings and not included in social events. I then contacted human resources.

What confused Melissa was that she was greatly respected by the patients. She was always attentive and went out of her way to check their charts to ensure everything was in order. Many visiting doctors respected her. If Melissa had a problem, it was that she was too efficient and attentive. However, management finally fired her for "negligence." All the while Melissa knew she was not only being scapegoated but had been set up to appear negligent. She was blamed for many of the complaints and hospital violations that were not being attended to. She was shocked how after ten years of employment, with a record of hard work and impeccable ethics, she could be dismissed so abruptly. Melissa's case shows that no matter how efficient and effective an employee is, issues unrelated to work (in this instance Melissa's "gayness") can become more pervasive than job performance. When Melissa contacted an attorney, she was told, as expected, that there was no substantial evidence that could constitute proof of unjustified dismissal.

Work Groups

How can we possibly understand how those in a work environment will sacrifice the people they supervise or will victimize and abuse other employees and coworkers—even to the exclusion of getting the work done. "It doesn't matter if you have a new and innovative idea; your ideas don't count here!" Of all the masters, Wilfred Bion (1959) is one of the few whose research on group psychology helps us make "sense of the senselessness." His work provides a methodology for understanding cult-like behaviors in groups, the pressure for people in groups to act like sheep and fuse and collude with certain leaders/ bosses. In many of my earlier contributions, I have applied Wilfred Bion's formulation of group psychology to the study of cross-culture, how people in groups bond together and identify with destructive leaders (Lachkar, 1992, 2008a, 2008b, 2008c, 2011, 2013). This also applies to the workplace. More than any other psychoanalyst, Bion understands the primitive, unconscious mechanisms operative in groups.

Bion clarified the relationship that exists between the individual and the group in his seminal work based on the main construct of two types of groups: the Work Group and the Basic Assumption Group. I characterize Bion's Work Group as the thinking, task-oriented group, people whose primary concern is to focus on the task at hand and the achievement of goals. It is the group in which primitive defenses such as control, domination, envy, and competitive rivalry do not impede, infect, or intrude into the group's capacity to reach its objectives.

The Basic Assumption Group, on the other hand, opposes new ideas and allows primitive defenses to get in the way of the group's goals. This group is characterized by cult-like behaviors dominated by irrational/delusional thinking, group myths, and bonding through collective group fantasies. There is a tendency to idealize the boss or group leader and never challenge or stand up to him in any way. Often these bosses or group leaders instill fear into their subordinates and threaten that those who speak up or express contrary opinions will be fired. As a result, members of the Basic Assumption Group form dependent, parasitic ties with one another. In order to release the tension and mounting anxiety they feel, they find a scapegoat into whom to project all their unleashed feelings of frustration.

Red Flags

Good workers who fall within the matrix of the corporate abuse system complain of consistently being criticized, having their job responsibilities taken away, and being assigned meaningless, makeshift tasks or "busy work" to perform on a daily basis. Some of these employees are given nothing to do at all and then written up for poor performance. The bully boss is obvious. However, not all workplace abuse involves the boss who is constantly on an employee's back. There is also the silent bully boss who ignores and avoids. Here are some of the signs of a bully boss and an abusive work situation:

- A boss who constantly yells at workers and picks on the same people in front of others or acts in a threatening or dismissive manner when there are no witnesses.
- A boss or powerful person who seeks out a scapegoat, thereby inviting others, who are eager to make sure the boss is aware of their "loyalty," to project their frustrations onto this person as well.

- A boss who constantly blocks someone's promotions, doesn't listen to requests, or repeatedly puts one on hold. "I came up with a great idea to enhance the method of getting donations, but when I brought it up to my boss, he tells me he will think about it and let me know. Of course he never does."
- The boss and coworkers who give an employee senseless, meaningless busy work, meant to undermine the employee's performance and to make him or her feel worthless and unneeded.
- The boss who heaps constant bullying and abuse, both overt and covert, on an employee.
- A supervisor who sabotages an employee's good work or claims it as his own.
- A boss, supervisor, or coworkers who deliberately ignore certain individuals at work and make sure that they are kept "out of the loop."
- A supervisor who overloads employees, sets unreasonable deadlines, and requires many hours of overtime work without additional pay. (Note: if, despite the long hours, the average wage dips below the federal minimum wage, legal action is allowable.)
- A supervisor who attacks a worker personally and calls him names.
- A boss, supervisor, or coworkers who make jokes about an employee.
- A boss or supervisor who consistently gives an employee equipment that does not function properly, such as the oldest computer in the building or a faulty printer.
- A boss who places an employee in dangerous positions, such as at a front desk area that recently has been the scene of an armed robbery, without initiating adequate security measures.
- A boss who puts an employee in a workplace area that does not have adequate heating, cooling, and ventilation.
- A boss or coworkers who consistently tell an employee that the empty seat next to them is taken, with the result that the employee ends up sitting alone in the back or must get a chair from another room, thus always feeling like the one left out.
- Department members who e-mail everyone about where they are going to for lunch or tell others that there is a celebration for a coworker's birthday except for the victim of their abuse, whom they deliberately want to exclude and embarrass.

Reverse Superego

The healthy superego is the voice of morality, providing the basic guidelines that help the child distinguish between right and wrong. The reverse superego is a term I originated to describe what happens to a child who despite doing good deeds gets punished instead of praised (Lachkar, 2008a, 2008c). The reverse superego is the result of inhibited development of a healthy superego. It creates ambivalence and confusion so that the child has trouble recognizing good from bad, right from wrong, and deserving from not deserving. In the corporate world, the same can hold true for excellent workers who do not get the awards and recognition they deserve, while others whose work is inferior are rewarded. As one disillusioned and disappointed worker explained:

> Whatever I do at my job, it is never good enough. I am actually being pun-
> ished for finding typos in some of the executives' reports. It is so crazy-making
> because that is the very reason I was hired. They are all so worried I will shame
> them. Now I feel very anxious and shaky. I am not myself, and have migraine
> headaches. When I walk into a room I stumble. I have no confidence, and
> feel as though I am constantly walking on eggshells. I am becoming forget-
> ful and am starting to doubt myself. I keep having to check on work I have
> done and retracing my steps to make sure I'm not doing something wrong.
> It is never clear what my role is. I was supposed to be an executive assistant
> administrator. Instead I spend half my time running errands, doing perfunc-
> tory things like picking up packages from the supply room. Often I am told
> that the package I was sent to retrieve was already picked up, like my bosses
> are sending me on a fool's errand. I am afraid to confront my bosses, fearful of
> getting them pissed at me or losing my job. When I fix everyone's typos, find
> ways to streamline procedures, or determine areas where we can save money,
> instead of getting a thank-you, my bosses give me a dirty look as though to
> say, "Who do you think you are?" Yet, I have saved them thousands upon
> thousands of dollars and much humiliation because I catch their errors before
> they are circulated.

THE CASE OF AMY

Amy Johnson, an attractive woman in her mid-fifties, worked for a large corporation managing sales representatives handling one of the many lines of
hospital equipment the corporation manufactured. As a sales professional
with a great deal of previous experience and stellar references, she was hired
with a guarantee of promotion. She worked with all male counterparts, who
were of varying ages and backgrounds. Hers was an outside sales management
position, and most often she worked from her home when she wasn't traveling
alone or with the reps—organizing and running sales meetings and occasion-
ally meeting and working with her supervisor.

At first there was no apparent animosity. However, there was always the
underlying resentment that she was the sole female on the sales management
team and had degrees and experience that far outweighed those of her colleagues. The best example of the sales staff's exclusion of Amy was during management meeting lunches. The only topic of social conversation was sports,
mostly basketball and football. Not one word was ever addressed to Amy, nor
was there any attempt to include her in the conversation. She realized this was
an obvious display of harassment. At other management meetings, farting was

a common amusement among these "grown" men. Periodically, there would be meetings to which Amy was not invited, the only sales manager that was left out; these included meetings with members of the sales team, 75 percent of whom were male. For the first few years at this company, she shrugged off the behavior of her colleagues. She kept to herself, ignoring their hurtful behavior and the jokes and innuendos about women that occurred during management meetings. She focused on her work and overlooked the many comments about the female reps' undergarments, their sexy appearance, and the constant scrutiny of all female employees of the corporation. As the years moved on, Amy realized how traumatized and distraught she was. She finally sought help from a therapist, complaining of migraine headaches, insomnia, and depression and admitting that she felt abused, mistreated, and ignored by other sales managers and corporate management.

After working for the company for more than ten years, Amy still was a top performer. One day, out of nowhere, her boss became an overbearing micromanager, which made it very difficult for her to continue to function at a high level. The shock came when she read her semi-annual evaluation, which indicated that she was negligent, not a good team player, judgmental, and non-compliant in many areas. She was called before upper management and warned about her poor performance. Finally she went to the "complaint department," human resources, which also comprised all males. "I knocked, but there was 'nobody there.'" Amy persevered and kept knocking on the door until she finally hired an attorney. She had kept immaculate records, full of anecdotal proof and sufficient evidence to win her a big settlement. Other women were not so lucky. They felt they had no than recourse when they were notified that their services were no longer needed.

Queen Bee Syndrome: Women Beware!

A new syndrome is emerging in the workplace. The Queen Bee (Drexler, 2013) is an alpha female who will go to great lengths to maintain control and power. She treats all subordinates critically, but females bear the brunt of her abuse. She is the prototypical female bully. I would speculate that the Queen Bee is often extremely narcissistic and is only out to accomplish her self-serving purposes, using childish tactics to keep other females from advancing. These are the women who oppose the rise of other females because they are obsessed with attaining dominance and authority and fearful of anyone who can surpass them in ability or popularity. They need to prove they can do the job just as well as males can. It has been found that women who achieve success in male-dominated environments are more inclined to oppose the rise of other women (Drexler, 2013).

Susan felt that because she was younger, more attractive, and more competent than her Queen Bee boss, her boss envied her and was constantly on her back.

Susan recalls how she showed up at work wearing a new outfit for a performance appraisal session with her boss, who commented, "Oh, here you are asking for a raise and you keep buying new clothes! Who are you trying to impress?"

THE CASE OF CATHY

Cathy, a sales representative for a large manufacturing company, had been interviewed by a male manger, who was immediately impressed and hired her on the spot. Cathy had very good interpersonal skills, knew how to pull off a sale, and was also very attractive. Misfortune came when the manager who hired her was himself fired and replaced by Ms. Ellis, a stiletto-wearing, high-powered woman who immediately took control. Cathy sensed from the beginning that there would be trouble ahead, and every day went to work with an ominous feeling. After weeks of being ignored or put down for everything she said and did, including how she dressed, Cathy felt she had no choice but to go to the human resource department.

She tried to explain to the woman in human resources how she was being mistreated and abused, that she often didn't hear about a meeting until it was too late to attend, then would get a surge of angry e-mails from colleagues asking why she wasn't there. When she complained about being excluded, her boss would respond with fake innocence, saying that she didn't know what happened and hadn't meant to leave Cathy off the e-mail list or that her secretary must have made a mistake. Cathy also told the woman in human resources that she desperately wanted the new boss's approval and that she had approached her with a great idea to enhance sales. Said Cathy, "When I presented the idea to my boss, I could tell she resented me and even had a feeling that she envied me for being younger and for being a Harvard graduate. She indicated she was extremely busy and would think about it, then abruptly picked up her cell phone and acted as though I didn't exist. I couldn't understand why no one in the company would ever take my side or defend me. I finally realized they were terrified of this 'Queen Bee.' I later discovered that so was the lady in the human resources department. I ultimately had to find another job because the situation continued to get worse, and no one seemed to be able to do anything about it. I ended up sounding like a whiner and a chronic complainer."

There is also a male equivalent of the Queen Bee. Most people who work in institutions and corporations are familiar with malicious, narcissistic bosses. The King Bee is an alpha male who uses his power to control, manipulate, and strip the workers of their will to work, as well as their creativity and desire for upward mobility. The King Bee devalues any new thoughts, creative endeavors, or entrepreneurial achievements. He demands to be the center of attention. If any success is achieved, it must be because of him and his magnificence, and he will claim ownership of the achievement.

THE CASE OF MR. FRANK

Mr. Frank came into the therapist's office carrying two bulging legal-size brief-cases. As he sat down, he said he might need a double session. He had been stifling his feelings for years and never told anyone about the kind of abuse he was getting at the $100 million corporation at which he worked. After years of loyal service and after raising more than $8 million for the company, he had asked for a raise. The King Bee's response was, "What for? You didn't do any-thing. All that money came from my efforts." At that point, Mr. Frank opened his briefcases, revealing piles of article clippings from magazines and newspa-pers, and other promotional materials he had created for the company as part of his money-raising efforts. "I need time off. I work endless hours for my boss and am always on call for his numerous complaints and constant demands. He is so cheap he refuses to buy a new computer and printer. He doesn't say a word when I bring in money or a new client; then when things are slow he blames me. My wife is ready to divorce me. We need to put a down payment on another house so I can live closer to work and shorten my two-hour commute every day. But he doesn't give me any credit. To him I'm a nobody."

The previous cases are examples of employees who are good, resourceful, entrepreneurial, and yet get punished by their Queen and King Bee bosses. It is difficult when a hard-working employee—whether it be in corporate America, an institution, a governmental agency, or a hair salon—comes to therapy with a complaint of workplace abuse. We can't control the abuse and aggression, but we can help our patients learn not to identify with the mistreatment—the bad boss/parent who never offered praise or reward for being good and dutiful.

My boss reminds me of my mother. Whatever I do is not good enough. I was a very dutiful child, just as I am a very dutiful employee. Whenever I got good grades, cleaned my room, took care of my younger siblings, I got a tongue-lashing. Most kids get rewarded. She would always complain I wasn't doing enough, wasn't good enough, and had no right to complain, that I should count my blessings for having a roof over my head. Here I am, an assistant department manager who works long hours and does more than is expected. Instead of being appreciated and invited to sit in on the management meet-ings, I get only criticism and put-downs. My boss neglects me, never praises me, leaves me out of meetings where I might get any credit, and treats me as if I am invisible. I can't sleep, I have nightmares and wake up every morning with terrible headaches.

To this the therapist can respond:

Anybody would have the same reaction. No mother, caretaker, or boss has the right to mistreat and neglect a child or an employee. Given your background of emotional abuse, one can understand how there can be a tendency to iden-tify or over identify with the "bad boss mother," but you must be careful not to personalize this. All you can do is what you have been doing. Try to stay focused. You need to know that in spite of what your boss says or how he treats you, you are doing a good job!

In the previous vignette, note that the therapist does not advise the patient to quit his job. As long as these primitive defenses mechanisms are operative, it is not a good time to make major decisions about one's career or lifestyle because ego dysfunctionality can impair the capacity to think rationally.

SUMMARY

This chapter illustrates that good workers and smart people can become of victims of abusive bosses. Part of understanding the abuse that occurs in the corporate world involves group psychology, which explains what happens when other workers band together in complicity with destructive bosses. Bion outlined two kinds of groups—the work-oriented group and the regressed group. The latter involves those whose goals and purposes become contaminated by such primitive defenses as control, domination, envy, jealousy, victimization, subordination, and oedipal rivalry. These primitive defenses become the replacement for "getting the job done," causing workers to lose focus on their goals. Why are good workers often punished and the bad ones praised? I use my concept of the reverse superego to explain why bad becomes "good" and good becomes "bad"—a corporate Mad Hatter's Tea Party. This chapter also discussed the gender-based destructive behavior of the Queen Bee boss and her King Bee counterpart. In many instances, corporations or institutions aren't set up to listen to and follow through on legitimate complaints and instead turn the complaint against the complainer.

Chapter 10

⚔

Treatment Suggestions
and Techniques

All the world's a stage
and all the men and woman merely players.

—Shakespeare, As You Like It

When it comes to listening to and analyzing complaints, therapists must be aware of the type of complaint being voiced, for there are vast variations on the theme. There is a difference between a patient showing concern for something that is genuinely disturbing to him/her and a patient who complains merely for the sake of complaining. Wilfred Bion's (1967) concept of alpha function versus beta elements helps decipher the latter phenomenon, which, simply stated, signifies a complainer without a complaint. An alpha function complaint has meaning. It is a digested thought, informed by a genuine desire to find a solution. On the other hand, a beta element complaint is a complaint without a conscious thought behind it—meaning that the complainer bonds with pain as part of maintaining a negative attachment or a negative transference with the therapist. Who better to apply to for guidance on dealing with patient complaints than Salman Akhtar (2013), who has transformed the traditional "talking cure" into a "listening cure." His valuable methods include four different kinds of listening approaches, which set out with great proficiency and precision the multiple facets of what seemingly is a simple therapeutic skill.

Dipping further into the vast pool of literature on listening, we must take into account the works of Heinz Kohut (1971, 1977) regarding emotions that communicate an "accurate" empathic understanding of how the patient feels and why he or she should feel that way. Kohut and his self-psychology cohorts stress the ability to empathize with the patient as a precondition to interpretation—replicating what the patient feels, or what Kohut refers to as empathic immersion.

The therapist must also listen to the silences and the non-verbal body language. There are different kinds of silences that emanate from part of human mind that has no words, the unmentalized experience; part of the human mind that has words that are hidden; and part of the human mind that speaks through non-verbal communication.

Here are some examples of the various ways to listen and
respond to complaints:

- *Objective:* "Your mother punished you and disciplined you, but she did not abuse you."
- *Subjective:* "I believe your mother abused you, but maybe you have other feelings about what happened."
- *Empathic:* "I can understand how traumatic this must have been for you."
- *Intersubjective:* "Now you feel that I am abusing you when I set limits and boundaries, just as your mother tried to do with you."
- *Introspective* (listening with the third ear; Reik, 1948): "Let's take a look at how this abuse has impacted your life."
- *Listening to the Silence:* "You either are at a loss for words or you don't want to talk about it."
- *Non-Verbal:* "I can tell by the way I get sleepy in sessions with you that you are letting me know that you feel a sense of deadness inside."
- *Body Language:* "I can tell by the way you tap your toe toward the end of the session that you are anxious to leave."

AFTER THE LISTENING

What about the therapeutic procedures and techniques needed after we have "listened"? I always think of therapeutic techniques as having a parallel to music and other art forms. It's not just what one says, but how one says it. The words and the manner of saying them must be orchestrated carefully in order to make the desired impact. Voice tone, change in dynamics, eye contact, and body language are all part of the mix.

We must always remain aware of the pivotal role therapists play in the success of the interaction that takes place during therapy. I think of a therapy session as a theatrical play, with the therapist assigned a specific role. The ever-present therapeutic dilemma is, How does one enact this designated role and not lose one's authenticity? This is a question often asked by supervisees. One of my supervisees told me she felt phony and trapped into having to become a self-mirroring object for a very narcissistic woman with whom she developed a very negative transference. "I don't want to be her container, her self-object. This is not who I am." I reassured her that assuming this role was in no way being phony; it was a therapeutic tool. To another supervisee, who happened to be a musician, I said, "It is similar to the conductor who has to be able to understand the nature of the music being performed and the abilities and range of all the instruments involved before he or she can orchestrate intelligently."

I believe that while we are acting out our parts, we must never lose sight of the fact that we are simultaneously performing a vital therapeutic function. Our authenticity lies in our ability not only to adapt innovative and varied theoretical positions but also to adapt and adjust them to each patient's distinctive personality. Do we become Freud when we interpret a patient's aggression? Do we become Klein when we become the good or bad breast? Do we become Winnicott when we become the "being" or the "doing" object mother? Bach is always Bach and Beethoven is always Beethoven, no matter how they are played and interpreted. The same holds true for the pioneering masters of psychotherapy, regardless of how we interpret their techniques using our own unique methods.

I remember a very specific moment in a dance class with master teacher Carmelita Maracci. I was extremely nervous because she was very critical, and I was not sure that I was at a level to meet the professional standards of her class. Suddenly, in the middle of a Bach adagio movement, in walks my immigrant, Polish-Jewish, overweight mother, who stomped heavily to a chair and plopped down. Everyone paused and looked at me. After a momentary silence, our teacher stated, "Look at Joan's mother. When she comes into a room, she makes a statement! The rest of you all look like prancing little nymphs." That was the moment when I understood that dance performance could carry over to my therapeutic work.

Patients come to therapy because they have fears and anxieties and are looking for someone to trust, someone who can offer a safe, containing environment that makes them feel secure. The persona of the therapist is of utmost importance, beginning with the initial contact on the phone or in person. The therapist should exude a feeling of confidence and professionalism that invites trust. It takes very little time for the individual or couple to get a sense that the therapist is in charge, has a sense of authority/confidence, is warm and inviting, yet is not an easy target to manipulate. Whether it is a student who is walking into a college classroom, a patient being seen in the emergency room for a broken arm, a music student going for a lesson, or a couple seeking help with their troubled relationship, the person in charge must radiate a sense of authority (not to be confused with grandiosity or omnipotence, but a little of that is good). In my book *The Many Faces of Abuse* (1998b), I pay homage to the famous violin virtuoso Isaac Stern, who claims, "There are three qualities a musician must embody. The first is confidence, the second is empathic attunement and the third is enough arrogance to carry it off" (p. 151).

Therapeutic Techniques, Tools, and Functions

This section focuses on therapeutic tools, functions, different ways to listen and respond after listening, and other techniques that include transference, countertransference, couple transference, projective identification, dual projective identification, reverse superego, and the languages I created specifically for dealing with narcissistic and borderline personality disorders.

The treatment techniques emphasized in this chapter are primarily common psychotherapeutic methods applicable for both individual and couple therapy. However, psychoanalytic technique and knowledge of theory are meaningless unless they are artistically and creatively executed. Just as with any form of artistic expression, therapy requires interpretation that should be expressed with meaning, feeling, and emotion. I have many years of experience supervising therapists who seem to have the idea that speaking in a soft, modulated voice will calm the patient, so no matter what transpires in the session, they do not alter this range. Actually, the affective experience must meet and match the mood of the patient to ensure an effective response that will keep the therapy alive—and the therapist awake! Moreover, the therapist must speak with passion and conviction at times and opt for silence and introspection on other occasions. Your empathic interpretation should fit the circumstances.

Table 10.1 provides a summary of the primary functions of the therapist.

A keen and ready sense of humor is a very important attribute for the therapist. One patient was feeling very frustrated because she had been avoiding practicing her instruments and finalizing a musical composition she was working on. At the end of the session, she remarked how she hated to go back to her studio to face all the "little superegos" glaring at her (the piccolos, flutes, and oboes), rubbing in her guilt. As she left my home office, she saw my baby grand piano (which I had not touched for a while) and remarked, "Oh, there is your piano!" To which I replied, "There is my big superego, always staring me in the face!" We laughed conspiratorially, which alleviated some of her tension.

TABLE 10.1

Therapeutic Functions

Therapeutic Tool	Function
Empathy	Therapist as bonding/weaning mommy
Listening	Therapist as holding/environmental mommy
Understanding	Therapist as "being" versus "doing" mommy
Introspection/thinking	Therapist as interpreter
Containment	Therapist as mirroring object
Silence	Therapist as self-object
Humor	Therapist as container (hard object)
Creativity	Therapist as transitional object

TABLE 10.2
Bad Internal and External Objects

Bad Internal Objects	Bad External Objects
Wronged self	Rejecting object
Insatiable self	Abandoning object
Craving self	Betraying object
Lost self	Depriving object
Betrayed self	Unavailable object
Rejecting self	Withholding object
Abandoning self	Painful object (the mother of pain)
	Idealized object
	Sadistic object

In Chapter Two, we discussed Fairbairn, who expanded Klein's idea of the good and bad breast into multitudinous types of internal objects (see Table 10.2). These include the rejecting object, the depriving object, the abusive object, the abandoning object, and the unavailable object. First, we must analyze the attachment formation. If, for example, a woman only hooks up with unavailable men, we can presume she is attached to an unavailable object. If she stays with someone who consistently betrays her, we can presume she is attached to the betraying object. The words the patients use often reflect the unspoken voice of these internal objects.

I am reminded of a patient who went back to a dress store to return a dress after the salesperson said there would be no problem. When she handed the salesperson the receipt and was told the dress was not returnable, her angry complaints exploded all through the mall. In session, she was still livid. "All people are horrors. They're all betrayers. They don't deserve to live on this planet. This woman made me a promise and she lied to me." I responded to her internal betrayer. "We cannot control all the betrayers out there, like this salesperson who lied to you. But we can control our internal betrayer." She snapped back, "Are you accusing me of betraying myself?" My reply: "I am reminding you of all the promises you've made to yourself that you have not kept. You should be pleased to know that although we can't control the betraying saleswomen, we can control this inner betrayer by listening to our own inner voice."

Fairbairn: Attachments to Internal/External Objects

Complaints may be reflected in statements and questions such as the following:

- Why am I always being rejected?
- Why am I always being abandoned?
- Why am I always getting involved with unavailable men?

- Why am I always getting betrayed?
- Whatever I get is never enough.
- How come everyone else gets more than I do?

GUIDELINES FOR THE THERAPIST

1. Set out terms of treatment at the first meeting. This includes payment arrangements, handling of insurance, policy for cancellation, set times, short- or long-term goals, and number of sessions.
2. Remind the patient about confidentially, and that whatever is shared by the couple outside session can be shared in session at the discretion of the therapist (email messages, telephone calls, etc.).
3. Don't be afraid to confront the aggression. Speak directly to the aggression with technical neutrality and by making clear, definitive statements. Be empathic toward the pain and the patient's vulnerabilities, but avoid getting drawn into the couple's battle.
4. Maintain eye contact.
5. Avoid talking too much.
6. Be awareness of separateness. Do not lump their dynamics together, as in "You both feel shame." Be specific: "You feel shame while your husband feels guilt."
7. When there is a severe amount of splitting, the focus should be on the couple's ability to function rather than on their "happiness."
8. Focus on the splitting: "I really don't want to be here. I want out of this marriage."
9. Stress the important functions of the roles patients play as wife, husband, and parent, rather than stressing the feelings: "She doesn't cook anymore or take care of the house."
10. Beware of couples' "feelings," which are often defenses (withdrawal/detachment) rather than actual feelings.
11. Listen for the theme, and be aware of repetitive themes. The subject and the feelings may change, but the theme is pervasive (betrayal, abandonment, or rejection fantasies).
12. Summarize what occurred at the end of each session. What was most meaningful—the "significant fact"?
13. Help the couple recognize "normal" and healthy dependency needs. "Today we talked about your aggression and how this becomes a replacement for feelings. To be vulnerable makes you feel shameful, little, and small, and it surprised you to know that it is the healthy part of you. As much as you want more intimacy with your wife, you were not aware how your aggression frightens her and makes her withdraw. Today you seemed to show more awareness that your vulnerability can actually make her feel safer and closer to you."

TREATMENT POINTS

1. See the couple together before transition into individual therapy (to form a safe bond), and avoid moving into individual work until the couple is ready (too early a separation can induce a "rapprochement crisis").

2. Encourage expression of ideas even if they are oppositional. "I always feel as though I have to walk on eggshells whenever I tell her something that bothers me."

3. Advise couples in the paranoid/schizoid position that this is not a good time for them to make major life changes because primitive defenses are operative and the ego becomes dysfunctional (impaired capacity to think and make rational decisions).

4. Be aware that each partner experiences anxiety differently, and respect these qualitative differences. One person's complaint is another person's attack.

5. The therapeutic alliance can be seriously threatened by an individual or partner that is predominantly narcissistic because of the tendency to flight/flee and become isolated and withdrawn. In the case of narcissistic/borderline couples, provide the borderline with empathic responses as the bonding with the narcissist is being accomplished.

6. Continually reevaluate and reiterate the treatment goals (why did the couple enter therapy in the first place?).

7. Avoid asking too many questions at the first session. Don't waste time on in-depth interrogation and obtaining lengthy histories. Start right in. The history and background information will automatically unfold within the context of the therapeutic experience and the transference.

8. Avoid self-disclosure, touching or consoling the patient, or making concessions.

9. Listen and be attentive. Speak with meaning and conviction, and maintain eye contact as you address the issues directly.

10. Use short, clear sentences, keep responses direct, and mirror and reflect sentiments with simple responses and few questions.

11. Keep in mind a "normal couple" or "ideal couple." This image will sharpen your focus and prevent you from getting tangled up in the couple's psychological "dance."

12. Explain how one partner may project a negative feeling into the other, but try to understand why the other identifies with what is being projected (focus on the dual projective identification).

13. Recap the dynamics at the end of each session, keeping aware of the qualitative differences. Avoid statements like, "You both feel attacked when you tell each other about your complaints." It is preferable to say: "When your husband complains, you (the narcissist) feel that your sense of specialness is threatened, and you (the borderline) feel a threat of abandonment when your wife complains."

THE CASE OF MR. AND MRS. V

Mrs. V: I want out of this marriage.

Therapist: Then why are you here?

Mrs. V: I don't want to be here.

Therapist: But you are here.

Mrs. V: I feel stuck. I can't afford to get a divorce, and I want out.

Mr. V: She is no longer a wife. She doesn't cook or go out with me socially and is very withdrawn.

Therapist: Oh!

Mrs. V: I am withdrawn because he has a terrible temper. He always yells at me and attacks me over the littlest thing.

Therapist: So you get scared.

Mrs. V: Scared! I get terrified. My parents used to yell and scream at me and even pull my hair.

Therapist: Does your husband physically attack you?

Mrs. V: No. He just gets angry and very controlling.

Therapist (to Mr. V):   I hear your wife saying she is very afraid of you.

Mr. V: Yes, I know, and that is why we are here.

Therapist: So, are you willing to work on controlling your anger?

Mr. V: Yes, but I don't know how. In Iran, where I grew up, everyone in my family would fight, so I never learned how not to.

Therapist: Yet you say in your business as a contractor you show control and patience with your customers, and that's a tough job.

Mr. V: Yes. People get very emotional when it comes to their homes, but I manage to keep my cool.

Therapist: So it shows you have the capacity to control your emotions. (the cross-cultural hook)

Mr. V: Yes, but that is different. When I come home, I just want to relax and be myself.

Mrs. V: Being yourself means taking out all your stress on me?

Therapist: Well, if you can be patient and control yourself when you are with your customers, you can do it at home. Your wife is just as important as your customers.

Mr. V: Ummm. I think you're right. I do love my wife and want things to work out.

Mrs. V: But I'm not happy.

Therapist: What I am about to say may sound strange to you, but for now the focus should not be on "happiness." I want you both to function as a couple, to concentrate on enacting your "roles" as husband and wife—just as you play your contractor role and I play mine as therapist.

Mrs. V: I don't want to do that. It sounds phony.

Therapist: I can understand how it sounds phony. But what you are doing is more phony, withdrawing and behaving as though you are not here, wishing you were somewhere else. So what choice do you have?

Mrs. V: (smiles for the first time as if there is a glimmer of hope) Yes, I will try. Because my daughter has an eating disorder I will do it for her.

Therapist: Sounds good. See you both next week.

Mr. V: Thank you, doctor.

Discussion

Whenever I ask a couple to focus more on their ability to function in their current roles rather than on their being happy, I'm often met with a response that I am suggesting that they act in a phony manner. "That just not me. Are you asking me to pretend?" This kind of intervention can only take place when the therapist is convinced that the patient is acting defensively. In the case of Mr. and Mrs. V, I used the cross-cultural hook to show him that if he has the ego strength to perform his role and control himself with his customers he can also function the same way at home. Bonding with the couple allows them to use their daughter's eating disorder as further motivation to function together and play out their roles as a couple.

THREE PHASES OF TREATMENT

In many of my earlier publications, I discuss the three development stages that couples work through. These phases, based on the theoretical constructs of Melanie Klein (1957) and the work of Donald Meltzer (1967), stress the importance of mental geographical confusion (zonal space) on movement from one psychic space to another. Within these phases, there is continual movement back and forth from states of fragmentation to that of wholeness and integration as couples work their way from the paranoid-schizoid position to the depressive position. The therapeutic task is to gradually wean the couple away from the relationship dominated by such primitive defenses as shame/blame, envy/jealousy, and domination/control to a position of self-development and responsibility (Lachkar, 1992, 2008a, 2008c, 2011, 2013).

Phase One—The Phase of Darkness: A State of Oneness (Fusion/Collusion)

In this first phase of couple treatment, complaints run amuck. V-spots explode everywhere! It is a phase during which couples live intrapsychically, inside the emotional space of the other. It is a state of fusion or oneness: "I am you and you are me." It is the shame/blame phase where attacks against the other are relentless, with each partner insisting the other is at fault for all the short-comings in the relationship and seek to retaliate. There is much stonewalling, blaming and shaming, and often envy or rivalry concerning the accomplish-ments of the other. It is a phase in which dual projective identification occurs, as one partner projects a negative feeling into the other and the other identifies or over-identifies that which is being projected. There is little awareness of the inner unconscious forces that invade and intrude upon their relationships. Instead, primitive defenses such as splitting, projection and projective identi-fication, magical thinking, and denial take center stage. Needs and feelings are often attacked and blown out of proportion. It is in this phase that the therapist has the opportunity to filter through the complaints to determine which are normal and legitimate complaints as opposed to those that are used for evacu-ation. "I do what my wife wants me to do but she still keeps complaining. If it is not one thing it is another. She is insatiable." "I think your wife is telling us how deprived she feels and whatever you give her cannot satisfy her" (identifi-cation with the depriving object). This state of fusion is often expressed in the form of "the dance."

> I complained to my boyfriend that I was upset.
> He then got upset about my being upset.
> I then got upset that he was upset about my being upset.
> He then got upset that I was upset about him being upset.
> Then I started to feel guilty, as though I never should have complained in the first place.

Phase Two—Complaints as a Transition to Separateness: Two-ness

This second phase marks the emergence of "two-ness," a glimmer of awareness of two separate emotional states, a sense of more trust and dependency on the therapist. In phase two, there is more tolerance for ambiguity, budding insights into unconscious motivations (internal objects), ability to see the therapist as someone who is helpful, and the beginning of bonding with the therapist and a weaning away from parasitic dependency toward mutual interdependence. The transitional space of phase two is where the partners become acquainted with their internal objects and become aware of how these objects make one overreact or distort. This phase is also where detoxification and transformation occur. It is almost like Noah naming the animals. If the patient is angry, the therapist helps him see he is disappointed. If the patient is depressed, the therapist helps the patient realize that he is in mourning. If the patient is feeling helpless, the therapist helps the patient become aware that he is feeling vulnerable or dependent.

Phase Three—State of Reason: Awareness of Two Emerging Separate Mental States (Dependent and Interdependent)

This phase marks the beginning of the depressive position; the ability and willingness to express sadness, feel remorse, and make reparation for one's wrongdoings. There is the desire to "repair" the damage, to embrace guilt, mourn, and take responsibility. It is a time of diminished primitive defenses and greater tolerance for uncertainly, ambiguity, vulnerability, and healthy dependency needs. The complaints become transformative during this period of healing and listening non-defensively to one another's hurts. It is important to let the couple know that feelings of sadness and remorse are normal.

> Mr. W called and said he needed to come in for a session, that all the work he has done in conjoint therapy has made him feel worse. "I feel sad, I feel depressed. I go around teary-eyed. I feel terrible about how I made my wife suffer all these years." To this the therapist responds, "Ah, Mr. W, what you are experiencing is healthy and normal. You are going through normal states of mourning and dealing with loss and coming to terms with some of your wrongdoings. You are sad, not depressed. Did you think things were better when you and your wife were attacking and blaming each other like two fighters in a boxing match?"

THE CASE OF MR. AND MRS. H

Mr. and Mrs. H have been married for 15 years. Mrs. H initiated the appointment because of her husband's constant threats about getting a divorce. This case brings up many therapeutic challenges. First, it illustrates how the therapist moves from dealing with "threats" within the relationship to how these threats enter into the therapeutic couple transference. It also brings up the issues of splitting, the idea of being in the marriage and out of it at the same time (as in the case of Mr. and Mrs. V). Furthermore, it shows the importance of ego functioning and reality testing. What a complaint means to Mr. H may be entirely different than what a complaint means to Mrs. H.

Therapist: Greetings. Who'd like to start?

Mr. H: Why don't you start?

Mrs. H: Why don't you start?

Mr. H:	Go ahead, you start.
Mrs. H:	Okay, I'm here because my husband keeps threatening me with getting a divorce.
Mr. H:	No, I don't threaten her. I mean to tell her that if she doesn't stop complaining and nagging I am out the door.
Mrs. H:	I take that as a threat.
Therapist:	I hear what you are saying. He is still here, which means he is still in the marriage. Yet he states that if you don't stop what you are doing he's out.
Mrs. H:	Yes. Don't you call that a threat?
Therapist:	No, I don't call it a threat.
Mrs. H:	Okay then, what do you call it?
Therapist:	In psychological terms, this is known as splitting.
Mr. H:	Are you calling me schizophrenic?
Therapist:	Heavens no. This means that there are two parts of you, one that stays married and the other that wants out of marriage.
Mr. H:	What's so wrong about that?
Therapist:	It's wrong because it is not realistic.
Mrs. H:	I know exactly what you are saying. I tell him that all the time he can't be in and out of it at the same time. What am I? An In-N-Out Burger?
Therapist:	No, you certainly should not be threatened either, but your husband did say that you complain too much. Since you are here and you are still married, let's address these "complaints."
Mr. H:	Boy, does she ever complain! I have a Jewish mother, so I know what kvetching is. But my wife can outdo any of them. She complains when I don't put the dishes in the dishwasher, she complains when I don't bring her flowers, she complains when I forget to take out the trash. She complains when I pick the kids up late from school. She complains that I don't give her enough attention.
Therapist:	Mr. H, do you think there is any legitimacy to these complaints?
Mr. H:	No. I bring home the bacon and am a good provider.
Therapist:	That's about money. What about emotional needs?
Mrs. H:	Thank you! Finally someone is addressing my needs. He thinks because he brings home the bacon, he is off the hook about being a caring and thoughtful husband.
Therapist:	I see two things going on. First, Mrs. H, I don't see anything wrong with your needs. They sound perfectly normal to me. What does

concern me is the communication. Because of your frustration, your voice sounds attacking and commanding, and therefore it's hard to tell that you are expressing your real and legitimate needs. In addition, I am concerned about the roles you play. Suddenly you become the dominating parent, and your husband an unruly child.

Mr. H: Exactly. I am reduced to a nothing, as if she has cut off my balls.

Therapist: But then when you feel castrated your only recourse is to threaten to run away like a little boy.

Mr. H: You got me there. Then what do you want me to do, doctor?

Therapist: First of all, I want you to know that you are not running away now. You are here and that is a positive sign.

Mrs. H: I'm thrilled he is here. I hope he continues to come.

Therapist: The first step is to recognize that this relationship needs help.

Mr. H: But I really don't want to be here. In fact, I'm not sure I will come next week.

Therapist: Now you are doing the same with me, threatening the work we are doing. Just as one cannot be in a marriage and out of it at the same time, as your wife stated, one cannot be in and out of therapy at the same time. The adult part of you, I'm sure, knows that. But the little boy part of you wants to run, and I'm not even complaining. I am here to express the needs of this relationship.

Mrs. H: I'm laughing because you really nailed it.

Therapist: So, in closing what was meaningful to you in this session?

Mr. H: You go first.

Mrs. H: Okay. I guess I will have to watch my tone of voice and not come across like a kvetch (like his mother) or a nag and not take his threats too seriously because, look, he's still here!

Mr. H: I guess if I don't want to get my balls cut off any more, I will have to keep coming. (Everyone laughs.)

Therapist: Great! See you both next week.

Discussion

This session had all the therapeutic elements. The therapist segued into the couple transference, showing that what Mr. H does with Mrs. H is reenacted in the treatment. The therapist very deliberately threw in the remark that, unlike his wife, she was not even complaining. This left a window of opportunity open to explore that something much deeper was going on than his wife's barrage of complaints. The therapist may have brought up the splitting defense mechanism a bit too early, but she knew she had to transition quickly from the arena of complaints to that of defenses. Mrs. H was more receptive than her husband. As conjoint treatment progressed, Mr. H became increasingly aware of how his threatened withdrawal from the marriage had not so much to do with his wife's complaints. In fact, he even confessed to having a mother who kvetched all the time and revealed more about how he felt suffocated and stifled by his mother and how a repressed part of him needed a freer leash to do things he could never do as a child.

SUMMARY

This chapter on treatment techniques, procedures, and approaches draws mainly on object relations, self-psychology, and on newer contemporary theories such as mindfulness, mentalization, and dialectic behavioral therapy as an integrative approach. Object relations is a most valuable construct for managing couples within the context of their primitive defenses offering the therapist the opportunity to get into "the dance" with the couple. Transforming the projective/introjective process to dual projective identification allows further understanding of how each complainer identifies or over identifies with the complaint of the other, making normal needs and feelings into bad foreign objects that assault and attack the psyche. During the three phases of treatment, the couple moves from states of fusion to states of separateness, allowing healthy needs and feelings to replace complaints.

Closing Thoughts

This book would not be complete without taking into account gender difference and the societal pressures that impact our psyches—and our complaints. Today's therapists cannot afford to be complacent. We need to be open to the fast-paced changes occurring not only in therapeutic techniques but also in society as a whole. Take, for example, the way contemporary society views homosexuality. Until recently, even the American Psychology Association considered homosexuality to be a mental illness. Gay, lesbian, and transgender individuals had to lead double lives to keep their "secret" in order to be accepted by their peers. Years ago it would have been unthinkable that homosexual partnerships and marriage would be sanctioned by society and the government, or that two females or two males could adopt a child. There has also been a significant increase in the number of single-parent households as the marriage rate has decreased and the incidence of divorce has risen. All these changes have completely transformed the image of the traditional American family.

The role of females has also shifted dramatically since World War II. Because of the pioneering "mothers" of feminism like Gloria Steinem and Betty Friedan, who radicalized the feminist cause and stressed the equality of men and women, no longer is it the norm for the men to go off to work while women concentrate on tending to the children and domestic duties. Women have become empowered in the workforce, while the number of house-husbands and stay-at-home dads has risen noticeably. In today's economic environment, it has become almost necessary in many instances for both genders to work, although women complain that the brunt of the household chores and childrearing responsibilities still fall to them rather than their male partners. Women feel beleaguered because men can continue to pursue their endeavors without the disruption of menstrual cramps, ticking biological clocks, pregnancy, kids needing to be picked up from school, menopause, night sweats, and the like.

Despite the rise of feminism and the ongoing effort to ensure that women are granted equal rights in the workplace, women still tend to idealize men and fall prey to the seduction of men. It is almost a given that men and women will respond differently to life's vicissitudes. Author John Gray (2012) says it all in *Men Are from Mars, Women Are from Venus*. This enormously popular—although not scientific—book outlines the different ways in which men and women respond to emotional needs. In the case of love, he states that men tend to withdraw, take time out, need "space," and get distracted, whereas women react more impulsively and emotionally.

> I called to tell him I love him. There was no response. I later called to tell him I missed him and got no response. I know he loves me, but why can't he say, "I love and miss you, too?" So I asked him, and he said he was not thinking at the time. His mind was on the Red Sox and Yankees game. I then said, "So the game is more important than me?" To this he replied, "That is a typical female response! Where is the logic? What does my watching a baseball game have to do with how I feel about you?" To this I blurt out, "That doesn't answer the question. Why didn't you respond?" To this he simply replies, "Because I am a guy!!"

It does not take a social scientist to understand the different influences parents have regarding raising their sons and daughters. Typically, boys are raised not to cry or to show emotion, whereas weeping is not only acceptable for girls but is often thought to be a charmingly feminine trait. The inherent differences between the sexes are obvious, but we still need to explore beyond the biological to the subtleties of their emotional, verbal, and nonverbal interactions. I am reminded of a stoic military father who would beat his son whenever he complained or cried but would shower his daughter with hugs and kisses when she cried.

The findings of Kernberg (1975) show that men tend to be more sadistic and women more masochistic, and that male domination has its etiology in gender roles. Kernberg traces his findings to early adolescence, when young girls often fall in love with an idealized, unavailable, or deeply disappointing man, which influences their future love life. Men are invested in developing a sense of manhood or separateness by repudiating the mother and pushing her away. In *The Bonds of Love* (1988), feminist psychoanalyst Jessica Benjamin substantiates Kernberg's findings that male domination has its roots in a gender role, whereby women are raised to be submissive and prescribed to become primary caretakers and nurturers, making them far more able to maintain an identification with the maternal object.

Society has made great strides in learning to accept and appreciate the differences among its denizens—however, unfortunately, bigotry still exists toward both homosexual and interracial individuals and unions. Although women are much freer to express themselves and pursue educational and career opportunities, an element of sexism remains in personal and work relationships. There may be a few more chips in the "glass ceiling," but it's still intact. Some women who prefer and actively choose to be stay-at-home moms, asserting that feminism and being home with their children are not mutually exclusive ideas, find there is a stigma attached to their decision, that their contribution to society is devalued. "Don't you get bored? Why don't you work? It is so much more rewarding than sitting home all day doing nothing." Furthermore, women disproportionately experience sexual misconduct, sexual violence or abuse, gender discrimination in the workplace, and poverty. This inequality is an important factor in creating a politics of engagement.

To sum it all up, there is still plenty to "complain" about and plenty of work to be done to achieve a happy balance that ensures a more equal, more satisfying, and harmonious life for all.

Glossary

>≫<

Attunement
Attunement is the rhythm of the heart and soul as it blends with another person. According to Winnicott (1965), it is that beautiful moment of the mother–infant ecstasy of togetherness against the backdrop of dialectic tensions of the dread of separateness. The infant and mother are one in total harmony, bliss, and synchronicity. Whether it involves the dancer and the pianist, the musician and the conductor, the painter and his canvas, or the patient and the analyst, there are two types of attunement to which I refer: (1) experiencing the moment of togetherness and (2) sensing the rhythm and timing of the other.

Borderline Personality
This personality disorder designates a defect in the maternal attachment bond as an over-concern with the "other." Many have affixed the term "as-if personalities" to borderlines, who tend to subjugate or compromise themselves. They question their sense of existence, suffer from acute abandonment and persecutory anxiety, and tend to merge with others in very painful ways in order to achieve a sense of bonding. Under close scrutiny and stress, they distort, misperceive, have poor impulse control, and turn suddenly against self and others (attacking, blaming, finding fault, and seeking revenge).

Containment
A term employed by Wilfred Bion (1961) to describe the interaction between the mother and the infant. Bion believed all psychological barriers universally dissolve when the mind acts as receiver of communicative content, which the mother does in a state of reverie by using her own alpha function. Containment connotes the capacity to transform the data of emotional experience into meaningful feelings and thoughts. It is based on the mother's capacity to withstand the child's anger, frustrations, and intolerable feelings and behaviors long enough to decode or detoxify them into a more digestible form.

Countertransference

Countertransference refers to a process by which feelings toward a patient become distorted if the patient stirs up some feelings that interfere with the therapist's ability to maintain technical neutrality. The clinician suddenly develops a personal emotion (e.g., such as sexual attraction, hatred, envy, or disgust) and these feelings can create a negative therapeutic alliance. At this juncture, the therapist needs to seek consultation.

Couple Transference

I devised this term to describe what happens during treatment when the couple jointly projects onto the therapist some unconscious fantasy. Couple transference does for the couple what transference does for the individual but is slightly more complex: "*Now you are doing the same thing with me that you do with your husband!*" Couple transference interpretations are derived from the analyst's experience and insights and are designed to produce a transformation within the dyadic relationship. The couple transference refers to the mutual projections, delusions, and distortions or shared couple fantasies that become displaced onto the therapist. The notion of the "couple/therapist" transference opens up an entirely new therapeutic vista or transitional space in which to work. It is within this space that "real" issues come to life. A borderline husband says to the therapist: "*Now you're just like my wife—selfish, greedy, and only caring about yourself.*"

Cultural V-Spot

The cultural V-spot is a collectively shared archaic experience from the mythological or historical past that evokes painful thoughts and memories for the group (e.g., burning of the temple, loss of land to Israel, or the expulsion of Ishmael to the desert with his abandoned mother Hagar).

Depressive Position

This is a term devised by Melanie Klein (1948) to describe a state of mourning and sadness in which integration and reparation take place. Not everything is seen in terms of black and white in this state; there is more tolerance, guilt, remorse, self-doubt, frustration, pain, and confusion, and one assumes more responsibility for one's actions. There is the realization of the way things are, not of how things should be. As verbal expression increases, one may feel sadness, but also a newly regained sense of aliveness.

Dual Projective Identification

Whereas projective identification is a one-way process, dual projective identification is a two-way process that lends itself to conjoint treatment. One partner projects a negative feeling into the other, who then identifies or over-identifies with the negativity being projected: "*I'm not stupid! Don't call me stupid!*"

Ego
The ego is part of an intrapsychic system responsible for functions such as thinking, reality testing, and judgment. It is the mediator between the id and superego. The function of the ego is to observe the external world, preserving a true picture by eliminating old memory traces left by early impressions and perceptions.

Envy
Klein (1957) made a distinction between envy and jealousy. Envy is a part-object function and is not based on love. She considers envy to be the most primitive and fundamental emotion. It exhausts external objects and is destructive in nature. Envy is possessive, controlling, and does not allow outsiders in.

Folie à Deux
In general terms, folie à deux refers to Melanie Klein's (1957) notion of projective identification, whereby two people project their delusional fantasies back and forth and engage in a foolish "dance." The partners are wrapped up in a shared delusional fantasy, and each engages and believes in the outrageous scheme of the other. Usually the term applies to both oppositional and collusive couples. In some cases, there is triangulation, a three-part relationship in which two people form a covert or overt bond against another member.

Guilt
Guilt is a higher form of development than shame. Guilt has an internal punishing voice that operates at the level of the superego (an internalized, punitive, harsh parental figure). There are two kinds of guilt: valid guilt and invalid guilt. Valid guilt occurs when the person should feel guilty. Invalid guilt comes from a punitive and persecutory superego.

Internal Objects
Internal objects emanate from the part of the ego that has been introjected. They are part of an intrapsychic process whereby unconscious fantasies that are felt to be persecutory, threatening, or dangerous are denounced, split off, and projected. Klein (1957) believed that the infant internalizes good "objects" or the "good breast." However, if the infant perceives the world as bad and dangerous, the infant internalizes the "bad breast."

Jealousy
Jealousy, a higher form of development than envy, is a whole-object relationship whereby one desires the object but does not seek to destroy it or the oedipal rival (father and siblings, those who take mother away). Jealousy, unlike envy, is a triangular relationship based on love, wherein one desires to be part of or included in the group, family, clan, or nation.

The Language of Empathology and the Language of Dialectics
Both narcissists and borderlines require their own "special" form of communication. This led me to invent the language of empathology for the narcissist and the language of dialectics for the borderline. Motivated by the works of Heinz Kohut, Wilfred Bion, and Marsha Linehan, I originated these languages to fulfill the need for empathic understanding for the narcissist and the splitting mechanism for the borderline and to make communication more "user friendly." These languages provide a wider range of therapeutic space, especially in addressing effective communication with different kinds of narcissists and borderlines, including "the narcissist the artist" and the "cross-cultural borderline."

Manic Defenses
The experience of excitement (mania) offsets feelings of despair, loss, anxiety, and vulnerability. Manic defenses evolve as a defense against depressive anxiety, guilt, and loss. They are based on omnipotent denial of psychic reality and object relations characterized by a massive degree of triumph, control, and hostility. Some manic defenses work in the ego.

Mirroring
This is a term devised by Heinz Kohut (1971, 1977) to describe the "gleam" in a mother's eye, which mirrors the child's exhibitionistic display and the forms of maternal participation in it. Mirroring is a specific response to the child's narcissistic-exhibitionist displays, confirming the child's self-esteem. Eventually these responses are channeled into more realistic aims.

Narcissistic/Borderline Relationship
These two personality types enter into a psychological "dance," in which each partner consciously or unconsciously stirs up highly charged feelings that fulfill early unresolved conflicts in the other. The revelation is that each partner needs the other to play out his or her own personal relational drama. Engaging in these beleaguered relationships are developmentally arrested people who bring archaic experiences embedded in old sentiments into their current relationships.

Narcissistic Personality
Narcissists are dominated by omnipotence, grandiosity, and exhibitionist features. They become strongly invested in others and experience them as self-objects. In order to preserve this "special" relationship with their self-objects (others), they tend to withdraw or isolate themselves by concentrating on perfection and power.

Object Relations
Object relations is a theory of how unconscious internal feelings and desires, in dynamic interplay with current interpersonal experience, relate to and

interact with others in the external world. This is an approach to understanding intrapsychic and internal conflict in patients, including projection, introjection, fantasy and distortion, delusions, and split-off aspects of the self. Klein (1957) developed the idea of pathological splitting of "good" and "bad" objects through the defensive process of projection and introjection in relation to primitive anxiety and the death instinct (based on biology). Object relations derives its therapeutic power by showing how unconscious fantasies/motivations can reflect the way a person can distort reality by projecting and identifying with bad objects.

Paranoid Schizoid Position

The paranoid schizoid position is a fragmented position in which thoughts and feelings are split off and projected because the psyche cannot tolerate feelings of pain, emptiness, loneliness, rejection, humiliation, or ambiguity. Klein (1957) viewed this position as the earliest phase of development, part-object functioning, and the beginning of the primitive, undeveloped superego. If the child views mother as a "good breast," the child will maintain good, warm, and hopeful feelings about his or her environment. If, on the other hand, the infant experiences mother as a "bad breast," the child is more likely to experience the environment as bad, attacking, and persecutory. Klein, more than any of her followers, understood the primary importance of the need for mother and the breast.

Part Objects

The first relational unit is the feeding experience with the mother and the infant's relation to the breast. Klein (1957) believed that the breast is the child's first possession. However, because it is so desired it also becomes the source of the infant's envy, greed, and hatred and is therefore susceptible to the infant's fantasized attacks. The infant internalizes the mother as good or bad or, to be more specific, as a "part object" (a "good breast" or "bad breast"). As the breast is felt to contain a great part of the infant's death instinct (persecutory anxiety), it simultaneously establishes libidinal forces, giving way to the baby's first ambivalence. One part of the mother is loved and idealized, while the other is destroyed by the infant's oral, anal, sadistic, or aggressive impulses. In clinical terms, Klein referred to this as pathological splitting. Here a parent is seen as a function of what the parent can provide—for example, in infancy the breast and in later life money, material objects, and so forth (*"I only love women who have big breasts!"*).

Persecutory Anxiety

This is the part of the psyche that threatens and terrifies the patient. It relates to what Klein (1957) has referred to as the primitive superego, an undifferentiated state that continually warns the patient of imminent danger (often unfounded).

Paranoid anxiety is a feature associated with the death instinct and is more persecutory in nature. It implies the kind of anxiety from the primitive superego that is more explosive and volatile than from the more developed superego.

Projective Identification
This is a process whereby one splits off an unwanted aspect of the self and projects it into the object, which identifies or over-identifies with that which is being projected. In other words, the self experiences the unconscious defensive mechanism and translocates itself into the other. Under the influence of projective identification, one becomes vulnerable to the coercion, manipulation, or control of the person doing the projecting.

Psychohistory
Psychohistory does for the group what psychoanalysis does for the individual. It offers a broader perspective from which to view cross-cultural differences. Using psychoanalytic tools and concepts, psychohistory allows a better understanding of individuals, nations, governments, and political events—very much as a therapist analyzes the couple as a symbolic representation of a political group or nation (DeMause, 2002a, 2002b, 2006a, 2006b, 2007).

Reparation
This is the desire for the ego to restore an injured love object by coming to terms with one's own guilt and ambivalence. The process of reparation begins in the depressive position and starts when one develops the capacity to mourn and tolerate and contain the feelings of loss and guilt.

Reverse Superego
Whereas the healthy superego is a moral structure that goes through life distinguishing between right and wrong and good and evil, the reverse superego does the opposite. It is a concept I devised when writing an article for *Inspire* on "The Twisted Mind and Its Reverse Superego" (Kobrin and Lachkar, 2011) to describe that what happens when one is praised for being bad and punished for being good. An example of this would be countries that encourage mistreatment of women. At the domestic level, it might sound something like, "*He is so envious of me and my accomplishments. Instead of celebrating my success, my promotion, my awards, he goes out with the guys, making me feel like a nothing.*"

Schizoid Personality
The central features of schizoid personalities are their defenses of attachment, aloofness, and indifference to others. The schizoid, although difficult to treat, is usually motivated, unlike the passive-aggressive. However, because of ongoing detachment and aloofness, the schizoid personality lacks the capacity to achieve social and sexual gratification. A close relationship invites the danger

of being overwhelmed or suffocated, for it may be envisioned as relinquishing independence. The schizoid differs from the obsessive-compulsive personality in that the obsessive-compulsive feels great discomfort with emotions, whereas the schizoid is lacking in the capacity to feel the emotion but at least recognizes the need. Schizoids differ from the narcissist in that they are self-sufficient and self-contained. They do not experience or suffer the same feelings of loss that borderlines and narcissists do (*"Who, me? I don't care; I have my work, my computer, etc.!"*).

Self-Objects
This is a term devised by Heinz Kohut (1971, 1977). A forerunner of self-psychology, the term refers to an interpersonal process whereby the analyst provides basic functions for the patient. These functions are used to make up for failures in the past by caretakers who were lacking in mirroring and empathic attunement and had faulty responses for their children. Kohut reminds us that psychological disturbances are caused by failures of idealized objects, and for the rest of their lives, patients may need self-objects that provide good mirroring responses.

Self-Psychology
Heinz Kohut (1971, 1977) revolutionized analytic thinking when he introduced a new psychology of the self that stresses the patient's subjective experience. Unlike with object relations, the patient's "reality" is not considered a distortion or a projection, but rather the patient's truth. It is the patient's experience that is considered of utmost importance. Self-psychology, with its emphasis on the empathic mode, implies that the narcissistic personality is more susceptible to classical interpretations. Recognition of splitting and projections is virtually non-existent among self-psychologists.

Shame
Shame is a matter between the person and his group or society, whereas guilt is primarily a matter between a person and his conscience. Shame is the defense against the humiliation of having needs that are felt to be dangerous and persecutory and is associated with anticipatory anxiety and annihilation fantasies. *"If I tell my boyfriend what I really need, he will abandon me!"*

Single and Dual Projective Identification (Conjoint Treatment)
In single projective identification, one takes in the other person's projections by identifying with that which is being projected. Dual projective identification is a term I originated in which both partners take in the projections of the other and identify or over-identify with that which is being projected (the splitting of the ego). Thus, one may project guilt while the other projects shame. *"You should be ashamed of yourself for being so needy! When you're so needy, I feel guilty!"*

Splitting

Splitting occurs when a person cannot keep two contradictory thoughts or feelings in mind at the same time and, therefore, keeps the conflicting feelings apart, focusing on just one of them.

Superego

The literature refers to different kinds of superegos. Freud's (1923) superego concerns itself with moral judgment (i.e., what people think). It depicts an introjected whole figure, a parental voice or image that operates from a point of view of morality, telling the child how to follow the rules and what happens if he or she does not. It covers the "dos, don'ts, oughts, and shoulds" and represents the child's compliance and conformity with strong parental figures. Freud's superego is the internalized image that continues to live inside the child, controlling or punishing. Klein's (1927, 1957) superego centers on the shame and humiliation of having needs, thoughts, and feelings that are felt to be more persecutory and hostile in nature and invade the psyche as an unmentalized experience.

Transference

Transference is a process whereby the patient transfers an emotion, feeling, or past relationship object bond to the therapist, re-creating it within the therapeutic process. It is often an unconscious mechanism that can thwart or distort the patient's seeing the therapist realistically. *"You are using me and taking advantage of me just like my father did."* Transference differs from projection in that this is where the patient cannot tolerate some part of the self and projects it onto the therapist. *"I don't like being used; now I make you into a user."*

V-Spot

The V-spot is a term I devised to describe the most sensitive area of emotional vulnerability that gets aroused when one partner hits an emotional raw spot in the other. It is the emotional counterpart to the physical G-spot. The V-spot is the heart of our most fragile area of emotional sensitivity, known in the literature as the archaic injury, a product of early trauma that one holds onto. With arousal of the V-spot comes the loss of sense and sensibility; everything shakes and shifts like an earthquake (memory, perception, judgment, and reality). It is a way of meticulously pinpointing the precise affective experience.

> No you are not depressed; you are feeling sad.
> No you are not insane; you are feeling ambivalence.
> No you are not angry; you are feeling betrayed and disappointed.
> No you are not suicidal; you feel hopeless and helpless.
> No you are not stupid; you are feeling anxious.

Whole Objects
The beginning of the depressive position is marked by the infant's awareness of his mother as a "whole object." As the infant matures and as verbal expression increases, he achieves more cognitive ability and acquires the capacity to love her as a separate person with separate needs, feelings, and desires. In the depressive position, guilt and jealousy become the replacement for shame and envy. Ambivalence and guilt are experienced and tolerated in relation to whole objects. One no longer seeks to destroy the objects or the oedipal rival (father and siblings, who take mother away) but can begin to live amicably with them.

Withdrawal versus Detachment
Detachment should not be confused with withdrawal. Withdrawal is actually a healthier state because it maintains a certain libidinal attachment to the object. When one detaches, one splits off and goes into a state of despondency. Children who are left alone, ignored, or neglected for long periods of time enter into a phase of despair (Bowlby, 1969). The child's active protest for the missing or absent mother gradually diminishes, and the child no longer makes demands. When this occurs, the child goes into detachment mode or pathological mourning. Apathy, lethargy, and listlessness become the replacement for feelings (anger, rage, betrayal, and abandonment).

Bibliography

Adams, K. A. (2012). Japan: The sacrificial society. *Journal of Psychohistory, 40*(2), 89–111.

Adams, K. A., & Hill, L. (1997). The phallic female in Japanese group fantasy. *Journal of Psychohistory, 25*(1), 33–66.

Akhtar, S. (2013). *Psychoanalytic listening.* New York: Karnac Books.

Allen, W. (Director). (2006). *Scoop* [Motion picture]. UK: BBC Films.

American Psychiatric Association. (1994). *Diagnostic and statistical manual of mental disorders [DSM-IV]* (4th ed.). Arlington, VA: Author.

Banner, L. (2012, August 5). Marilyn Monroe, the eternal shape shifter. *Los Angeles Times,* p. A26.

Benjamin, J. (1988). *The bonds of love: Psychoanalysis, feminism, and the problem of domination.* New York: Pantheon.

Berry, S. (2007). *House of Abraham: Lincoln and the Todds, a family divided by war.* New York: Houghton Mifflin.

Berton, P. (1995). Understanding Japanese negotiating behavior. *ISOP Intercom, University of California Los Angeles, 18*(2), 1–8.

Berton, P. (2001, May). *Japan on the psychological couch.* Presentation, University of Southern California at Los Angeles, Emeriti Center.

Berton, P., & Lachkar, J. (2001, June). *German and Japanese reactions to the acts during World War II: A psychoanalytic perspective.* Paper presented at the International Psychohistorical Conference, Amsterdam.

Bion, W. (1959). *Experience in groups.* New York: Basic Books.

Bion, W. R. (1962). *Learning from experience.* London: Heinemann.

Bion, W. R. (1967). *Second thoughts. Selected papers on psycho-analysis.* New York: Jason Aronson.

Bion, W. R. (1970). *Attention and interpretation.* London: Tavistock.

Bion, W. R. (1977). *Seven servants. Four works by Wilfred R. Bion.* New York: Jason Aronson.

Bowlby, J. (1969). *Attachment and loss* (3 vols.). New York: Basic Books.

Brown, B. (2010). *The gift of imperfection: Let go of who you think you're supposed to be and embrace who you are.* Center City, MN: Hazelden.

deMause, L. (2002a). The childhood origins of terrorism. *Journal of Psychohistory, 29,* 340–349.

deMause, L. (2002b). *The emotional life of nations*. New York: Karnac Books.

deMause, L. (2006a). The childhood origins of the holocaust. *Journal of Psychohistory, 33*, 204–222.

deMause, L. (2006b). If I blow myself up and become a martyr, I'll finally be loved. *Journal of Psychohistory, 33*(4), 300–307.

deMause, L. (2007). The killer mutterland. *Journal of Psychohistory, 34*, 278–300.

Dicks, H. (1967). *Marital tensions. Clinical studies toward a psychological theory of interaction*. New York: Basic Books.

Doi, T. (1973). *The anatomy of dependence*. Tokyo: Kodansha International.

Drexler, P. (2013, March 6). The tyranny of the queen bee. *The Wall Street Journal*. Retrieved from http://online.wsj.com/news/articles/SB1000142412788732388430 4578328271526080496

Endleman, R. (1989). *Love and sex in twelve cultures*. New York: Psychic Press.

Fairbairn, W.R.D. (1940). Schizoid factors in the personality: An object relations theory of the personality. New York: Basic Books.

Fonagy, P., & Bateman, A. (2006). Progress in the treatment of the borderline personality disorder. Mechanisms of change in mentalization-based treatment of borderline personality disorder. *British Journal of Psychiatry, 188*, 1–3.

Foster, R., Moskowitz, R., & Javier, R. (1996). *Reaching across boundaries of culture and class*. Northvale, NJ: Jason Aronson.

Freud, H. (2013). *Men and mothers: The lifelong struggle of sons and their mothers*. London: Karnac Books.

Freud, S. (1923). *The ego and id*. New York: Norton.

Freud, S. (1930). *Civilization and its discontents* (Standard ed., Vol. 20, pp. 77–174). London Hogarth Press.

Freud, S. (1953). Creative writers and day-dreaming. In J. Strachey (Ed. & Trans.), *The complete works of Sigmund Freud* (Standard ed., Vol. 9, pp. 141–153). London: Hogarth Press. (Original work published 1908).

Freud, S. (1955). Notes upon a case of obsessional neurosis. In J. Strachey (Ed. & Trans.), *The complete works of Sigmund Freud* (Vol. 10, pp. 153–318). London: Hogarth Press. (Original work published 1909).

Freud, S. (1957). On narcissism: An introduction. In J. Strachey (Ed. & Trans.), *The complete works of Sigmund Freud* (Vol. 14, pp. 69–102). London: Hogarth Press. (Original work published 1914).

Freud, S. (1979). Group psychology and the analysis of the ego. In J. Strachey (Ed. & Trans.), *The complete works of Sigmund Freud* (Vol. 18, pp. 65–143). London: Hogarth Press. (Original work published 1921).

Gay, P. (1988). *Freud: A life for our times*. New York: Norton.

Goodman, S. (2012, February 6). The mistreatment of women in Moslem countries. Retrieved from Family Security Matters website: www.familysecuritymatters.org/publications/id.11369/pub_detail.asp

Gottman, J. (1995). *Why marriages succeed or fail*. New York: Simon & Schuster.

Gray, J. (2012). *Men are from Mars, women are from Venus*. New York: Harper Collins.

Grotstein, J. (1981). *Splitting and projective identification*. New York: Jason Aronson.

Grotstein, J. (1987). *Meaning, meaningless, and the "black hole." Self and international regulation as a new paradigm for psychoanalysis and neuroscience: An introduction*. Unpublished manuscript.

Grotstein, J. (1993). Boundary difficulties in borderline patients. In L. Bryce Boyer & Peter Giovacchini (Eds.), *Master clinicians: On treating the regressed patient* (pp. 107–142). Northvale, NJ: Jason Aronson.

Hare, R. D. (1993). *Without conscience: The disturbing world of the psychopath among us.* Guilford Publications. New York.

Hartmann, H. (1958). *Ego psychology and the problem of adaptation* (D. Rapaport, Trans.). New York: International Universities Press.

Hoffman, D. (Director). (2012). *Quartet* [Motion picture].USA: The Weinstein Company.

Iga, M. (1986). *The thorn in the chrysanthemum.* Berkeley, CA: University of California Press.

Johnson, F. (1994). *Dependency and Japanese socialization: Psychoanalytic and anthropological investigations into amae.* New York: New York University Press.

Kaiman, J. (2012, February 24). Lin inspires China—to a point. *Los Angeles Times.* Retrieved from http://articles.latimes.com/2012/feb/23/world/la-fg-china-lin-20120224

Kernberg, O. (1975). *Borderline conditions and pathological narcissism.* New York: Jason Aronson.

Kernberg, O. (1976). *Object relations theory and clinical psychoanalysis.* New York: Jason Aronson.

Kernberg, O. (1980). *Internal world and external reality.* New York: Jason Aronson.

Kernberg, O. (1985a). *Borderline conditions and pathological narcissism.* New York: Jason Aronson.

Kernberg, O. (1985b). *Internal world and external reality: Object relations theory applied.* New York: Jason Aronson.

Kernberg. O. (1992). *Aggression in personality disorders and perversions.* New Haven, CT: Yale University Press.

Kernberg, O. (1998). *Love relations: Normality and pathology.* New Haven, CT: Yale University Press.

Kernberg, O. (2013, September 8). *New developments in the treatment of severe personality disorders.* Conference sponsored by the New Center for Psychoanalysis, Skirball Museum, Los Angeles.

Kivy, P. (2011). *The possessor and the possessed: Handel, Mozart, Beethoven, and the idea of musical genius.* New Haven, CT: Yale University Press.

Klein, M. (1927). Criminal tendencies in normal children. *International Journal of Psychoanalysis, 42,* 4–8.

Klein, M. (1948). Mourning and its relation to manic states. In *Contributions to psychoanalysis 1921–1945* (311–338). London: Hogarth Press.

Klein, M. (1957). *Envy and gratitude.* New York: Basic Books.

Klein, M. (1975). Love, guilt, and reparation. In R. E. Money-Kyrle (Ed.), *The writings of Melanie Klein: Vol. I. Love, guilt and reparation and other works 1921–1945* (pp. 306–343). New York: The Free Press.

Klein, M. (1984). Narrative of a child analysis. In R. E. Money-Kyrle (Ed.), *The writings of Melanie Klein* (Vol. 4). New York: Free Press.

Kobrin, N. (2010). *The banality of suicide terrorism: The naked truth about the psychology of Islamic suicide bombings.* Dulles, VA: Potomac Books.

Kobrin, N. (2013a, May 23). The mind of the terrorist is the mind of his mother [Web log post]. Retrieved from http://blogs.timesofisrael.com/the-mind-of-the-terrorist-is-the-mind-of-his-mother/

Kobrin, N. (2013b). *Penetrating the terrorist psyche.* New York: MultiEducator.com.

Kobrin, N., & Lachkar, J. (2011, April 6). The twisted mind: Inspire Magazine No. 5 and its reverse superego. Retrieved from Family Security Matters website: www.familysecuritymatters.org/publications/id.9168/pub_detail.asp#ixzz2hIHTUxNY

Kobrin, N., & Lachkar, J. (2012). *Tears real or fake*. Unpublished manuscript.

Kohut, H. (1971). *The analysis of the self*. New York: International Universities Press.

Kohut, H. (1977). *The restoration of the self*. New York: International Universities Press.

Lachkar, J. (1985). Narcissistic/borderline couples: Theoretical implications for treatment. *Dynamic Psychotherapy, 3*(2), 109–127.

Lachkar, J. (1986). Narcissistic/borderline couples: Implications for mediation. *Conciliation Courts Review, 24*(1), 31–43.

Lachkar, J. (1992). *The narcissistic/borderline couple: A psychoanalytic perspective on marital conflict*. New York: Brunner/Mazel.

Lachkar, J. (1993a). Paradox of peace: Folie à deux in marital and political relationships. *Journal of Psychohistory, 20*(3), 275–287.

Lachkar, J. (1993b). Political and marital conflict. *Journal of Psychohistory, 22*(2), 199–211.

Lachkar, J. (1998a, July). *Aggression and cruelty in cross-cultural couples*. Paper presented at the Psychohistory Congress, Paris.

Lachkar, J. (1998b). *The many faces of abuse: Treating the emotional abuse of high-functioning women*. Northvale, NJ: Jason Aronson.

Lachkar, J. (2000). *Slobodan and Mirjana Milosevic: The dysfunctional couple that destroyed the Balkans*. Unpublished manuscript.

Lachkar, J. (2001). Narcissism in dance. *Choreography and Dance: An International Journal, 6*, 23–30.

Lachkar, J. (2002). The psychological make-up of a suicide bomber. *Journal of Psychohistory, 29*(4), 349–367.

Lachkar, J. (2004a). *The narcissistic/borderline couple: New approaches to marital therapy*. New York: Taylor and Francis.

Lachkar, J. (2004b, September). Women who become undone. The many faces of abuse, review by Aimee Lee Ball. *Oprah Magazine*, pp. 300–305, 327.

Lachkar, J. (2006). The psychopathology of terrorism: A cultural "V"-spot. *Journal of Psychohistory, 34*(2).

Lachkar, J. (2008a). *How to talk to a narcissist*. New York: Taylor and Francis.

Lachkar, J. (2008b, May 9). *Psychopathology of terrorism*. Paper presented at Rand Corporation, 3rd Annual Conference Terrorism and Global Security, Santa Monica, CA.

Lachkar, J. (2008c). *The V-spot: Healing the "V"ulnerable spot from emotional abuse*. New York: Roman and Littlefield.

Lachkar, J. (2009). How to talk to a borderline. *The Therapist*. California Association for Marriage and Family Therapists (CAMFT), San Diego, CA.

Lachkar, J. (2011). *How to talk to a borderline*. New York: Taylor and Francis.

Lachkar, J. (2013). *The disappearing male*. New York: Jason Aronson.

Lasch, C. (1979). *The culture of narcissism*. New York. Norton.

Linehan, M. M. (1993a). *Cognitive behavioral treatment of borderline personality disorder*. New York: The Guilford Press.

Linehan, M. M. (1993b). *Skills training manual for treating borderline personality disorder*. New York: The Guilford Press.

Mahler, M. S., Pine, F., & Bergman, A. (1975). *The psychological birth of the human infant.* New York: Basic Books.

Martin, P., & Bird, H. M. (1959). Marriage patterns: The "lovesick" wife and the "cold sick" husband. *Psychiatry, 22,* 242–249.

Masaaki, I. (1981). 16 ways to avoid saying no. Tokyo: *Nihon Keizai Shimbun* [Japan Economic Journal].

Mason, A. (1981). The suffocating superego. Psychotic break and claustrophobia. In J. Grotstein (Ed.), *Do I dare disturb the universe?* (pp. 140–166). Beverly Hills, CA: Caesura.

Mason, P. (1998). *Stop walking on eggshells: Taking your life back when someone you care about has a borderline personality.* Oakland, CA: New Harbinger.

Masterson, J. F. (1981). *The narcissistic and borderline disorders: An integrated developmental approach.* New York: Brunner/Mazel.

McCormack, C. (2000). *Treating borderline states in marriage: Dealing with oppositionalism, ruthless aggression, and severe resistance.* Northvale, NJ: Jason Aronson.

McDougall, J. (1995). *The many faces of Eros: A psychoanalytic exploration of human sexuality.* London: Free Association Books.

Meltzer, D. (1967). *The psycho-analytic process.* London: Heinemann.

Miyamoto, M. (1994). *Straitjacket society: An insider's irreverent view of bureaucratic Japan.* Tokyo: Kodansha International.

Nathanson, P., & Young, K. (2006). *Legalizing misandry.* Montreal, Canada: McGill-Queen's University Press.

Nowrasteh, C. (Director). (2008). *The stoning of Soraya M.* [Motion picture]. USA: Mpower Pictures.

Ogden, T. H. (1986). *The matrix of the mind. Object relations and the psychoanalytic dialogue.* Northvale, NJ: Jason Aronson.

Raine, A. (2001). *Violence and psychopathy.* New York: Springer Science Business Media.

Reik, T. (1948). *Listening with the third ear.* New York: Farrar, Straus.

Rule, A, (2000). *The stranger beside me* (Rev. ed.) New York: New American Library.

Seinfeld, J. (1990). *The bad object: Handling the negative therapeutic reactions in psychotherapy.* Northvale, NJ: Jason Aronson.

Soderbergh, S. (Director). (2013). *Behind the candelabra* [Motion picture]. USA: HBO.

Stein, J. (2013, May). Millennials: The me me me generation. *Time, 181*(19), 26–34.

Stout, M. (2006). *The psychopath next door.* New York: Broadway Books.

Svoboda, E. (2009). Field guide to the pack rat: Closet cases. *Psychology Today.* Retrieved from www.psychologytoday.com/articles/200901/field-guide-the-pack-rat-closet-cases

Vaknin, S. (2007). *Obsessive-compulsive personality disorder* (OCPD). Retrieved from http://samvak.tripod.com/personalitydisorders29.html

Vaknin, S. (2011). *Schizoid personality disorder* [216 videos]. Retrieved from the YouTube website: www.youtube.com/watch?v = vu802wwef

Vaknin, S., & Rangelovska, L. (Eds.) (2007). *Malignant self love—Narcissism revisited.* Prague, Czech Republic: Narcissus.

Winnicott, D. W. (1965). *The maturational process and the facilitating environment.* New York: International Universities Press.

Index

66–8; obsessive-compulsive 71–2; paranoid 73–5; passive-aggressive 71; passive aggressive defined 7, 59; passive-aggressive redefined 59; pathological 68–9; schizoid 72–3; therapeutic tools 150; versus antisocial 106

Borodin, Alexander 57

bosses 110, 141–5; bully 139, 140; idealize 139; Japanese male 125, 126; loyalty 118, 125, 139; *see also* King Bee; Queen Bee

Bowlby, John 33–4, 38; detachment versus withdrawal 33

breasts: good 109, 132, 151; loss of 102–3; *see also* bad-breast mother

bully 111; boss 139, 140; dismissive 138; female 142; silent 139

C

Castro, Ariel 48

child neglect 38, 70, 88, 144

Chinese: honor 124–5; war crimes against 117

clinical depression; versus states of mourning and loss 98, 101–3

complaints: common xiv, xvi, 8–11, 15, 17, 40; distinguishing real from non-legitimate 6–8, 17; listening to at the cultural level 118–23; psychodynamics and culture 116–18; psychosomatic 10–11; real from pseudo 17; withholding 87

conjoint therapy 13, 20, 24, 26, 31, 38, 78, 96, 157, 160

containment: defined 165; Bion 165

containment listening 4, 6; Bion 6

controlling mother 122–4

corporate abuse 137; basic assumption group, 139; primitive defenses regressed groups, scapegoats, work group 1381–39;

corporate level complaints 137–45; bosses 110, 141–5; bully 139, 140; idealize 139; Japanese male 125, 126; loyalty 118, 125, 139; red flags 139–40; reverse superego 140–1; work groups 138–9; *see also* King Bee syndrome; Queen Bee syndrome

countertransference: defined 166; and transference listening 4, 6, 132, 150

couple transference 64, 78, 81, 95, 96, 97, 129, 131, 159; defined 166

cross-cultural complaints 114–16, 135; and psychodynamics 116–21

cross-cultural hook 118, 121, 123, 124, 126, 127, 128, 131, 132, 135, 154, 155

cultural V-spot 115; defined 166

D

deadbeat dads 106, 108–9

depressive position xvi, 22, 23, 97–8, 100, 103, 157; analectic 88; associated complaints 104; common characteristics 104; defined 166; Klein 166; narcissist 50; passive-aggressive 91

deprivation 12–13; early 43; entitlement 35; Fairbairn 23, 24; good and bad breast 109; Mrs. P 21; passive-aggressive 93

depriving object 24, 151, 156

detachment: Bowlby 33; children 88, 173; narcissist 72–3; schizoid 72, 89, 170; versus feelings 152; versus withdrawal 33, 173

Diagnostic and Statistical Manual of Mental Disorders (DSM-IV) 71, 79, 91

dialectic behavioral therapy (DBT) 17, 35, 36, 37, 160

DiMaggio, James 70, 110

Disappearing Male syndrome 125

disappearing object 25

distinguishing real complaint from non-legitimate complaint 6–8, 17

Dicks, Henry 79; *Marital Tensions* 78

Don Juan syndrome 66–7

dual projective identification 20, 101, 150, 153, 156, 160; defined 166

E

East/West cultural distinctions 113–36; child rearing practice xv, 113, 118, 125; controlling mother 122–4; cultural V-Spot 115, 166; group mind-set 121–24;

pathological artist versus malignant artist
    56–7
persecutory anxiety 73, 106, 165; defined
    169–70; Klein 169
persecutory superego 2, 79, 106, 167, 172
primitive anxiety 169
promiser xiii, xvi; borderline 66–7; passive-
    aggressive 67
projective identification 48, 103; artist 53;
    Bion 36; borderline 74; defined
    170; dual 20, 101, 153, 156, 160;
    Klein 2, 17, 18, 20, 21; Kohut 2;
    malignant borderline 69; passive
    aggressive 93; pathological
    borderline 68
psychodynamics: cultural complaints
    116–18; Freud 18–19; Klein
    20–1; reparation 23; theoretical
    contributions 17–38
psychohistory 114; defined 170
psychopath 107, 109–11; associated
    complaints 111; characteristics
    10, 107, 110–11, 115; sadistic
    105; versus schizoid 105, 109
psychosomatic complaints 10–11

Q

Queen Bee syndrome 142–3

R

Raine, Adrian: *The Biology of Violence*
    109–10
Ramirez, Richard 109
Rape of Nanjing 117
Reik, Theodor 12, 15, 134, 148; ego 2;
    Listening with the Third Ear 2
rejecting object 24, 151; Fairbairn 23
reparation 22, 117, 157; defined 170; Klein 23
reverse superego 13, 140–1, 145; defined 170
robotic relationship xvi, 77–90; overly
    emotional wife and robotic
    husband 79–81
Rule, Ann: *The Stranger Beside Me* 110

S

sadistic object 25, 48, 151
sadistic superego 50, 97

scapegoats xvii, 40, 59, 125, 137, 138, 139
schizoid personality 2, 22, 72–3, 79, 89–90,
    106; defined 170–1; paranoid 74,
    117, 153, 155; robotic 88; saving
    face xv; 116
self-hater 97, 98, 103–4; and group
    98–101
self-objects xiv, 25; defined 171; Kohut 29;
    narcissist 40, 88
self-psychology 135; defined 171;
    Kohut 3, 28, 148; objective
    listening 4
self-saboteurs 91–111; clinical depression
    versus states of mourning and
    loss 98; depressive 97–8; group
    and the self-hater 98–101;
    passive-aggressive 91–5
serial killers 109, 110
September 11 69; *see also* 9/11
severe anxiety 25
shame 5, 20, 33, 59, 135, 152, 167, 173;
    anticipatory and annihilation
    anxiety 171; /blame 24, 31, 156;
    borderline 68; cross-cultural
    aspects 117; culture 117–18,
    124, 127–8; defined 171; and
    honor 116, 128; and guilt 20, 24,
    35, 120, 152; Japanese women
    120, 132; Klein 172; narcissist 94;
    nationalistic 116; self-saboteurs
    91; superego 172; treatment of
    women 128
Sharia law 116
Sheen, Charlie 56
silent (non-verbal) listening 5–6, 14, 63
single and dual projective identification
    (conjoint treatment) 13, 20, 24,
    26, 31, 38, 78, 96, 157, 160;
    defined 171
Smith, Anna Nicole 70
sociopaths 104, 105, 107–9, 111;
    characteristics 106; complaints
    associated with 108; narcissist 48;
    superego 107, 109
splitting 3, 20, 21, 23, 36, 37, 65, 106,
    132, 152, 157, 158, 159–60;
    defined 172
Stein, Joel 11
Steinem, Gloria 161
Stern, Isaac 149
The Stoning of Soraya M. 129

Stout, Martha: *The Psychopath Next
Door* 110
subjective listening 3–4
suicide bombers 73, 115
superego 2, 11; antisocial 61, 106;
        antisocial narcissist 49; big
        150; borderline 106; critical
        104; culture 136; defined
        172; depressive 97; depressive
        narcissist 50; Freud 172; guilt
        117; id 31; internalized 24;
        Klein 2, 22, 172; lack of xvi,
        49, 106, 107, 109; little 150;
        OCD 79; persecutory 79, 106;
        primitive 22; prohibitive 37;
        punitive 50, 97; psychopath 107,
        109; sadistic 50, 97; reverse 13,
        140–1, 145, 150; sociopath 107,
        109; well-integrated 71

T

Takeo Doi 121–2
Time magazine 11
transference: defined 172; and
        countertransference listening 4, 6
treatment of women 128–32
treatment suggestions and techniques
        147–60; after the listening
        148–52; attachments to
        internal/external objects 151–2;
        Fairbairn 151–2; guidelines for
        the therapist 152; therapeutic
        techniques, tools, and
        functions 150–1; three phases
        of treatment 153–7; treatment
        points 153
true self 27, 28, 38, 117, 124

U

unavailable object 7, 24, 151; Fairbairn 23

V

Vaknin, Sam 125
validating environment 21, 36
victim 9, 13, 59, 65, 66, 67, 68, 69–70,
        71, 91, 93, 95, 108; antisocial
        narcissist 49; artist 75; cultural
        125; depressive xvi, 50, 97, 98;
        group 100; malignant narcissist
        48; psychopath 110, 111;
        sociopath 109, 111; work groups
        138, 140, 145
Vivaldi, Antonio 57
V-spot xiv, 18, 30, 34, 36, 38, 156;
        borderlines 76; cultural 115;
        defined 172; kvetching 133–4;
        narcissism, 46; trigger 60, 93

W

war crimes: German 115, 117; Japanese
        115, 117
whole objects 32, 167; defined 173
Williams, Robin 70
Winnicott, Donald 27–8, 38, 53, 78, 100;
        attunement 165; false self 27,
        117; true self 27, 117
withdrawal 35, 88
withdrawal versus detachment 33, 152;
        defined 173
withholder xiii, 78, 87–8
withholding object 25, 151
women, treatment of 128–32
work groups 138–9; red flags 139–40

For Product Safety Concerns and Information please contact our EU
representative GPSR@taylorandfrancis.com
Taylor & Francis Verlag GmbH, Kaufingerstraße 24, 80331 München, Germany

www.ingramcontent.com/pod-product-compliance
Lightning Source LLC
Chambersburg PA
CBHW050710280326
41926CB00088B/2916